CONFESSIONAL SUBJECTS

REVELATIONS OF

GENDER AND POWER IN

VICTORIAN LITERATURE

AND CULTURE

Susan David Bernstein

The University of North Carolina Press

Chapel Hill and London

Frontispiece: Sir John Everett Millais, *The Vale of Rest*, 1858/9.
Oil on canvas.
(Courtesy of the Tate Gallery)

Library of Congress Cataloging-in-Publication Data

Bernstein, Susan David.

Confessional subjects: revelations of gender and power in
Victorian literature and culture / Susan David Bernstein.

p.   cm.   Includes bibliographical references (p.   ) and index.

ISBN 0-8078-2313-9 (cloth: alk. paper)

ISBN 0-8078-4624-4 (pbk.: alk. paper)

1. English prose literature—19th century—History and
criticism. 2. Confession in literature. 3. Women and literature—Great Britain—History—19th century. 4. English
literature—Women authors—History and criticism.
5. English fiction—19th century—History and criticism.
6. Anti-Catholicism--England—History—19th century.
7. Great Britain—Civilization—19th century. 8. Power (Social
sciences) in literature. 9. Sex roles in literature. I. Title.

PR788.C56B47   1997   96-23854

828'.80809353—dc20   CIP

01 00 99 98 97   5 4 3 2 1

IN LOVING MEMORY
OF MY PARENTS,

Barbara Melman Bernstein
Sidney Bernstein

CONTENTS

PREFACE

The genesis of this project unfolded nearly ten years ago when Michael Ryan suggested my name for a 1986 MLA panel on the reception to Lacan in the United States. I participated in this session with a paper that later became an article entitled "Confessing Lacan." Although this book focuses on Victorian uses of confession, my thinking about confession and power actually began with speculations about Jane Gallop's and Stuart Schneiderman's first-person anecdotes in writing about Lacanian psychoanalytic theory. I was intrigued with the different rhetorical effects of this personal criticism, which I labeled a "confessional mode" because of the way autobiographical disclosure functions as an intrusion where the subject attention shifts from Lacan's texts to the narrating subject. It seemed evident in my reading that both Gallop in *Reading Lacan* and Schneiderman in *Jacques Lacan: The Death of an Intellectual Hero* deployed this version of confession as a rhetorical strategy, yet I found Gallop to be more self-conscious, more canny, than Schneiderman about the relationship between power and signification. I observed that Schneiderman's brand of confession revealed his allegiance to his own literary confessional fathers—before Lacan—that is, to Augustine and Rousseau, inasmuch as Schneiderman's "I" reigns supreme throughout his discourse. Yet Gallop's confessional interruptions, shaped by feminist theories, often dislodge the traditional opposition between subject and object, and through that unanchoring, Gallop draws attention to the power relations between analyst and analysand, between confessor and confessional subject.

But my point here isn't to replay these early arguments, although I must admit it is difficult to resist the compulsion to repeat all of my analytical journeys in moving from then to now, from my first reflections on confessional discourse to the present book. A preface seems a space to gather and place the various filaments that texture an intellectual project. Such an undertaking is necessarily untenable because of the complicated life—and the lives that are also part of this fabric—that any piece of scholarly work entails. My reading of Gallop and Schneiderman reading Lacan marked an early recognition of how confessional modes replicate gendered power relations, yet my abiding fascination with different forms of confession—from my childhood when I accompanied a Catholic friend to church on Saturday afternoons and waited while she disappeared into the confessional booth—has been too extensive and too varied to chart. In terms of the daily acts of confidences that people make, I have observed the power and pleasure tied up with such everyday confession on both sides. The burden of someone's disclosure of a transgression—the difficulty of what to say or do, whether to comply with the agreement to secrecy—is in fact an uneasiness with the kind of power that confession bestows on its interlocutor. By the same token, imparting such charged information can also be understood as an act of power where such divulgence can reorganize the listener's perceptions of the world, of social relationships, and of the individual who makes the confession. Someone tells me of his unusual domestic relations, but I am instructed not to disclose this knowledge to any of our mutual acquaintances because it could affect his professional status; someone else tells me of her extramarital affair, but I am not to repeat this information, especially since the husband presumably doesn't know. Why am I targeted with this intelligence, gossip which I both crave and fear? What kinds of responsibilities does this confidence entail and how does the very notion of obligation tend to mystify the power dynamics and the politics of confession? And, finally, what discrete forces foster this impulse to confess in the first place? Why not keep quiet?

For the very question of power is where all my reflections on confession—contemporary and historical, literary and otherwise—return. I want to underscore here the timeliness of this subject of confession in our culture that multiplies the occasions of personal disclosure with an astonishing rapidity, most recently on television talk shows and in the cyberspace of the Internet. It is by now a commonplace that we live in a confessional age, a narcissistic society where we confess and are bombarded with the confessions of others at every turn. I decided to locate my study of confession in the Victorian age, one celebrated, if differently, by both Foucault and Freud, as a historical era that reworked and expanded the institutional and discursive practices of confession from the church to medicine, law, urban sociology, and the family. This secularization of confession redistributed the church father's power to other patriarchs: the medical man, the solicitor, the criminal or sociological investigator, the father and the husband. But who and what were their confessional subjects?

My attention in this study fastens on the entwined issues of power and gender in Victorian representations of confession. If Freud's earliest psychoanalytic writings on hysteria address this interplay, so does Foucault's formulation of Victorian discourses on confession in *The History of Sexuality*. In terms of mid-nineteenth-century documents on confession, I turn to anti-Catholic propaganda chiefly because of its explicit engagement with questions of gender, sexuality, and power. While these accounts of lecherous priests who prey on young women within the hallowed walls of the confessional box are as "fictional" as the four novels whose confession scenes I also examine, all of these representations emphasize the ways in which power dons specific social features. In other words, confession never occurs outside of particular relationships marked by privilege and dependence, authority and vulnerability; confession is also discursively situated, framed within overlapping discourses.

For example, Victorian medical discourses on insanity undercoat the acts of transgressive disclosure on the part of heroines in the four novels I examine—*Villette, Lady Audley's Secret, Daniel Deronda, Tess of the d'Urbervilles*—whose confessions are also to be understood as narrations of truth. Such is the inconsistent condition of these women as confessional subjects, a paradox of Freud's speculative permutations, his divided explanations on his theories of seduction where female patients tell the truth of their sexual assault, but a truth to which Freud finally attributes—and then valorizes—psychological validity. I capitalize on this double rhetoric where truth is fiction, and fiction is truth, where confession is testimony, both self-incriminating and accusatory. Equity is a fiction, too, and the definitions and lines of power are more numerous, more intricate, and less stable than either Freud's theory of psychological power or Foucault's theory of discursive power allow.

In my analogies with contemporary popular culture in this retrospective on how I came to write a book on confession, I am also reminded of one of my favorite after-school entertainments, a television game show of the 1960s, *To Tell the Truth*. The program's chief appeal resided in its convincing performances of truth, not necessarily in truth itself, as two impersonators competed with the third guest, whose story all three must enact to persuade the celebrity panel to vote for them. I mention this program because in all of the representations of confession my book surveys and analyzes, the probity value is less important, less discernible, than the performative value, that is, the ways in which "truth" is displayed, the ways in which confession is syntactically and symbolically constructed.

I refer to this television show also because I want to recognize a connection between confession and pleasure, something that Foucault discusses. For Foucault, the power of the confessor who "questions, monitors, watches, spies, searches out, palpates, brings to light" affords an inquisitive pleasure. But such pleasure in confession is not wholly the reserve of the one who receives the secret. Foucault also asserts that the one confessing likewise derives enjoyment in the power of self-exhibition, the power of making scandal, of resisting normative behaviors. My own position on Foucault's observation that "perpetual spirals of pleasure and power" permeate confessional discourses on sex is far less sanguine, given that I am far more struck by the pain rather than the pleasure that attends the forms of domination that impinge on confessional subjects. Yet I still recognize a generalized pleasure in our culture that comes with watching and making confession, as long as confession remains a remote spectacle, where the viewer and the viewed are sufficiently cushioned from the powers of valuative dissection and correction.

I also want to make mention of recent popular culture because I had entertained a conclusion to this book that surveyed the construction of confessional subjects today, namely, the public obsessions with representing confessions of Amy Fisher, Tonya Harding, and Susan Smith, American women whose transgressions have earned them celebrity status in the media. Lady Audley in Braddon's Victorian sensation novel could easily be a precursor to these contemporary deviant women who assault or murder in order to protect what they envision as their most salient opportunities for monetary gain. In some cases, this material advantage is attached to heterosexual relations, to the economic and social status that a union with a particular man might offer. As Chapter 3 argues, this version of a crime of passion fits the case of Lady Audley, who attempts murder and commits arson, fraud, and bigamy in order to cling to a lifestyle of luxurious ease, one so different from her penurious childhood. But in other cases, Lorena Bobbitt, the twenty-four-year-old woman who in 1993 severed her sleeping husband's penis after being subjected repeatedly to his rape, is a more apt figure for stories of Victorian heroines who execute or fantasize about committing violent acts of retaliation against men who have abused their power over them. All of these examples call into question cherished notions about motherhood, about marriage and the unstinting sexual and emotional availability of the ideal wife, or her counterpart, the woman as whore. The important historical link here is that confessing women still involves a gendered and sexualized discourse of transgression and reprisal, as in Victorian England.

Instead of reworking these recent portrayals of confessional subjects— women who disclose violations and the substance of these misdeeds—I want only to gesture toward the analogy to suggest that the ambiguities of power surrounding acts of self-revelation in Victorian narratives have not been resolved by any means, even if the terms and degrees of the representations of transgressive women have shifted. George Eliot's novel is uncertain about whether the egotistical Gwendolen deserves the marital torture she endures under the dominion of her wretched husband, whether she deserves the plot's death-in-life sentence for her attempt to retaliate physically against Grandcourt's brutality. And what do we think about Susan Smith? How has the media construed her as both unredeemable villain, the premeditated murderer of her young children in order to snare the son of a wealthy man, and a much abused woman, the victim of incest and the casualty of a social services system that proved inept at helping her deal with such blatant travesties? Within these confessions of transgressions, therefore, are testimonies of wrongdoing directed against women often by virtue of the ways in which their gender is held hostage to privileges of masculine authority. I defer further analysis of the discursive forces that so shape the presentations of these modern-day confessional subjects to another place and time, as I turn instead to Victorian culture and its alloyed treatment of confession, gender, and power.

In reviewing the trajectories and tributaries of my thinking on this subject, I find I cannot offer a linear route of how I moved from "Confessing Lacan" to *Confessional Subjects*. Likewise, I am unable to provide a complete inventory of all the people and organizations facilitating my encounters with these questions on confession. This partial acknowledgment will have to suffice. To the Tate Gallery I am grateful for permission to use a reproduction of *The Vale of Rest* by John Everett Millais to grace the cover design of this book. An earlier version of Chapter 5 appeared as an essay, "Confessing and Editing: The Politics of Purity in Hardy's *Tess of the d'Urbervilles*," in *Virginal Sexuality and Textuality*, edited by Lloyd Davis and published by SUNY-Albany Press. To the Graduate School at the University of Wisconsin, I appreciate the financial support from summer fellowships in 1990, 1991, and 1993 that enabled my research and writing. In the spring of 1994 the Program for the Study of Women and Gender at Rice University provided me with a library and with colleagues whose participation in my colloquium on confession and gender aided me in reshaping the overall direction of this project.

Given the different permutations on confession I have pursued these past ten years, speculations that nourished the present book, my debts are as varied as the diversity of supports and challenges I received from teachers, colleagues, friends, and family. Those who either read portions of the manuscript at different stages or who discussed its issues include Helena Michie, Robyn Warhol, Allen Grossman, Kathryne Lindberg, Jill Dolan, Elaine Marks, Olga Valbuena, Martin Danahay, Mary Jean Corbett, Ellen Goodell Michel, Daniel Kleinman, Leora Zeitlin, Kathy Retan, Robbie Kahn, Daria Donnelly, Nora Mitchell, and Theresa Rebeck. Helena Michie merits particular thanks for introducing me to the pleasures of Pre-Raphaelite art on book jackets, for her careful critiques of the early embodiments of this study, and for generously revisiting it during my semester in Houston. To my dear friend Leora Zeitlin, with whom I first encountered the novels of George Eliot in college under our teacher Phebe Chao's guidance, I convey a special indebtedness for her meticulous reading of my chapter on *Daniel Deronda*; Leora offered crucial perspectives for understanding the complicated and conflicting histories that have constructed Zionism from the middle of the nineteenth century to the end of the twentieth century.

At the University of Wisconsin, I have been fortunate in my research assistants, David Welshhans, Celena Kusch, Cindy Hangartner, and Seanna

Oakley, all of whom eased the rigors of bibliographic detective work. My colleagues in Madison who deserve special recognition for their painstaking commentary on various portions and aspects of the manuscript are Dale Bauer, Sargent Bush, Betsy Draine, Susan Friedman, and Sarah Zimmerman. Throughout this undertaking, Dale Bauer's spirited readings repeatedly tested the clarity of my own convictions; I am also grateful to Dale for her confidence in the consequence of my essay "Confessing Feminist Theory," which, although not a formal part of this book, articulates a significant facet of my thinking on confessional rhetoric. Susan Friedman's support and ready counsel were matched by the wealth of her invaluable remarks, especially on Chapter 1. Sarah Zimmerman warrants my warm appreciation for her assistance in my most recent revisions of the manuscript; Sarah managed to read through chapter after chapter in fairly short order as she offered judicious comments that have aided me in bringing into full relief the connections between and across the specific instances of confessional subjects this book explores. I also thank Barbara Hanrahan, my editor at the University of North Carolina Press, for her extraordinary efficiency and integrity. Sian Hunter White and Alison Tartt carefully shepherded the book through the editing stages; my thanks to them. Marcia Reddick and Laura Stempl Mumford deserve my gratitude for their essential contributions during the final stages of preparation.

My ultimate recognition goes to my family: to my parents Barbara and Sidney Bernstein, whose lives did not extend long enough to witness the publication of this book, but who did mark with pride its early incarnations; to my brother Jonathan Bernstein, whose practical support has made this work possible, even a welcome distraction, at times when work seemed impossible; to my partner Danny Kleinman, who has given so abundantly to me during the making of this book, with tangible and intangible contributions ranging from tofu gumbo to taxonomies of confession; and finally to my daughter Flora Claire Berklein, whose expressed desire, at the age of three, to write her own book has been my most cherished compensation for all the doubts and misgivings—to confess momentarily—that have accompanied the intellectual joys of labor that somehow resulted in *Confessional Subjects*.

CONFESSIONAL SUBJECTS

INTRODUCTION

CONFESSION AND GENDER

A Process of Power

And yet what must be spoken must also remain secret. Isn't this contradiction one that
arises out of the . . . clos(et)ed space of the confessional discourse? It must not be spoken
everywhere, but is privileged by the coupled place of the inquisitor-victim, confessor-
confessant, analyst-analysand, master-slave. Isn't it this reversal of recent years that
now makes sexual discourse marketable and, perhaps in everyday life, liberating? . . .
Aren't the confessions of today made as much, if not more, for those in the position
of the dominated than for those in the position of domination?
—Frances Bartkowski, "Epistemic Drift in Foucault"

This book is a study of an array of Victorian disclosures about domination and
a method of reading I develop through a feminist theory of confession. My
epigraph from Frances Bartkowski's work on Foucault usefully underscores
the political contradictions of gender in the "clos(et)ed space of confessional
discourse." This "clos(et)ed space" of disclosure and concealment is also a
"coupled place of the inquisitor-victim," one that accentuates the heterosexualized power relations that so often frame acts of confession. Bartkowski
nonetheless allows for the restricted potential of confession as "liberating," as
a discourse "for those in the position of the dominated." Whereas confession is
a discourse of power, power is not necessarily and not only an adverse form of
domination. Indeed, Foucault suggests that power, as a mode of action, can
also mean an opening up of possibilities.

Throughout *Confessional Subjects: Revelations of Gender and Power in Victorian Literature and Culture*, I take the position that confession is largely a site
of coercion, especially given its early institutional authority, the father confessor. But I also contend that any system of domination is marked by contradictions, by points of inconsistency and ambivalence within a governing
ideology, within a pervasive scheme of representation. Viewing women as
"confessional subjects" exposes one of these discrepancies inasmuch as confession typically implies guilt and responsibility, a kind of dubious or con-

straining agency. In the larger cultural context of Victorian England in which women are not accorded by law or by custom much opportunity to act on their own behalf, such agency seems ironic at best.

Accordingly, I find confessional modes in general, as well as the specific Victorian scenes of confession I pursue in the following chapters, to be ambiguous with respect to a coherent political stance. By the same token, I am reluctant to schematize literary genres and narrative styles through the subversion/containment binary that has become increasingly prevalent in cultural criticism. This manner of reading, where literary texts exhibit signs of resistance to or compliance with mainstream ideology, masks rhetorical complications and political contradictions difficult to decipher through such easy oppositions.[1]

For instance, it would be reductive to estimate as either subversion or submission the blank space in *Tess of the d'Urbervilles* that figures the heroine's honeymoon confession of her sexual impurity, seemingly the consequence of an act of rape. As I shall explore later, issues of Victorian censorship and the conventions of audience and authorship shape, among other things, Tess's confession of sexual violation, a subject that is simultaneously represented and concealed. One value of this equivocal confession is its indication that any resistance—in this case, resistance to an overestimation of female virginity and an underestimation of sexual violence—is incomplete and fragmentary, an activity revealing the contrariness of power. Throughout this book I refrain from reading resistance per se in acts of women confessing, although I do recognize within these confessions elements of testimony or bearing witness to inequities that define the transgression and the transgressor and that compel and mediate confession itself.

Following Foucault, I see confession as an effect of power, "an obligatory act of speech."[2] At the same time, power is an effect of discourse; it can be located through the presumption of narrative authority, the ability to control and to circulate stories. Beyond Foucault, I ask how cultural constructions of gender, that is, the equation of domination with masculinity and submission with femininity, are embedded in the rhetorical folds of confession. For in Hardy's novel the silence of a female character's confession also bespeaks a masculine entitlement to write her history. Of a piece with Tess's foreclosed confession, her voice is quelled repeatedly beneath her husband's version of her autobiography. This crucial power dynamic directs my attention to the speculations of Foucault on confessional discourse.

By now, Foucault's formulations about sexuality—the discursive construction of sex—are well known; less rigorous attention has been paid to his theory of confession. By "confession" Foucault means that any narrative of transgression is a product of power, that it is never simply the unmediated outpouring of sin from the sinner to the absolver. To confess means to be folded into a network of surveillance and control in which the truth of the confession merely replicates the truth of domination. In order to understand this "truth," one must take into account social constructions of identity that bestow and curtail privilege. While I focus on gender and its social and symbolic meanings in my exploration of Victorian confession, additional facets of identity—class, nationality, race, sexuality, religion—figure into my readings. An abiding question of my study is how particular social categories of selfhood frame each act of confession, given Foucault's attention to power.

Foucault also stipulates that where there is power, there is resistance. If the act of confession signifies the working of power, what activity in relation to confession signifies a resistance to power? Is such resistance even thinkable given Foucault's panoptic model of domination that constitutes the discourse of confession? Is this equation of power and resistance a flimsy panacea in a theory that does not easily allow for concepts of agency, opposition, social progress? Such gendered arrangements of power inform the dyadic structure of confession itself between (female) confessant and (male) confessor, between the confessing subject compelled to narrate a story of transgression and the authorized audience of this tale who determines its meaning and the speaker's absolution, treatment, or punishment.

In therapeutic accounts of sexual violation a century ago—narratives that formed the foundation of Freud's so-called seduction theory—the analysts as well as the assailants were men. These male analysts likewise had the professional power to read and relay the confession, in other words, to preserve patriarchal privilege. Freudian readings of deviance characterized women patients as neurotics who either repressed erotic responses to male sexual aggression or who imagined their own desires in the form of fantasies of sexual overtures from, for the most part, fathers, brothers, or male acquaintances of the family. Much recent feminist work has concentrated on Freud's abandonment of his original seduction theory that held as actual events the sexual offenses Freud's female patients remembered through analysis. Nevertheless, the shift from reality to fantasy in the revised seduction theory did not disturb an emphasis that the patient was aberrant, a victim of some psychological pathology that turns mundane sexual episodes into nightmares.

In the decades of the nineteenth century prior to the advent of Freudian psychoanalytic theory, such narratives were practically unspeakable; a century later such narratives abound. Although it is tempting to see this distinction as a mark of social progress for women, I also see the proliferation of confession today as an effect of power whereby cultural forces permit and police representations of sexuality—specifically, the transgressions of sexuality that "confession" implies—into discourse. Perhaps it seems an anachronism to invoke the late-twentieth-century controversy surrounding recovered-memory therapies of sexual abuse to introduce a study of Victorian confession. Even so, the range of questions that structure this contemporary debate underpin representations of confessional subjects in nineteenth-century culture. In today's version, there seems more latitude for questioning "truth" and its construction: the truth of the therapist's practice, the truth of the client's memories, the truth of the imputed assailant's denial. As Leigh Gilmore usefully observes, confession, along with its production of truth, is a "relational" endeavor.[3] Ultimately, though, I am less concerned with the veracity of such narratives than with the consequences that these representations promote.

In the updated mode of confession known as psychotherapy, power dynamics continue to frame this form of truth production. A *New York Times Book Review* feature article on the "recovered" versus "false" memory syndrome controversy asserts that the truth status of such narratives as either memory or fantasy has much to do with what the reviewer calls "a process of influence."[4] The reviewer in fact understands this process through two commonplaces: people are susceptible to suggestion; people need to please an authority, to believe an expert, to submit to a master. Given that these narrated memories tend to feature younger females as victims of sexual abuse and older males as the violators, I prefer to think not in terms of a neutral "process of influence," but instead in terms of a gendered process of power. In other words, I place this debate today in the realm of Foucault's theory of confession, signification, and power.

No matter the social and legal differences between Victorian and contemporary conditions of women in western cultures, women's narratives of sexual offenses against them continue to function as "confession." Since confession typically means the revelation of one's own transgressions, how is it that such reports—what might otherwise be labeled "testimony"—persist as confession? Again, this qualification rehearses cultural arrangements of power that favor the stories of the empowered over the disempowered, or, for example, the privileging of men's words over women's. While there was considerable opposition to this perspective, Anita Hill's testimony in the U.S. Senate in the fall of 1991 was largely treated as confession, as the uncovering of her own psychological, moral, and political failings. Many interpreted Hill's narrative of her sexual harassment in the workplace by a man in a position of power as her own distorted fantasies of events that never occurred, the fabrication of a politically manipulated, sexually repressed, or "scorned" woman.[5]

This confessionalizing of women's accounts of others' sexual infractions seems remarkably similar to the recovered/false memory controversy, to Freud's seduction theories, and—as this project ultimately traces—to nineteenth-century narratives that transform the wrongs done to women into their own wrongdoings. As Jeremy Tambling remarks in a recent study of confession and literature, "In the confessional, the sins of women are always highlighted."[6] A crucial premise of this study of confessional modes and confessional sites in Victorian culture is that any attempt by the disempowered to describe abuses and violations on the part of the empowered gets locked into a system of confession whereby such disclosure itself becomes a violation, a transgression of propriety. From Victorian narratives and the case studies of Freudian psychoanalysis to more recent debates over stories of sexual abuse, narratives of male license at the expense of disempowered women continue to constitute a conflicted and contested discourse. Thus testimony starts to look like confession where the very act of telling becomes a transgression.

Confessional Subjects examines the cultural codes of gender difference that shape assorted confessional narratives. In organizing my study of confession around gender differences I also want to invoke Judith Butler's notion of "gender trouble." Butler argues against reifying the binary opposition of man / woman as she repeatedly theorizes the indeterminacy of gender across a range of discourses.[7] Moreover, Butler contends that the emphasis on simple gender divisions reinforces the structure of power relations where one gender and sexuality—masculinity and heterosexuality—is dominant, the "other" gender and sexuality—femininity and homosexuality—is subordinate. My reliance on the conventional gender binary in this study results from my overall definition of confession as a discourse that does fortify traditional structures of power in Victorian culture. The textual moments where a female character's confession poses a kind of challenge or testimony to forces of domination are often places where habitual notions of femininity seem to falter.

For the truthfulness of confession is complicated not only by the power relations that frame its production, but also by its representation of a transgression, one that implicitly or explicitly associates sexuality with violence in women's narratives. In Foucault's argument, sex furnishes "the theoretical underside of confession" to explain all manner of anomalies and transgressions of dominant ideology: "There was scarcely a malady or physical disturbance to which the nineteenth century did not impute at least some degree of sexual etiology."[8] For Foucault, sexual pleasure is confession's privileged topic. I maintain that in selected Victorian texts female characters confess acts figured as sexual because these acts encompass a struggle over domination. In the material I examine, the transgression that qualifies women's confessional modes is twofold: first, confession addresses the subject matter of female sexuality and desire; second, confession depicts domestic scenes of violence.

Let me elaborate on this focus on violence and on the domestic in scenes of confession. By "violence" I mean primarily acts of force, stark expressions of domination, sometimes with sexual implications. These acts of violence, like the confession scenes themselves, are inevitably tethered to the so-called private spheres of home and family, domestic spaces that reproduce cultural notions of social order. In three of the four novels I explore, female characters confess to male characters who hold a familial relationship, typically the most viable candidate for patriarch. These confessions of violence—from frenzied passions to physical brutality—occur in domestic quarters, that is, away from public scenes of confession like the church stall, courtroom, or medical examining room.[9]

Teresa de Lauretis has written that representations of violence and of the family are inseparable from notions of gender.[10] Drawing on the work of René Girard, de Lauretis observes that by definition of cultural standards, the subject of violence is masculine, the object of violence is feminine. A main concern of this project is the complicated rhetorical and political maneuvers by which a female character seems to occupy both positions of subject and object of violence. In the chapters that follow, I am interested in how women are held accountable in their narratives for acts of violence committed against them. To speak of "domestic violence" here might again seem an anachronism in the context of Victorian culture, yet I use these words to underscore the importance of the familial and the national, on one hand, and the structures of domination and subordination, on the other. For the instances of confession that I follow also encode wider cultural anxieties about the stability of masculine authority and feminine submission within the English home and nation; "domestic violence" is meant to invoke this uncertainty of larger power relations.

Perhaps the term "confession" itself seems historically misplaced in the Victorian era. The failure of the Oxford movement to reinstate Roman Catholic ritual in England suggests that confession is a rather un-Victorian activity. This repudiation also reveals a general cultural discomfort with overt self-expression and public display; such disavowal of the revelatory clarifies why confession scenes in Victorian texts frequently take on sensational rhetorical effects. In *Repression in Victorian Fiction*, John Kucich remarks on this antipathy toward confession as "the nineteenth-century cultural decision to value silenced or negated feeling over affirmed feeling, and the corresponding cultural prohibitions placed on display, disclosure, confession, assertion." Kucich's work on the specific meanings of "repression" in Victorian culture distinguishes "a general Victorian tendency to make matters of intense feeling—primarily, but not exclusively, sexual feeling—matters of secrecy and self-reflexiveness, and to withhold them from speech and action."[11] This position illuminates the heated agitation in mid-century England against Catholicism and its rituals of display and disclosure like confession. However, Kucich does not take into account class and gender politics that complicate such cultural repression and secrecy around "sexual feeling." For nineteenth-century repression not only functions as a psychological condition or an English middle-class manner of feeling and rhetorical style, but also constitutes a habitual silencing that safeguards patriarchal privilege. In this cultural sense, confession might be regarded as the spectacle of the repressed, the textuality of the silenced; in the context of Victorian culture, women's confessions are inevitably sensational narrative events, even if the content of the confession remains inscrutable.

Given the vexed nature of this Victorian discontent with expression and exhibition, Joseph Litvak's work on theatricality in the English novel provides a useful figure for the Victorian confessions that interest me here. Collapsing Foucault's distinction between a society of spectacle and a society of surveillance, Litvak combines these categories into "spectacles of surveillance" as he claims that as a society of surveillance, Victorian culture enacts its own spectacular practices.[12] I would portray each scene of confession in the chapters that follow—whether staged in anti-Catholic pamphlets or in domestic fictions—as a "spectacle of surveillance" that suggests the gendered parameters of home rule.

The succeeding chapters show how these contradictions frame women and sexual violence precisely as "confessional subjects." My readings attend to the social, psychological, and linguistic forces that constitute what I mean by gendered confession. Each chapter records the violence of confession itself, that is, the cultural offense of women narrating accounts of abusive power; each chapter also charts rhetorical disorders where confessional passages attempt to represent a sexualized transgression. While Victorian codes obscure the disclosure of sexual violence toward women in some of these narratives, each confession does trace the economic and psychological oppression of women. *Confessional Subjects* explores how women are positioned discursively as "confessional subjects," how narrative representations of violation necessarily subject women to authorized interpretations, readings that reproduce the network of social, political, and physical tyranny that foster these violations.

I survey a range of scenes of confession in four novels: *Villette* (1853); *Lady Audley's Secret* (1862); *Daniel Deronda* (1876); and *Tess of the d'Urbervilles* (1891). Only with *Villette* do I focus on a woman's confession that falls under the auspices of religion and beyond the boundaries of home; Lucy Snowe's confession is undomestic in two senses: its setting in a Catholic church and on foreign—that is, non-English—soil. Where this confession scene differs in kind from those in the later three novels, my treatment of it also differs since I read *Villette* primarily for its resonances with contemporary anti-Catholic discourse. I have chosen these four novels in part because their publications span the latter half of the nineteenth century, in part because they inscribe a trajectory from the prolixity of a sensation confession to the invisibility of a premodernist confession, in part because they demonstrate collectively how confession is a process of power where transgressions against women are depicted as women's transgressions. Of the four, only the most recent, only the one written by a man, distinctly deals with the subject of sexual violence, that is, Tess's confession of her rape. As a blank space on the page, the vexed representation of this sexual transgression illuminates the ideological and rhetorical contradictions of depicting such scenes of brutality. One might wonder why Tess's excised story of sexual violence against her is persistently labeled in the novel as "confession," something that implies her own culpability for an act in which she is overpowered.

Frequently the substance of the confessions made by female characters in the other novels seems unrelated to sexual transgression. Here it is useful to bear in mind that in Victorian culture any expression of passion is troped as sexual desire.[13] Such passion may be construed as a yearning for bodily ease, material comfort, or emotional sustenance; it may be portrayed as a craving for material finery like fancy dresses and jewels or a lavish meal or a spiritual soulmate; or it may be configured as an intense, even violent, opposition to prohibitions—often by men in familial positions of power—to these desires. Thus in *Villette* Lucy Snowe's confession to a Catholic priest marks an attempt to refuse the systematic repression of her passionate need for companionship. In *Lady Audley's Secret*, Lady Audley's confession of bigamy, among other crimes, is a protest against the miserable condition of women who are compelled to prostitute themselves through the legitimate sex market of marriage in order to secure material ease. In *Daniel Deronda*, Gwendolen's confession of a desire to murder her husband also discloses the sexualized violence of male domination in her marriage. The instances of confession that I explore in Victorian culture and fiction contribute to what Foucault terms an "endless mill" of talking sex; at the same time, they also pose uneven protests against sexualized victimage.

I would like to forecast and elaborate upon the diversity of my theoretical and methodological approaches to these Victorian texts. Since I define confession as a heterogeneous genre, a discourse that runs across different institutional spaces from the church to the family, from medicine and the law to the novel, I employ both historical and theoretical methodologies, always with an accent on gender politics. My overall approach is best described as theoretical; more specifically, I utilize deconstruction, Lacanian psychoanalysis, and feminist theories. Yet my readings also register the crucial importance of the historical and cultural conditions structuring these textual representations of confessions. The qualification Regenia Gagnier makes of nineteenth-century British autobiographies also applies to confessions inasmuch as both are "rhetorical projects embedded in concrete material situations."[14] Consequently, my opening two chapters lay the foundation for my use of theoretical models that elucidate the rhetorical structures of confession within a particular cultural framework. Chapter 1 focuses on the theoretical paradigms of Foucault and Freud; Chapter 2 situates the novels themselves within a mid-nineteenth-century cultural setting in order to better understand the political and social resonances embedded in fictional acts of confession. I want to stress at the outset that any historical analysis is meant to be suggestive rather than comprehensive. Much fascinating research, for instance, remains to be done on Victorian documents of women "confessing"—or testifying—across different discourses and institutional spaces, including courts of law and medical examining rooms.[15] While each of my chapters gestures variously—sometimes in more sustained ways, sometimes only fleetingly—toward history, this attention furnishes a critical backdrop for my overall emphasis on the symbolic, rhetorical, and linguistic dimensions of confession as a relational act of power.

As Mary Poovey has said, "Every text participates in a complex social activity," and this "cultural work" reproduces the abiding ideology of its social and historical context just as it also reveals the contradictions and "unevenness" within this dominant system of representation.[16] By attending to the multiple signifying effects of the texts I consider here, it is possible to chart how violence and women, how violent women as "confessional subjects," can be read as transgressive and as transgressed against. Because I am interested in signification and the construction of meaning in these scenes of confession, not as a unified process, but rather as complex and contradictory, and in excess of any presumed intention, poststructuralist theories inform my own reading practices here. As a whole, my explorations of four Victorian novels move from a predominantly historical analysis informed by theory with *Villette* and with *Lady Audley's Secret* in Chapters 2 and 3, to more sustained theoretical evaluations, yet accented by historical events, of *Daniel Deronda* and *Tess of the d'Urbervilles* in Chapters 4 and 5. By employing these different interpretive approaches, I more fully explicate the varied facets of the social practices of confession in Victorian culture, that is, its institutional, psychological, and linguistic aspects.

In Chapter 1, "Theorizing Confession, Gendering Confession," I both analyze the master theories by Foucault and Freud on Victorian confession and I assess these theories on discourse, sex, and power in terms of the unequal relations of gender. For Foucault, confession means the policing and subjugation of illicit sexual desires; for Freud, confession means the treatment and cure—that is to say, the liberation—of repressed sexual desires. For Freud, confession signifies a triumph over resistance and repression; for Foucault, confession is part of the paradoxical apparatus of repression itself. My particular concern here considers how each theorist constructs authority and power in the dyadic relationship of confessor and confessing subject. Since neither Foucault nor Freud explicitly considers the category of gender, I also contemplate feminist responses to these "master" constructions of confession; some feminists read confession as a possible site for protesting patriarchal force, while other feminists view the unlikelihood of such potential within a discourse so mired in advantages historically associated with men. In charting the gender politics of different theoretical paradigms of confession, this chapter also contemplates alternatives to the "containment versus resistance" dichotomy often featured in recent cultural criticism. Here I explore the possibilities and liabilities of redefining confession as "testimony," a form of self-disclosure that carries some promise of the rhetorical agency and opposition available to speaking subjects.

My approach in Chapter 2, "Histories and Fictions of Victorian Confession," is informed by the interpretive strategies of new historicism and cultural criticism. Working chiefly with historical materials lambasting Catholic confession in mid-century England, I explore ways propaganda against the Roman church characterized the enterprise of confession as an assault on the sanctity of English domesticity. Framed by the Oxford movement and the advent of Freudian psychoanalysis, the Victorian era witnesses the dispersal of confession so that virtually any narrative of transgression can be labeled "confessional." While the first chapter addresses confessional discourse through the medical institution of psychoanalysis, this chapter focuses on troubling depictions of Catholic church confession in the Victorian imagination. To draw a connection between popular representations of confession and nineteenth-century gender ideology, I explore anti-Catholic narratives circulating around Great Britain at mid-century that construe the confessional booth as a scene of violation where women are seduced, raped, and otherwise initiated into sexual service by father confessors. Granted the fictional, contrived, and motivated nature of these—or any—confessions, the anti-Catholic representations of the confessional also highlight a recondite cultural truth: the inevitably sexualized nature of female domestic servitude to male economic, social, and physical might.

An emphasis on female social, material, and sexual vulnerability in scenes of confession informs the analysis that follows of the four Victorian domestic novels. Taken together, these readings explore female characters as confessional subjects who are variously regarded as immoral, insane, rhetorically inexplicable. Embarking on explicitly fictional accounts of women as confessional subjects, I conclude Chapter 2 through a consideration of Brontë's *Villette*, in which Catholicism functions, according to British domestic ideology, as a mixed trope for illicit sexual and self-expression. By the same token, the unchecked license to intimacy of the father confessor serves as a vehicle to critique patriarchal domestic—both British and familial—power.

Chapter 3, a reading of confession in Braddon's sensation novel *Lady Audley's Secret*, studies the way Lady Audley's confessional narrative both deploys and critiques the tropes of deviant femininity most prominent in Victorian culture: the madwoman and the prostitute. To bring out the figure of the prostitute embedded in Lady Audley's confession, I juxtapose contemporary depictions of prostitution in England drawn from mid-century sources, including articles in the *Westminster Review* on the public debate over prostitution and Henry Mayhew's interviews with London prostitutes published in the *Morning Chronicle*. While this sensation heroine confesses her own transgressions, her story also situates her depravity in the context of the economic and social subjugation of a lower-class woman. The language of "fallenness" in Mayhew's investigation of prostitution and in Braddon's sensational confession scene illuminates the material conditions implicit in Victorian notions of degenerate femininity. This sensation novel's spectacular confession of Lady Audley's overt criminality offers a dramatic contrast to the covert and conflicted confessions of female characters in the later Victorian fictions of Eliot and Hardy. Whereas Lady Audley does confess to bigamy, arson, and murder, the confessions of Gwendolen, Leonora, and Tess are far more recondite, their agency as transgressors less evident than the domestic violences against them that these oblique confessions uncover. Given the rhetorical complications of these confessional modes, I utilize poststructuralist theories in these later chapters to explore the symbolic dimensions of gendered domination.

In the fourth chapter I scrutinize the ideological work of subjection in women's confessions of marital and maternal transgressions in *Daniel Deronda* in contrast to a different and empowering confession enacted between men, that is, Daniel's testimony of religious faith. The confessions of Gwendolen Harleth and Leonora Halm-Eberstein unfold scenes of male domestic domination—the physical, psychological, and economic tyranny of husband and father—begetting the violence of female defiance. With George Eliot's trademark in what has become known as psychological realism, I follow Lacan's symbolic operations of power through the paternal metaphor in my attention to the twin confessions that display the spectacle of two female characters' interiority. I use the Lacanian concept of the paternal metaphor, or symbolic domination, with inflections from Foucault's theory of signification and power to demonstrate how gendered domination works best through substitution, absence, and invisibility. To historicize the gendered power dynamics behind both women's confessions of familial subjugation, I locate the current event of the Jamaican uprising of 1865 to which Eliot alludes as an extended metaphor for the domestic terrorism that tacitly undergirds Gwendolen's marriage and sparks her confessed desire to murder her husband. At the same time, I show how ideas of race inflect Eliot's notion of a national inheritance encoded in the scenes of Jewish confession of faith between men, testimonies of identity that lead to the removal of the Jewish characters from England altogether.

Continuing with this interest in the metaphorics of power that structure women's confessions, Chapter 5 explores the ideological and rhetorical complications of representing the subject of sexual violence in *Tess of the d'Urbervilles*. Where both women's confessions and transgressions in *Daniel Deronda* are cryptic and convoluted in contrast to Lady Audley's adamant self-expression and agency, in Hardy's novel we witness a spectacular vanishing point of women as confessional subjects. Mirroring Tess's agency in her rape, Tess's confession is negated, foreclosed from textual representation, yet its rhetorical and narrative effects are prodigious. I also consider how Hardy's treatment of Tess's rape bolsters a relationship between the corrupt text, marred by editorial demands, and the fallen Tess, a correspondence Hardy's prefaces to the different editions of the novel encourage. Tess's account of her rape, registered through a textual void, conveys the cultural prohibition against a woman narrating sexual transgressions, regardless of whether she is the agent or the object. In part this proscription accounts for the slippage between rape and sex, between testimony and confession, where a woman's rape inevitably sexualizes her—and where she is held responsible for this illicit sexuality—so that a narrative of this event necessarily constitutes a confession. Again, this transformation illustrates the cultural contradictions of confessional discourse that assigns Victorian women moral responsibility without agency.

Since power mediates both textuality and sexuality, the chapter investigates an analogy between Hardy's prefatory claims about his text's purity and the novel's claim of its heroine's purity despite, respectively, editorial and sexual defilements. This avowal is anchored in a metaphor of power that Derrida labels "white mythology," the assertion of a natural, intrinsic state prior or external to forces of domination. Hardy's rendition of such a mythology of purity—whether textual or somatic—attempts to separate power and sexuality from Tess's rape and its consequences.

As a whole, these chapters demonstrate the complexity of power relations, particularly in relation to social differences, embedded in Victorian domestic confessions. Beyond this focus on the ways gendered confession reproduces and reveals cultural configurations of domination and subordination within familial relationships, my readings survey the rhetorical complications of representing violence through acts of confession and testimony. One of the reasons I find "confession" as a notion drawn from the religious ritual significant is its stress on the institutional and political structures that shape acts of witnessing transgression. At the same time, the coordinates of confessor and confessee, authorized audience and speaking self, are crucial to bear in mind in any examination of subjectivity. Here I again note the twofold meaning of "confessional subjects" that my title suggests: the gendered subjects of women confessing and the substantive subject of confessing violations.

It is especially valuable to work through the intricacies of these Victorian confessional modes and moments because the diverse ambiguities surrounding this form of self-representation persist into the late twentieth century. The range of possible rhetorical positions and representational opportunities for confessional subjects in Victorian texts—from anti-Catholic invectives against confession as a site of sexual crimes against women to Lady Audley's explicit confession of reprisals against material and social oppressions to Tess's obliterated and appropriated narrative of sexual violation—have proliferated in recent times. Today we have confessional occasions in a vast variety of television talk shows, in a plethora of magazines and memoirs that capitalize on confession's interest in the sensational. Again, these media spectacles of confession both expose and generate violation and violence, such as the murder connected to an episode on *The Jenny Jones Show* in March 1995 when a gay guest confessed his "crush" on a heterosexual and homophobic male friend who subsequently killed him.[17] Such events again remind us that confession is a spectacle of surveillance, one that reinforces the dominant forms of subjectivity and polices the deviant.

As debates over recovered-memory therapy demonstrate, the political contradictions of confessing transgressions continue today. For it is possible to read the articulation of such "recovered" memories both as resistance to power and as submission to the heavily policed technology of confession orchestrated by a confessor-therapist in compliance with larger arrangements of authority circulating in the culture. In light of this attention, Victorian culture provides a resourceful realm for exploring the gendered dimensions of confession. Inhabiting a pivotal historical position that bridges religious and secular discourses, these accounts reveal the gendering of interpretive power, the difficulties of representation, the discursive displacements of sexual violence. On one hand, these Victorian narratives suggest that stories of transgression can impart a recondite testimony. On the other, these stories make manifest that responsibility and agency are often at odds where women are compelled into the events for which they are held morally, socially, and psychically accountable. My perspective revises this constraining agency of confession with an affirmative activity of testimony. Bringing social history, theories of power, and materialist feminist theory to bear on depictions of confession, the following chapters explore how these contradictions frame women and sexual violence as "confessional subjects."

THEORIZING CONFESSION,
GENDERING CONFESSION

The confession is a ritual of discourse in which the speaking subject is also the
subject of the statement; it is also a ritual that unfolds within a power relationship,
for one does not confess without the presence (or virtual presence) of a partner who
is not simply the interlocutor but the authority who requires the confession.
—Michel Foucault, *The History of Sexuality*

The woman is not the agent of any institutional power. She has no authority either to
exact penance or to interpret the situation according to norms that could, in effect,
increase the prestige of the institution she represents, hence her own prestige.
—Sandra Bartky, *Femininity and Domination*

To theorize confession from the vantage point of the late twentieth century
requires an encounter with its two master theorists Michel Foucault and Sigmund Freud.[1] For Foucault, confession means the police; for Freud, confession
means the talking cure. For Foucault, confession guarantees ideological control; for Freud confession overcomes psychological repression. Thus, according to Foucault's scheme, confession by any name at all—the religious sacrament of Catholic confession, the so-called unconscious discourse that emerges
through psychoanalysis, the medical history of the examining room, an admission of guilt extracted by a representative of the law—is still a form of subjugation. But in Freud's account, the divulgence through psychoanalysis of traumatic memories, often of sexual transgression, spells psychic liberation.

Despite these discrepancies, both Foucault and Freud understand confession as a dialogic event that occurs between confessor and confessant,
analyst and analysand.[2] In this interchange, both theorists assign enormous

power to the position of the confessor, "the interlocutor," as Foucault stipulates in the epigraph above, "the authority who requires the confession." Yet neither theorist explicitly considers the cultural components of this domination. Given that historically men have filled the shoes of confessors and that too often women are disempowered even before entering the scene of confession, one might well ask how the genders of confessor and confessant amplify or diminish the process of power that the confessional act unfolds. In what ways do these master theories of confession overlook, dismiss, or ignore such cultural configurations of power?

Another correspondence between Foucault and Freud is that both identify sex, particularly whatever is considered pathological, perverse, or illicit, as the privileged subject of confession. Foucault claims that especially in the nineteenth century "the principle of sex as a 'cause of any and everything' was the theoretical underside of confession." Allowing that this sexual etiology sometimes seems a bit overstated, Foucault theorizes that Victorian discourses on sexuality, chiefly Freudian psychoanalysis, understand the "ways of sex" to be obscure and obdurate, a kind of "principle of a latency intrinsic to sexuality." Such latency justifies techniques of extraction whereby the retrieval of confession becomes a modern, "scientific" practice.[3]

While sex seems at the root of all confession, the formulations of sex and sexual "pleasure" in Foucault and Freud are often oblivious to differences of male and female sexuality, that is, to the social differences that construct such divisions of sexuality and gender.[4] Yet these are cultural distinctions of power. As Gayle Rubin observes, "Sex is always political." In contrast to this idea that sex is mediated through the politics of historically specific institutions and cultural practices, Rubin defines sex essentialism as "the idea that sex is a natural force that exists prior to social life and shapes institutions" and that sex is "eternally unchanging, asocial, and transhistorical."[5] Neither Foucault nor Freud supports sex essentialism explicitly in their theories of sex; neither do they offer sustained critiques of the ways standards of sexuality are intertwined with cultural constructions of femininity and masculinity. The very category of sexual "pleasure" must be regarded in relation to not simply some vague idea of power but to historical and cultural manifestations of power relations like gender.

Foucault's Confession: Whose Power? Whose Pleasure?

Foucault's first volume of *The History of Sexuality* offers the most extensive theory of confession since Freud.[6] Reversing historical chronology, I begin with Foucault because of my interest in the relations of power that pattern confession, an interest that Foucault specifically addresses. Foucault defines the discourse of confession as an effect of power so that confession is "a ritual that unfolds within a power relationship." For Foucault, confession is a disciplinary device, an injunction to render into language what is often culturally unspeakable: "one confesses one's crimes, one's sins, one's thoughts and desires, one's illnesses and troubles; one goes about telling with the greatest precision, whatever is most difficult to tell." The conventions of confession typically define the "unspeakable" as sex. One feature of confessional discourse is its tendency to sexualize any transgression or aberration, to subsume any violation under the master category of sex. In Foucault's model, the deeds and desires of the flesh—what Foucault also refers to as "pleasures"—constitute sin and require surveillance and punishment.[7]

Why is sexual pleasure critical to Foucault's theory of confession? The "truth" of the disciplinary subject floats through this discourse on sex: confessions of the body serve as an index to character and individuality. Nonetheless, the emergence of this "truth" is an effect of power relations, something Foucault emphasizes repeatedly. The meaning of this "truth" is imposed by the confessor, the authority who enjoys interpretive privilege, and by the institution that frames the confession, an establishment of which the confessor is an agent. As a cog in this machinery of the power/knowledge complex, the "yoke of confession"[8] functions as a vise on the wayward social subject who may speak but cannot authorize this confessional narrative of sex.

Foucault stipulates that the act of confession itself is an act of power. Such deployment of power can be invisible where the confession seems to be freely given or it can be manifest where a confession is clearly a consequence of force: "When it is not spontaneous or dictated by some internal imperative, the confession is wrung from a person by violence or threat; it is driven from its hiding place in the soul, or extracted from the body."[9] Thus power in confession functions from below or above; it appears to be initiated by the confessant alone or it is externally exhorted and extorted by a confessor and by the institution under which confession is enforced.

For Foucault, the nineteenth century marks a watershed in the history of confession as an act of power. During this period with the secularization of confession through medicine and psychoanalysis, the scope of confession expanded from what the confessant knew and kept secret to "what was hidden from himself, being incapable of coming to light except gradually and through the labor of a confession." The confessional subject may speak a narrative of sex, but cannot authorize its meaning. Instead, the confession emanates from the body, from the unconscious, and, most significantly, from the confessor who is entitled to define the speaker of the confession: "Causality in the subject, the unconscious of the subject, the truth of the subject in the other who knows, the knowledge he holds unbeknown to him, all this found an opportunity to deploy itself in the discourse of sex."[10]

If this power that compels confession can be invisible, the force of the confessor can be silent: "the agency of domination does not reside in the one who speaks . . . but in the one who listens and says nothing." Foucault suggests here that domination is complete when it requires no visible effort to reinforce itself. The confessor is the actual agent of confession but the confessing subject appears to engine the self-regulation that absolution confers by virtue of simply making the disclosure: "the expression alone, independently of its external consequences, produces intrinsic modifications in the person who articulates it: it exonerates, redeems, and purifies him; it unburdens him of his wrongs, liberates him, and promises him salvation."[11]

The preponderance of masculine pronouns attached to the confessant in this passage inadvertently marks a gender difference that Foucault otherwise overlooks; confession is seldom so restorative for women. Certainly Foucault understands confession as a corrective measure that is effectively a form of ideological laundering, but my point here is that techniques of containment function differently for those outside the purview of a dominant social identity. Although Foucault acknowledges a heterosexual or straight-sex imperative to the policing of sexual pleasure through confession, he is often inattentive to an untroubled masculine standard that informs this theory. In *The Use of Pleasure*, the second volume of *The History of Sexuality*, Foucault does recognize that a masculine perspective dominates "the history of desiring man": "an ethics for men: an ethics thought, written, and taught by men, and addressed to men. . . . A male ethics, consequently, in which women figured only as objects."[12] Yet in the first volume, where his theory of confession is most fully diagrammed, this bias is implicit, a partiality that Foucault's own viewpoint shares. The salubrious effects of confession that Foucault lists may rehearse abstract assumptions about how confession is supposed to operate, about how it polices even as it appears to pardon. How might such suppositions differ in an analysis that underscores the gendered implications of a theory of confession where "women figured only as objects"?

According to Foucault, confession plays a crucial role in constructing and producing sexuality, in determining the standards of pleasure. Observes Foucault, "A dissemination . . . of procedures of confession, a multiple localization of their constraint, a widening of their domain: a great archive of the pleasures of sex was gradually constituted." Drawn from examinations of the bodies of the criminal and the diseased including prostitutes and hysterics, this "great archive" furnishes the material for sexology research. Male sexuality supplies a tacit standard, but female bodies stock the annals of medicine with data to determine pathology and degeneracy. Foucault refers to the "hysterization of women" as the displaced site of confession through the medical diagnosis of their bodies "as being thoroughly saturated with sexuality."[13] Through symptoms culled from examinations of women's bodies, medical men construct women's confessional narratives of sexual desire, sexual pleasure, and sexualized, unfeminine aggression. In other words, as Linda Williams remarks in her study of pornography, "techniques of confession . . . [were] applied first and foremost to female bodies."[14] Throughout the nineteenth century the "truth" of the subject is increasingly located through detailed visual investigations of female bodies.

I would like to turn now to Foucault's phrase "pleasures of sex" because it highlights a contradiction in his theory of confession. On the one hand, the confessional archive collates research on women's bodies; on the other, this investigation of the "pleasures of sex" presumes a masculine sexual teleology, what Williams calls the "hydraulics" of male desire. Foucault's repressive hypothesis unmasks the paradox of so-called Victorian prudery, whose effect is to channel sex into specialized discourses of confession. Yet this same precept also suppresses gender, sex, and class differences in the structure, substance, and outcome of confession.

The reason for this silence hinges on Foucault's concept of power; it is ubiquitous, affecting all disciplinary subjects alike, permeating all institutions without discriminating specific political agents: "There is no binary and all-encompassing opposition between rulers and ruled at the root of power relations."[15] With no central location, power is irreducible so that it is impossible to locate domination in gender relations. Even within the family, Foucault equivocates on the issue of power and thus fails to distinguish the political dimensions of familial roles. There is no subject outside or above Foucauldian power, a corollary in its totalizing scheme to the Freudian unconscious. Nancy Hartsock aptly axiomatizes Foucault's program, "Power is everywhere, and so ultimately nowhere."[16] Power seems to render all subjects agentless; all subjects are subjected to this power that seems, for all intents and purposes, to smack of transcendence. In fact, Foucault replaces the notion of subjectivity with the idea of the individual as an effect of power relations; neither does he define these power relations nor refine any differences between the ways individuals are constructed through them. Foucault's theory of power does not consider social categories like gender that are organized according to unequal power relations.[17]

For instance, what constitutes "pleasures of sex" has everything to do with power, with the way power encodes notions of gender and sexuality. Yet in Foucault's analysis of confession, sex—like power—is everywhere and nowhere, pervasive but unspecific. An anecdote from *The History of Sexuality* illuminates this elision in Foucault's theory of confession, power, and sex. Foucault tells of "a farm hand . . . somewhat simple-minded" who "obtained a few caresses from a little girl" in the form of "the familiar game called 'curdled milk.'" Foucault argues elsewhere that there is no outside to discourse, specifically to confessional discourses of sex, and that power functions through discourse. Nevertheless, in this account Foucault romanticizes "inconsequential bucolic pleasures" as "timeless gestures," as a carefree game routinely played by "village urchins" before the intrusion of the disciplinary, confessional discourses of sex, as if such "pleasures" endure separate from language and power. Assailing "the institutions of knowledge and power" for encumbering "this everyday bit of theater with their solemn discourse," Foucault laments such discursive interventions on "these barely furtive pleasures between simple-minded adults and alert children." At the same time, Foucault seems oblivious to his own deployment of pastoral discourse that glosses over the gendered power relations between the "farm hand" and the "little girl" of his story.[18]

In my reading of this anecdote I do not uphold the idea that sex is inherently dangerous—what Rubin calls "sex negativity," although admittedly sexual power, like any form of domination, can be deleterious.[19] Nonetheless, I think Foucault's tale of "inconsequential bucolic pleasures" does beg for commentary on the relationship between power, gender, and confessions of sex. Just as sexual practices are not natural or intrinsic, just as their representations do not exist as "timeless gestures" outside historical and social forces, pleasure is never "inconsequential" to power. This narrative of "the familiar game called 'curdled milk'" troubles Foucault's notion of evanescent power if one wonders whose "bucolic pleasures" this game serves. And once the role of domination is recognized, these pleasures can hardly remain "inconsequential."[20]

Foucault does acknowledge the power of class in this little narrative of sexual pleasure between an itinerant field laborer and a girl whose family clearly enjoys some economic stability by virtue of their alliance with the local authorities: "So he was pointed out by the girl's parents to the mayor of the village, reported by the gendarmes, led by the gendarmes to the judge, who indicted him and turned him over first to a doctor, then to two other experts who not only wrote their report but also had it published." Foucault's point here is to demonstrate the transformation of something like pure sex—those "timeless gestures"—into detailed documentation and analysis of illicit activity and medical pathology authorized by various institutions and discourses. The story is meant to condemn structures of confession that put sex into words as a ploy of power, in this case, the power of class. Yet Foucault mythologizes this scene as a benign, innocent, "everyday occurrence in the life of village sexuality." By doing so he overlooks other configurations of social power such as gender and age as well as the authorizing gaze of his own discourse that frames the description in the first place.[21]

Confessions of sex are not necessarily confessions of pleasure, especially when one takes into account social categories defined through domination and subordination, the very political arrangement that structures confessional discourse itself. Although Foucault recognizes religion and psychoanalysis as discourses that normalize sexual desires, he does not regard standards implicit in his own descriptions of sexuality. Given that confession reinforces power relations, it is no wonder that the "truth" of identity coincides with the identity of power: the subject that confession affirms is implicitly gendered masculine and heterosexualized male.

For both Freud and Foucault, as Williams puts it, "the confession of pleasure is organized according to male norms," criteria measured by "the frenzy of the visible."[22] Foucault affiliates visual surveillance, classification, and management of the body with the speaking of sex through confessional discourse. Accordingly, confession is part of a larger technology of self-regulation in which the organizing semiotic is the panopticon, a mechanism of visual power that is simultaneously omniscopic and invisible. While the role of the visible figures in Freudian concepts such as the "castration complex," in the process of psychoanalysis Freud stresses the forceful function of hearing, the auricular dimension that distinguishes religious confession as well. In addition, the surveillance system of confession as a form of policing in Foucault's work shifts with Freud to psychoanalysis as a form of curing.

Psychoanalysis and the Modern Confessor

Foucault's theory of confession is evasive on the question of whose power and whose pleasure is at stake. Although Freud seems to offer more pointed and direct answers to such inquiries, there are also contradictions in the way he formulates power and sexuality in the confessional site of the consulting room. For patriarchal power and masculine pleasure loom large in Freudian psychoanalysis. As one example, his construction of the oedipal complex makes evident the tremendous significance that the power of fathers assumes in psychic life. But in many instances power is attributed ambiguously, an equivocation that obfuscates encounters between analyst and analysand, between confessor and confessant.

In this secularized version of auricular confession the position of power is clear. The analyst constructs the repressed story of sex from the fragmentary traces—parapraxes, dreams, so-called "free" associations—the confessing subject provides. Even so, Freud theorizes complications in this distribution of power through the concept of countertransference, which puts in question the construction of confession as wholly the story of one subject. In this sense, psychoanalysis seems to underscore a collaborative condition of confession itself, whether between confessor and confessant, between what is conscious and unconscious, between institution and subject, or between competing discourses. Despite this theoretical acknowledgment of the diverse ways confession may be constituted, Freud persistently asserts that the professional analyst is the most privileged authority to interpret it.

Although Freud maintains that the work of psychoanalysis differs significantly from the religious ritual of confession, it is interesting that he himself first poses the resemblance, then urges the distinction repeatedly. In fact, the salient difference between Freud's "listening treatment" and Catholic auricular confession rotates around the very idea of power. Freud makes clear that the psychoanalyst's ability to read confession outstrips the father confessor's, that the analyst is by far the master confessor. The earliest associations between psychoanalysis and religious confession appear in "Studies on Hysteria," a series of essays Freud compiled with Josef Breuer from 1893 to 1895.[23] Having worked through a discussion of "hysterical conversion," the displacement of an affective thought onto somatic phenomena, Freud then emphasizes the compulsion to speak as "the normal, appropriate reaction to excitation caused by very vivid and irreconcilable ideas." Freud continues: "We meet the same urge as one of the basic factors of a major historical institution—the Roman Catholic confessional. Telling things is a relief; it discharges tension even when the person to whom they are told is not a priest and even when no absolution follows. If the excitation is denied this outlet it is sometimes converted into a somatic phenomenon . . . *hysterical phenomena of retention*." In this passage, Freud is building an analogy between his burgeoning practice and "a major historical institution" of confession. However, he indicates that neither priest nor penance is necessary for the chief benefit of confession to occur, for the "relief" that comes with "telling things."[24]

On the one hand, these words seem to suggest that no particular confessor, neither priest nor analyst, is required in this act that fosters mental and physical health. Instead, "telling things" to a "person" is rendered as natural as breathing air. On the other hand, the analyst's abstraction here as "person" is noteworthy when one considers that an analyst is in fact authorizing the analogy. This gap manages the psychoanalyst's quiet, invisible usurpation of the priest's role, with his interpretations replacing religious penance and absolution. After all, power is implicit in the very terms in which "telling things" is couched, since what constitutes "a normal, appropriate reaction" is a function of prevailing cultural conventions. The passage obscures external coercion with the notion of an internal or psychic "urge." By the same token, the abstraction of "telling things" elides the volatile subject of so-called abnormal sex, the content of the confessions to which Freud turns his masterful ear. This double use of abstractions affiliates power with sex in the correlation between Catholic confession and Freudian psychoanalysis.

Sex and power might seem muted beyond recognition in this passage, but traces of the standards of sexual pleasure and power supporting Freud's theory are still discernible. The release of pent-up tension describes what Freud elsewhere terms "abreaction," a crucial ingredient in Freud's system of the psyche.[25] A masculine erotic encodes this orgasmic depiction of abreaction that "discharges tension" so that "excitation" gains an "outlet." In this way even the act of "telling things" begins to resemble a sexual act based on male norms.[26]

The illustrations in "Studies on Hysteria" that follow this association between disclosures in the Catholic confessional and "telling things" in the consulting room expose the politics of gender that shape stories of sexual violation. These narratives, a series of miniature case studies, not only support masculine conventions of heterosexual behavior but also treat differently male and female subjects of such confessions. First, Freud describes an anorectic boy who does not eat, who vomits, and who finally relays in psychoanalysis an incident in which a man asked him to perform fellatio in a urinal: "He had run away in terror, and nothing else had happened to him. But he was ill from that instant. As soon as he made his confession he recovered completely." The next example involves a seventeen-year-old girl who "had her first hysterical attack . . . when a cat jumped on her shoulder in the dark. The attack seemed simply to be the result of fright. Closer investigation showed, however, that the girl, who was particularly good-looking and was not properly looked after, had recently had a number of more or less brutal attempts made on her, and had herself been sexually excited by them."[27]

Attributions of agency and accountability in these twin cases that demonstrate confession as cure reveal gendered assumptions about power and sexuality. No matter how provisional this position of action, the boy does "make [made] his confession," while the girl's story of transgression is absorbed into an agentless "closer investigation." The boy is granted, at the very least, grammatical agency in relation to his narrative in contrast to the girl's complete effacement in this regard. However, it is the girl who is tacitly held responsible for the sexual aggressions that befall her because she is "particularly good-looking"; her complicity with these violations is further implied in the assertion by the analyst that she "had herself been sexually excited by them." In the homosexual advance made by the man in the urinal, the agent of the transgression is stipulated, but this does not follow in the case of the girl. In fact, there is not a direct reference to the perpetrator of the violation or to its exact nature, which is equivocally described as "a number of more or less brutal attempts made on her." Instead, the language of this description locates the violence in the illness, in the "hysterical attack," rather than in the doubly suppressed "attempts" that precipitate it. The boy is accorded some agency over his confession, but none whatsoever in the sexual incident that occasioned his illness, a transgression clearly assigned to the man—homosexual by implication—in the urinal. The girl is silenced in the construction of a story of transgression, a transgression that is ambiguously attributed to herself. The unspoken standard of sexual behavior operating in these two case studies seems based on a heterosexual male model with the presumption that a girl both provokes and sexually enjoys "more or less brutal" aggressions.

During this period before 1897, Freud still regarded the repressed narratives, mostly drawn from women hysterics who claimed that they had been sexually transgressed, as historically true, although even then he privileged "psychical" over "material" reality.[28] As the preceding example illustrates, Freud was not interested in assigning responsibility to the ungendered aggressors of his female patient. Nor was he concerned with the question of sexual travesty or violation itself in these narratives of so-called "seduction" that surfaced in the course of the analysis. His field of attention encompassed and categorized psychic reactions to material sexual assaults. After 1897, with the invention of his concepts of infantile sexuality and the oedipal complex, Freud viewed sexual assaults, what he construes in the previous illustration as "more or less brutal attempts," as psychic phenomena as well. A widespread reading of Freud's "abandonment" or "revision" of his so-termed seduction theory is that this switch from material to psychic reality, a propensity evident even before 1897, served to safeguard the untoward authority of men, whether fathers or others relishing familial, social, and economic powers.[29] I mention this amplification of the seduction theory in the context of Freud's explicit comparisons between psychoanalysis and Roman Catholic confession because the later distinctions he draws between the two institutions accord increasingly greater powers to the psychoanalyst, to himself, the father of the latest innovation on the institution of confession. I am suggesting a correlation between Freud's articulated augmentation of the psychoanalytic confessor and his tacit protection of patriarchs.[30]

Some decades after the essays on hysteria that Freud co-authored with Breuer, Freud again distinguishes his practice from the religious sacrament. In "The Question of Lay Analysis" (1926), subtitled "Conversations with an Impartial Person," Freud reiterates the rule that the patient "keep nothing back intentionally that comes into his head, and then to put aside *every* reservation that might prevent his reporting certain thoughts or memories."[31] On this list of secrets to be disclosed are "intimacies," or what one would withhold from other people, as well as "other things that one would not care to admit *to oneself.*" The patient must adhere to "the demand made by analysis that he shall say everything."

At this point, the "Impartial Person," the imaginary partner in Freud's dialogic description of psychoanalysis, likens this command to speak secrets to religious confession. The narrator, the spokesman for psychoanalysis, responds: "We must reply: 'Yes and no!' Confession no doubt plays a part in analysis—as an introduction to it, we might say. But it is very far from constituting the essence of analysis or from explaining its effects. In Confession the sinner tells what he knows; in analysis the neurotic has to tell more. Nor have we heard that Confession has ever developed enough *power* to get rid of actual pathological symptoms."[32] The initial ambivalent response to the equation between Catholic confession and psychoanalysis resembles what Freud elsewhere calls the hysteric's "strange state of mind" where "one knows and does not know a thing at the same time."[33] To the extent that the paradox of this emphatic "Yes and no!" suggests hysterical discourse, this equivocal gap disguises the power over sexualized secrets that psychoanalysis asserts over the confession ritual of church fathers. After all, who determines the "thing" that "one knows and does not know"? The passage insinuates that religious confession bears only subordinate, superficial proximity, an "introduction. . . . very far from constituting the essence," to analysis.

The critical distinction here depends on the assertion that the sinner confesses what he knows, but "the neurotic has to tell more." This compulsion to "tell more" is both an effect of what Freud theorizes as the unconscious and a rule of the analytic session, "the demand made by analysis that he shall say everything." The domain of psychoanalysis and the sway of the analyst inscribe a much vaster empire than that of Catholic confession. If "the neurotic has to tell more," then certainly the analyst has to hear more, to know more, than the confessor. That this difference Freud inserts between confession and psychoanalysis concerns the mightier capacities of the latter emerges in the passage's concluding sentence whose implication is that psychoanalysis does have "enough power" because it cures "actual pathological symptoms."

Indeed, the changes in Freud's treatment of hysterics trace a movement from overt to covert means of coercing stories of sex. At first, hypnosis induces typically women hysterics to disclose a narrative of transgression, whether in words or acted through bodily poses, while under a trance. When Freud substitutes the dialogic talking cure, he first practices the "urging" method, probing patients for details about sexual fantasies. To facilitate the retrieval of this material, Freud incorporates physical contact, a technique of lightly touching his subject's forehead to capture "forgotten memories." Finally he arrives at free association: "Instead of urging the patient to say something upon some particular subject, I now asked him to abandon himself to a process of *free association*."[34] The patient is no longer put into an altered state or pressed—verbally or bodily—into talking about unpleasant or dangerous topics like sexual violation. Rather, the patient is required to yield to psychoanalysis, "to abandon himself to a process," a phrase that implicates the talking cure as a version of sexual seduction. The analyst's role might seem more passive, less intrusive. Yet this procedure in which the patient "abandon[s] himself" (or herself) to the analyst's decree to "say everything" expedites the uncovering of resistance, something necessary for excavating secrets, for bringing so-called unconscious material to light. This contradiction of posturing the analyst as active and passive, as—to use two of Freud's tropes—the surgeon's knife and a big ear, only masks the considerable powers that Freud elsewhere bestows on his medical science of confession.[35]

As a confessional institution, psychoanalysis reigns supreme; it is the substance, the thick volume to which confession is merely the "introduction." It has "enough power" to compel the neurotic to tell more than "he knows." It can even banish "actual psychological symptoms." When the "Impartial Person" submits to this explanation of a distinction between these competing versions of speaking transgression, the "Person" attributes the power to the analyst, not the institution or practice: " 'But I can well believe that as analyst you gain a stronger influence over your patients than a Father Confessor over his penitents, since your contacts with him are so much longer, more intensive and also more individual, and since you use this increased influence to divert him from his sick thoughts, to talk him out of his fears, and so on.' "[36] Where the analyst of the consulting room enjoys "a stronger influence" over patients than a Father Confessor does over penitents, the basis for this advantage depends on circumstances that accumulate into something like scenes of seduction, occasions of dubious persuasion. Not only are "contacts . . . so much longer, more intensive and also more individual," but also "this increased influence" empowers the analyst to "divert" the patient and "talk him out of his fears, and so on." In Freud's dialogic promotion of his dialogic practice, the indeterminate "and so on" forms another hysterical gap, a symptomatic gesture of ambiguity in the discourse of the "Impartial Person." The vestiges of professional propriety waver behind this discursive uncertainty, behind the unaccountable power, the unnarratable outcome of "this increased influence." The "stronger influence" of the psychoanalyst arises from his magnified scope of visual, aural, and silent sources of knowledge.

Armed with the cognizance of unconscious processes, the analyst becomes a detective par excellence, as Freud himself suggests: "He that has eyes to see and ears to hear may convince himself that no mortal can keep a secret. If his lips are silent, he chatters with his finger-tips; betrayal oozes out of him at every pore."[37] Not unlike Foucault's concept of the panopticon, the very conditions of psychoanalysis intimate an invincible structure of power exemplified by the analyst's collaboration with the patient's unconscious.

If Freud repeatedly implicates this power dynamic in the scene of psychoanalytic confession, Jacques Lacan explicitly masculinizes the concept of power in language and culture. According to Lacan's rereading of Freud, "the phallus is the privileged signifier."[38] In other words, meaning and authority in psychic life, in symbolic representation, defer to the masculine. Although Lacan asserts that this paternal power is illusory, he still insists on a remarkably unified, pervasive, and ahistorical construction of the function of the father. Thus Lacan theorizes the oedipal dialectic in terms of the father as law, as primary metaphor, as the gaze. Given Lacan's emphatic presumption of paternal authority, the psychoanalyst as *father* confessor, as phallic power, seems more compatible than Freud's disclaimers would allow.

Redirecting the Powers of Confession:
Feminism and Resistance

Freud's theory doesn't mince words about the superior powers that psycho-analysis and the analyst maintain in contrast to those of Roman Catholic confession and the father confessor. Foucault also recognizes confession under any institutional banner as a discourse of power. Yet Freud justifies this use of force in order to combat illness, despite the fact that the social construction of mental illness with which he argues is clearly an effect of power as well. To Foucault, however, confession is always an act of discipline and subjection, a discourse whose policing of sex guarantees domination, even if he is unclear about the makeup of this domination. For Freud, confession, as articulated knowledge of one's sexuality, is a form of self-empowerment; for Foucault, power constructs such confessional knowledge of oneself. For Freud, concealment and repression of sexuality disempowers the self as it constitutes psychic disorder; for Foucault, putting sex into discourse is part of an extensive, institutionalized network to police human behavior.

When one begins to inspect the nature of this power, to consider the social configurations of gender, for instance, that particularize confessors and confessional subjects, a series of questions arise. Given the male standards that implicitly define sexuality and power for both Foucault and Freud, can confession ever be empowering for, say, women? Are there ways to explore sexual identification, victimization, empowerment that aren't immediately rein-scribed within this web of policing, curing—that is, normalizing—the subject? Can confession function as resistance to, instead of containment of, a dominant ideology, a broad, systematic representation of power, gender, and transgression? Can narratives of transgressions that might be socially disempowering for the confessional subject—such as rape or incest—also emphasize usefully wrongdoings perpetrated against rather than by her? In other words, what is the relationship for feminist inquiry between confession and testimony, between repeatedly shoring up domination and attempting to rehearse its opposition by bearing critical witness to that domination?

To approach these questions, I want to consider various feminist responses to discourses of confession; some of these feminist negotiations are specifically referenced to Freud or to Foucault; others treat the politics of confession more generally. Such a survey of confession in terms of gender and power necessarily embarks on the subject of resistance, particularly since feminist theory is a discourse of resistance, a refusal of patriarchy, of unequal power relations based on gender. Are confessional subjects also subjects of resistance? In order to theorize resistance in the context of confessional discourse, I briefly revisit Freud and Foucault.

In Freud's theory of psychoanalysis, resistance is the formidable stumbling block to the therapeutic cure, a forceful phenomenon against which "the doctor must be distrustful and remain on his guard."[39] Resistance opposes the normalizing process of the psychoanalytic cure. In "Studies on Hysteria" Freud describes the analyst's efforts to dismantle the patient's resistance as if it required a military operation: "We can think of attacking the resistance before us afresh. . . . We force our way into the internal strata, overcoming resistances all the time."[40] Requiring belligerent force to oppose it, Freudian resistance is patently an illegitimate, pathological power.

According to Freud, resistance is part of the illness, an agent of the repression that has brought the patient to the scene of psychoanalytic confession in the first place. But "resistance" also encompasses any criticism of the analyst's interpretation, so the attempt to refuse this institutional discourse is subsumed under the category of pathology. In "Resistance and Repression," Freud categorizes the patient's "criticisms and objections" as "intellectual resistance": "It now appears as an intellectual resistance, it fights by means of arguments and exploits all the difficulties and improbabilities which normal but uninstructed thinking finds in the theories of analysis. It is now our fate to hear from this single voice all the criticisms and objections which assail our ears in a chorus in the scientific literature of the subject. And for this reason none of the shouts that reach us from outside sound unfamiliar. It is a regular storm in a tea-cup."[41]

The concept of resistance for Freud becomes a way to dismiss any objection to the analyst's reading, to Freud as master confessor of narratives of transgression, as diagnostician of the transgression.[42] This passage associates such "shouts" from inside the consulting room—the patient's resistance—with those from "outside," from "the scientific literature." In either case, this resistance is trivialized as "a regular storm in a tea-cup." Without resistance there would be no illness, no necessity for this medical version of confession. Resistance is what both compels and opposes the cure, the psychoanalytic intervention.

As for techniques to "overcome" resistance of woman patients to "erotic trains of thought," Freud implies in "Studies on Hysteria" that the physician must offer himself up as a "substitute for love": "I have already indicated the important part played by the figure of the physician in creating motives to defeat the psychical force of resistance. In not a few cases, especially with women and where it is a question of elucidating erotic trains of thought, the patient's co-operation becomes a personal sacrifice, which must be compensated by some substitute for love. The trouble taken by the physician and his friendliness have to suffice for such a substitute."[43] The passage suggests that resistance to speaking sex—confession's mainstay—can be undermined through the medical man appearing to be a surrogate lover, "a substitute for love." The gender politics of this scheme for "defeating" resistance seems dubious at best. Once again, resistance affords a pretense for exerting whatever powers an analyst might be able to marshal.

Unlike Freudian resistance as pathology, Foucault sees some redeeming, progressive potential in resistance, although he is hard-pressed to chart its appearance. For Foucault, resistance is a curious phenomenon that exists as both corollary and subordinate to power: "Where there is power, there is resistance, and yet . . . this resistance is never in a position of exteriority in relation to power." Because power is pervasive, Foucault argues, an absolutely binary relationship between ruler and ruled, between power and its opposition is inconceivable. As a result, Foucault imagines "a plurality of resistances" rather than an organized, consolidated resistance: "mobile and transitory points of resistance, producing cleavages in a society that shift about, fracturing unities and effecting regroupings, furrowing across individuals themselves, cutting them up and remolding them, marking off irreducible regions in them, in their bodies and minds." Like Foucault's notion of power, this passage suggests that resistance, with its "mobile and transitory points," is everywhere and nowhere. Despite this general ambiguity, Foucault's qualification of resistance implies its possibility, its location through the contradictions or "cleavages" of power.[44]

How does the idea of resistance as relational function in the context of confession which, as an activity of power, is also relational? How do feminists theorize resistance in relational terms? In the last decade, several feminists have addressed the question of confession and gender in the accents of Foucault's theory of discourse and power. Leigh Gilmore, whose study of women and autobiography argues that confession is the foundational discourse of self-representation, situates her understanding of confession in terms of Foucault's relational notion of power. Reluctant to grant confession for women oppositional value, Gilmore maintains that confession produces gender as a "truth effect," that is, confession reinforces sanctioned forms of femininity and masculinity. But at other points in *Autobiographics* Gilmore is able to defer this hesitation as she also views various confessional modes as "a canny raid on the discourses of truth and identity," something that suggests that confession can also launch smart skirmishes on the "truth effect" of gender.[45]

Other feminists are more eager to envision rhetorical resistances to a Foucauldian idea of confession. For Mary Lydon, feminist resistance to confession takes the shape of silence and equivocation. Reading Foucault's theory of confession in terms of gender relations, Lydon draws a connection between "the inquisitorial gaze" of the confessor whose privileged object is a woman's sexual body and "the clinical gaze" of contemporary Irish Catholic bishops who impart detailed information about female reproductive processes.[46] These church confessors disclose the "secrets" of female sexuality and thus control the interpretation of women's bodies. Consequently, Lydon recommends silence and semiotic evasion as subversive strategies for women to circumvent the power of confessors over narratives of sexuality.

Lydon's revision of Foucault on confession is important inasmuch as she recognizes the gendering of power relations between church fathers and confessing women, a disparity Foucault neglects. Even so, I am less enthusiastic about silence and rhetorical circumlocution as resistance, as would-be subversion of patriarchal power. The formulation suggests a kind of paradox: resistance implies agency; silence, at the very least, conceals agency. A recommendation of silence in place of confession only reasserts the blank spaces of women's stories, which others in privileged positions in relation to discourse can exploit by inserting their own versions. The distinction between silence as compliance and silence as resistance seems tenuous at best.

Not unlike Lydon's advocacy of semiotic evasion to forestall the knowledge/power machinery of male domination, some feminists even regard confession as a form of resistance. According to Hélène Cixous, confession promises to liberate female sexuality from phallocentric imprisonment. Cixous celebrates the female body as a revolutionary confession, as transgressive language that threatens to dismantle patriarchal hegemony: "Let the priests tremble, we're going to show them our sexts!" The "sexts" of écriture féminine supposedly diminish father confessors—and the prodigious institutions they represent—to mere quivering creatures. Cixous imagines an alterior space for "the impregnable language" of female confession that somehow escapes the gendered power relations structuring confession in the first place. This idea turns the pathology of Freudian resistance into an estimable insurrection. Consequently, Freud's famous hysteric is transformed into a radical and deconstructive feminist, her symptomatic body into sheer art: "You, Dora, you the indomitable, the poetic body, you are the true 'mistress' of the Signifier." Rather than the priest's mastery of women's bodies and words, Cixous's feminism extols Dora as the evasive, subversive "mistress" of language. Of course, Cixous usurps the role of the father confessor, the psychoanalytic patriarch, by herself mastering Dora's hysterical body with her own theory of narrative transgression.[47]

My own reservations with this rendition of feminist resistance begin with the problem of converting pathology—no matter how problematic its construction—into heroism. Whether elliptical or overt, whether a narrative of oppression or liberation, any confession is inevitably assimilated through relations of power. The institutions of confession channel the so-called secrets of women's bodies into a master narrative of sexual transgression. Yet Cixous's feminist imperative likewise excavates a mistress narrative from an untroubled essential truth that female bodies supposedly speak. These two positions on confession—as ultimately tyrannical or as vitally emancipatory—

are not as divergent as one might expect or wish, something Sarah Kofman suggests by using the tropes of Foucault to read the contradictions of Freudian theory for women: "the analytic treatment cannot be seen as a simple restitution of a woman's right to speech; it is also an attempt to 'tear' from them their secret, to make them 'admit' or 'confess' . . . an attempt not to give them speech but to extort speech from them. Woman is not only a patient, a hysteric; . . . she is always also a criminal, and the psychoanalyst is a policeman on the alert for the slightest clues that may betray her, or at best he is a *father confessor*."[48] Rather than viewing the hysteric of psychoanalysis as a potential idol of feminist subversion, Kofman makes patently clear here that women as confessional subjects are also objects of domination to be disciplined and punished.

Frances Bartkowski sees contemporary proliferations of confession, that is, narratives of sex, as a way of redefining the relations producing this discourse and as a way of establishing a dialogue between resistance and power. But "confession" always signifies a disclosure framed by the power structure of confessor/confessant; it recuperates any resistance into the master discourse of confession, a point Bartkowski also makes: "The confession of which Foucault speaks at length is an attempt to give voice to the resistance: yet what we (readers/confessors) hear are not the voices of women, children, homosexuals, perverts, but the voice of power as it institutionalizes, rationalizes, domesticates, and suppresses those very discourses by which it shores itself up." The possibility of resisting confession, of confession as a politically progressive form of resistance, seems more than unlikely given the prevalence of "the voice of power" over other voices.[49]

Likewise Biddy Martin finds little hope of liberation in confession as Foucault theorizes it. Nevertheless, Martin sees Foucault's work as a useful correction on some feminist confessions, the so-called transgressive narratives of cultural feminism that reify and celebrate the essentialism of female language, body, culture, knowledge: "Foucault's deconstructive methodology provides an immanent critique of a search for *the* authentic female voice or *the* sexuality, a warning against the commitment to any confessional mode as necessarily liberating, and a challenge to the notion that simply speaking or writing frees us in any simple way from patriarchy or phallocentrism."[50] As I have discussed elsewhere, confessional modes in contemporary feminist theory are self-proclaimed textual moments that contend to challenge the sovereignty of male (that is, objective, distant, abstract) academic discourse. Too often, these feminist first-person disclosures reinforce discursive power relations where a woman's "personal" knowledge replaces male authority but without due attention to the contingent, relational accents of this knowledge and to the rhetorical construction of the subject of this knowing.[51]

Despite this disavowal, I return to the question of whether confession can function as "resistance," whether it can effectively protest social injustice. After Foucault, I understand confession as a discourse of power and as a rhetorical process of assimilation of the transgressive into the normative. As such, I have difficulty envisioning its potential as political resistance to domination, as an act that threatens or alters existing structures of power. The frequent aspiration within recent literary studies to locate a progressive political impulse gravitates toward the search for the "subversive" that I have been scrutinizing. Regrettably, this desire usually resorts to a simple, fixed demarcation between power and resistance, between ideological containment and subversion, a tidy arrangement that Foucault's theory dislodges.

Notwithstanding all these disclaimers, I still hold that the promise of resistance is crucial to any engagement with issues of inequality and social change. If resistance cannot be neatly characterized as a coherent opposition to domination, likewise power cannot be depicted as an invariable force. In the context of a feminist project, "resistance" might mean nothing more ambitious than a determination to view women as active subjects.[52] But in terms of confession, the confessional subject's agency is questionable by definition. Nevertheless, one can imagine within a discourse that typically disempowers women a limited space for a different, contradictory narrative, one of witnessing acts of domination to which the confessional subject is subjected.[53] Rather than unalloyed resistance, I am envisioning a provisional and provocative attention to the power relations that pattern authority and that preserve an arrangement of privilege and punishment. By the same token, I want to move away from the stringent binary of containment/opposition whereby either a text is reductively dismissed as a tool of ideological control or, through some interpretive somersaults, the text is valued as a species of revolution.

As Susan Bordo usefully observes, resistance is contextual, historical, and social. In her direction against a "postmodern inclination to emphasize and celebrate resistance," Bordo warns that this tendency to romanticize the cultural challenge that texts pose only deflects attention from "continued patterns of exclusion, subordination, normalization."[54] In addition, Bordo qualifies Foucault's correlation of power and resistance as a description of social relations rather than a recipe for reading texts. And yet the conflict suggested by these social relations can materialize as a struggle over contrary forms of representation. After all, if the division between power and resistance is difficult to draw, the distinction between text/context, between discourse and social world is equally ambiguous.

Recognizing the political significance of preserving the possibility of resistant activity, if not pure resistance, I suggest that narratives of transgression present descriptions of domination that might be starting points for questioning the rhetoric and structure of power. It is here that I would like to consider the act of witnessing, something to which the term "testimony" rather than "confession" typically refers. Embedded within confession is at least the potential of testimony whereby the confessional subject describes vaster social inequities as well as the transgressions of others, those in positions of authority whose violations are most often construed as prerogative. In the discourse of confession, typically the speaker is the transgressor; in the discourse of testimony, usually the speaker is an onlooker, sometimes a witness to a crime committed against oneself or against those sharing the speaker's social identity. While "transgressor" suggests a position of action and "witness" one of passivity, testimony also upholds the idea that witnessing is an activity as well. Of course, the very notion of confession as a testifying act is preserved in the meaning of religious confession of faith rather than the confession of sin that governs the kind of discourse that Foucault critiques.[55] Such witnessing activity is not unencumbered by the politics of rhetoric, by cultural and historical forces of influence that shape any depiction.

It is possible to imagine an agency that is enabling even if framed by the limiting discursive and institutional structures of confession itself. Judith Butler's meditation on epistemological descriptions of gender identity embarks on a theory of agency useful to my purposes here. Taking into account its rhetorical construction, Butler understands agency in relation to the regulated and repetitive process of signification: "'agency,' then, is to be located within the possibility of a variation on the repetition."[56] In terms of gender ideology, Butler designates parody as the most advantageous mode of this modification on the reiteration of dominant ideas of gender identity. I want to retain Butler's model of an agency that constrains at the same time as it opens up "the possibility of a variation" on the redundancy of power relations that mark women as confessional subjects. Parody suggests a pointed revision on a subject. By the same token, testimony can be considered a perspective different from—but related to—confession as the act of making disclosures of trangressive acts.

Although I want to inflect a feminist theory of confession with the idea of testimony, I continue to use "confession" as a way of underscoring the networks of power that encompass any act of self-disclosure. By shuttling between "confession" and "testimony" I mean to complicate the either/or critical template on power relations so that a confessional subject is not only subdued and passive. Gilmore asks, "How does one confess an experience and subjectivity that are not fully assimilated to the rhetoric of confession?"[57] I would elaborate on this observation by asking: Within confession, what rhetorical positions or narrative movements suggest a different story, one that exceeds the folds of the official version of dominant ideology that confession rehearses? How might ideas of testimony open up ways to explore this possibility?

Confession as Testimony: The Power of Witnessing

In pursuing the relationship between testimony and confession, Shoshana Felman and Dori Laub's *Testimony: Crises of Witnessing in Literature, Psychoanalysis, and History* is illuminating. This collaborative study, written by a literary critic and a psychoanalyst, addresses the crucial roles of memory and testifying in relation to the Holocaust, a radical crisis in witnessing. Alive to the political components of testimony, Felman and Laub question the complicated affiliations between history and text, between a historical event that systematically destroyed its witnesses and various attempts to preserve through representation this catastrophic transgression. In building their theory of testimony, the authors repeatedly draw on a concept of confession. At times, the two terms seem to be synonymous, at other times, distinctly divergent. In the preface, for instance, Felman and Laub coordinate "the impossible, unspeakable confession" of Holocaust survivors in the film *Shoah* with the *"liberation of the testimony* from the bondage of the secret."[58] Confession is mute, silent, secret; testimony breaks the "bondage" of this silence and liberates the unspeakable.

In the chapters that Felman authors, she further distinguishes and valorizes testimony over confession. Confession is a complete, closed process with resolution through absolution; it "pretends to reduce historical scandals to mere sense and to eliminate the unassimilable shock of history." In contrast, testimony, although a "discursive practice," is "not a completed statement, a totalizable account" but rather where "language is in process and on trial." Felman stresses the fragmentary nature of testimony as "bits and pieces of a memory that has been overwhelmed by occurrences that have not settled into understanding or remembrance . . . events in excess of frames of reference." Unlike confession, testimony opposes legitimatizing, naturalizing discourses; it is radically "other," unassimilable into dominant modes of narrating experience. Felman also defines testimony as a transformative activity rather than as a systematic, conventional, and recuperative discourse such as confession: "The testimony is itself a form of action, a mode not merely of accounting for, but of going through, a change: as opposed to a confession, the meaning of the testimony is not completely known, even by its author."[59]

This last qualification about testimony's uncertain meaning sounds perilously close to Freud's own assertion that "the neurotic has to tell more" than what he knows, than what the confessant says in the religious ritual. As the book's subtitle announces, Felman's perspective on testimony is informed by psychoanalytic theory, that is, with a deconstructive turn to the unassimilable, unspeakable nature of bearing witness. Using the manifest/latent distinction that Freud makes in his theory of dream interpretation, Felman labels as "confession" the explicit narrative of the patient, while "testimony" refers to the unconscious material that surfaces in the course of the psychoanalytic dialogue. In this scheme "unconscious testimony" is privileged over "manifest confession"; testimony is defined as the radical displacement of confession. Consequently, the concept of "unconscious testimony" is a revolutionary contribution: "Psychoanalysis, in this way, profoundly rethinks and radically renews the very concept of testimony, by submitting, and by recognizing for the first time in the history of culture, that one does not have to *possess* or *own* the truth, in order to effectively *bear witness* to it; that speech as such is unwittingly testimonial; and that the speaking subject constantly bears witness to a truth that nonetheless continues to escape him, a truth that is, essentially, *not available* to its own speaker."[60]

I find this theory of testimony resourceful for alternative readings of confession, yet I have a few caveats to offer. It seems naive to rely on a psychoanalytic confidence that a would-be unconscious "truth"—whether the truth of historical acts of genocide or domestic acts of violence—will eventually come out in broad daylight without taking stock of the ideological and discursive forces that package such truths for widespread consumption. Absent from Felman's account is an analysis of power relations that organize acts of testifying, just as they do acts of confessing. If a witness is not capable of "possessing" or "owning" the truth of her experience, who is qualified to read this surprisingly uncomplicated sense of "truth"? The implication is that an institutionally authorized reader, trained in psychoanalytic theory, holds the power of interpretation over these crucial acts of witnessing traumatic violence.[61] But what is the nature of such institutional and discursive authority that can confer meaning on or determine "a truth that is, essentially, *not available* to its own speaker"? What is politically, rather than psychically, radical about a theory in which truths are "essentially" and emphatically inaccessible to the one who is positioned as witness? On the one hand, Felman seems to preserve the progressive capacity of witnessing by labeling it a "transformative activity." On the other hand, she repeatedly emphasizes the "unwittingly testimonial" character of speech and writing, a qualification that forecloses the possibility of agency and directed social protest. Privileging "unconscious" testimony does not acknowledge the cultural and symbolic structures of power that inevitably read and ratify such testimony.

Like Freud's neurotic, "speech" and "the speaking subject" may say more than it or she knows, but one must not overlook that such constructions still presume a subject of *more* knowledge without taking to task the basis for determining this superior knowledge. I realize that my formulation here of "a subject of more knowledge" paraphrases Lacan's epithet about transference-love in the consulting room where the patient views the analyst as "the subject presumed to know" ("le sujet supposé savoir"). As I have argued earlier, despite Lacan's attempt to destabilize all placeholders of power—

including the position of psychoanalyst—such masculine-inflected domination prevails in his account of subjectivity. I uphold the critical importance of gendered subjectivity, both feminine and masculine; yet any concept of subjects of knowledge must ponder the forms and relations of power determining such knowledge.

Whereas the confessor's power is tacitly gendered a masculine prerogative in the theories of Foucault, Freud, and Lacan, for Mary Daly testifying is a patriarchal privilege that women simply cannot share. Daly's brief reference to testifying occurs in the context of a discussion of Patty Hearst's trial in which her testimony had no validity without "male corroboration." With her trademark panache for lexical archaeology, Daly explores the etymology of "testify" from the Latin "testis," meaning to witness; at the same time, Daly observes that "testicle" is likewise from "testis." The significance of this linguistic coincidence, Daly concludes, is that "since women do not have testicles, they cannot really be qualified to testify—give evidence—in patriarchal courts." Despite Daly's resort to biological essentialism here, she does acknowledge the social conditions of power that mediate the act of bearing witness.[62]

Daly's point here is especially relevant to the nineteenth century, when women were usually not accorded the institutional authority to license them to grant religious absolution, to make a medical diagnosis, or to deliver a legal verdict. Women could confess, that is, they might testify against themselves, but rarely did they have the requisite cultural power to effectively bear witness. By the same token, for Sandra Bartky woman as confessor is a political oxymoron. Bartky's interest in confession focuses on the "emotional labor" of women's caregiving in which they are positioned culturally as consolers and nurturers rather than identified with the law or as authorized readers. Whether as confessional subjects or as audience for a man's confession "in the case of heterosexual intimacy," women are disempowered by the act of confession.[63] Accordingly, Daly and Bartky find testimony and confession to be acts in which women are forced to replicate their disenfranchised social status.

Bearing in mind these various feminist rejoinders on the gendered power relations that structure notions of testimony and confession, I would like to enlarge upon the more vital aspects of Felman's work. Of particular consequence is the potential political value of bearing witness to what is often rendered unspeakable or unnameable. Patterns of domination and rhetorical forms for representing disempowerment are historically and culturally variable. To delineate crimes of sex against them was typically unspeakable for Victorian women; to articulate such offenses continues to be, at best, a troublesome affair today. Such silence is habitually reasoned as part of a cultural trope of modesty, a British and privileged-class reserve on private or domestic matters. Yet given the negligible legal, political, and economic status of women throughout much of the nineteenth century, any semiotic stuttering on sexuality, domesticity, and violence seems feasible, whether or not it is deliberately drawn. In this light, Felman's idea of testimony, of witnessing heinous wrongdoing, as "not completely known, not even by its author," makes sense. By imbricating confession and testimony together, I mean to highlight the political dimensions that inevitably mark and constrain any embattled agent of documents—and here I make no distinction between so-called factual and fictive texts—of injustice. Nonetheless, the idea of testimony conserves the possibility of agency that both Foucault's and Freud's theories of confession undermine or disband altogether.

For Felman insists that there are always witnesses to historical occurrences even if atrocities like the Holocaust are intent on silencing and destroying such observers. In this sense, Felman stresses the violence of witnessing violence. Defined as an open-ended process, however, witnessing cannot ultimately be quashed. Like the Freudian unconscious, testimony "oozes out" despite efforts to repress a transgressive history. As a result, Felman sees the prospect of testimony everywhere, "implicated—sometimes unexpectedly—in almost every kind of writing."[64] By association, a confessional narrative—one that discloses the speaker's transgression—can also encode a witnessing narrative—one that unveils outrageous events of which the speaker is simultaneously positioned as overwhelmed victim and as vigilant narrator. To maintain that testimony is inherently incomplete allows space for divergent accounts, for competing perspectives. This possibility is useful to my way of understanding confession as a discursive site at which emerge varying vested interests in defining the transgressor, the transgressed, and the transgressive.

One of the most recent versions of the genre of witnessing political crimes is *testimonios*, narratives about egregious acts of power perpetrated across Latin America. This testimonial literature begins the work of replacing the politically unspeakable with "voices for the voiceless," a counterdiscourse to official, canonical representations of western colonialist culture.[65] Of particular interest, these *testimonios* tend to come from women, like Nobel Prize–winner Rigoberta Menchú, an Indian peasant whose story witnesses the government-sponsored violences against Guatemalan poor people.[66] And the power of the *testimonios* often reside in their painstaking details of the domestic devastations—the murders of children, mothers, the literal destruction of family and home—that these war crimes inflict. Like confession, *testimonios* are the consequence of a dyadic process between the confessional subject and an interlocutor, usually an ethnographer who assumes the role of editor or "midwife," as the literature occasionally terms this woman collaborator. Rather than reinforcing dominant modes of behavior and identity, in this case the midwife-confessor supposedly assists the speaker in exposing the transgressions of the governing against the governed, the brutalities of the dominant against the subordinate. Despite this charitable attempt to give prominence to the story of the individual whose testimony is in part her life story, the term "midwife" does not altogether disguise the fact that the *testimonio*, like confession, is still a mediated discourse where issues of cultural and linguistic authority emerge in complicated ways.

Perhaps a more significant divergence between western confessional narratives—religious and secular—and Latin American testimonial literature is the concept of subjectivity; for *testimonios* replace an emphasis on the spiritual, moral, and psychological condition of a discrete individual with the embodied and embattled welfare of an entire group of people. In this sense, *testimonios* are class-action documents speaking for the collective despite the designations of a particular proper name or historical person. Testimonial literature transforms objects—the marginalized or voiceless—into subjects as it also revises the very idea of the rhetorical and autobiographical subject.[67] This narrative form also attributes agency in redressing wrongdoing to those who are typically disempowered by virtue of the iniquities they recount.

In reading domestic scenes of transgression in various Victorian texts, I emphasize the ways in which the genre of *testimonios* functions as a rejection of master narratives.[68] As I draw on *testimonios* as an evocative genre for my own theoretical transformations of Victorian confessions, I also acknowledge some important differences. Testimonial literature is regarded as true and truthful; my angle on confession finds truth-value in representations of domestic violence, but does not engage in distinctions between truth and fiction per se. The designation of *testimonios* as "postfictional discourse" is suggestive in this regard because it gestures beyond and yet also embeds the idea of fiction.[69] *Testimonios* also have specific cultural roots in oral storytelling, unlike the confessional discourse I consider, yet this medium of communication that falls outside official channels of information is crucial to what I describe as "testimonial moments" and "testimonial margins" within confession. By testimonial moments and margins I mean the possibility of a rhetorical switchboard between the power of domination and an inchoative, contesting vantage point on narratives of transgression. I eschew "resistance" here because I am seeking something less discretely organized and articulated, whereas "moments" and "margins" impart the fleeting and limited nature of protest that such occasions of testimony signify.

Assembled in this chapter are many questions about confession and testimony as liberating, oppositional phenomena, particularly when gender is sifted into the power equation. To talk about confession and "resistance" in the same breath requires some acknowledgment of the liabilities of such struggle, given the way confession as a discourse and as a cultural institution tends to reinscribe authority and subjugation. Testimonial moments and margins recommend some kind of active motion on the part of confessional subjects even if to label such textual activity "resistance" seems implausible. Although I take issue with the psychoanalytic logic behind Felman's notion of "unconscious testimony," I would in any case like to maintain the idea of a *latency* of testimony—margins and moments of testimony—embedded within confession, particularly confessions of those who are disempowered, those who are culturally prohibited from speaking a different "truth." I understand the latency of these moments and margins to mean that which is provisional, partial, occluded.

I also appreciate that reading an underside or latent narrative of testimony alongside a confessional one cannot produce a unified and controlling "truth." Instead, such contingent testimony forms a series of observations from which one might begin to shade in areas of contradiction in the dominant discourses of confession, including the theories of Foucault and Freud, that are modulated by masculine authority and by male heterosexual standards—despite the varieties that this designation overlooks—of pleasure. Confession typically disempowers the speaker, but within this discourse that largely reinforces conventional power relations of domination/submission, especially in terms of gender, is a limited space for another contradictory narrative, one of witnessing, no matter how hemmed in this testimony is by unresolvable issues of power.

Just as testimony is delimited by the confessional, that is, by power relations that fortify subjects and narratives of violation, confession is also punctuated by the testimonial, by narratives of witnessing the transgressive. This doubling of confession and testimony is particularly important for confessional subjects, for variously disempowered "others"—and in the terms of this study, for women—categorized as subordinate to or outside of a privileged identity. As the chapters that follow suggest, the implicit testimonies encoded in these confessions address sexual, domestic, or economic transgressions that describe a power structure of male domination and female subordination. In turn, this description proposes difficulties about the legitimacy of such gendered power arrangements in domestic, sexual, and material relationships.

This chapter offers a theoretical starting point for an exploration of Victorian confession with its examination of the gendering of power and sex embedded within Foucault's and Freud's analytical work on confession. For both theorists, confession's authorized reader and confession's privileged subject are coded masculine, despite the lack of attention—and because of the negligence—Foucault or Freud devotes to this question. The designs of power that structure any scene of confession, any construction of violation, sexual or otherwise, are particularized by their historical location, by the specific cultural conditions and rhetorical forms in which gender bias is ideologically inscribed and institutionally reproduced. Foucault and Freud theorize different perspectives on confession—as the ideological police and as a psychic cure—in the latter part of the nineteenth century, the era of so-called "Victorian puritanism" from which both discover accounts of sexual violations. Given that gender politics—or the cultural authority of men—tended to discredit, discount, or pathologize women's testimonies of male transgression, such acts of witnessing were most often assimilated into the structure of confession, that is, accounts in which the speaker is held morally or unconsciously accountable for wrongdoings against herself. The mid-nineteenth century is also crucial in terms of the modern secularization and proliferation of confessional discourses as English culture reconsidered and discarded the religious sacrament of confession.

To appreciate the transgressive value of women as witnesses, Chapter 2 turns to a series of outlawed confessions, that is, depictions of religious confession construed by anti-Catholic propaganda circulating in Great Britain and North America in the 1850s. The emergence of the expanded powers of modern, secular confessors, like the medical man of psychoanalysis who knows what the confessant does not know but unconsciously reveals, is oddly foregrounded in this anti-Catholic discourse. In these Victorian accounts, women's confessions are indeed taken as truthful testimony, descriptions of the sexual, economic, and domestic violations that father confessors enacted often under the guise of the sacrament of religious confession itself. And yet these historical documents in which Englishwomen are allowed to speak the "truth" about patriarchal abuses were used to condemn and delegitimate the Church of Rome and the mid-century surge of Irish Catholic immigrants into England. With the theoretical landscape on confessional discourse that this chapter's gender commentary on Foucault and Freud offers, I now entertain histories and fictions of religious confession in Victorian Britain, stories that provide templates for imagining women as confessional and testimonial subjects.

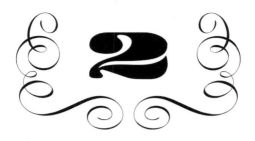

HISTORIES AND FICTIONS
OF VICTORIAN CONFESSION

Anti-Catholic Rhetoric and *Villette*

> To articulate the past historically does not mean to recognize it "the way it really was."
> . . . There is no document of civilization which is not at the same time a document of
> barbarism.—Walter Benjamin, "Theses on the Philosophy of History"

> Since it is constructed in a zone of contact with the incomplete events of a particular
> present, the novel often crosses the boundary of what we strictly call fictional literature—
> making use first of a moral confession, then of a philosophical tract, then of manifestoes
> that are openly political, then degenerating into the raw spirituality of a confession. . . .
> After all, the boundaries between fiction and nonfiction, between literature and
> nonliterature and so forth are not laid up in heaven. Every specific situation is
> historical.—Mikhail Bakhtin, "Epic and Novel"

In *Letter to the Women of England on the Confessional,* an anti-Catholic tract
published in London in the mid-nineteenth century, W. J. Brockman cautions:
"I know not another reptile in all animal nature so filthy, so much to be
shunned and loathed, and *dreaded by females,* both married and single, as a
Roman Catholic Priest or bishop who practices the degrading and demoraliz-
ing office of Auricular Confession." Brockman's warning typifies a perspective found in a spate of such cultural documents, namely that a dangerous
intimacy troubles the relationship between a woman and her father confessor,
the spiritual advisor who represents both a moral and sexual threat in his
reptilian "animal nature so filthy." According to Brockman's vision, the confessional "means . . . to bring chiefly the female mind beneath their [father

confessors'] deadly and mysterious control."[1] Despite its unmistakable status as propaganda against Roman Catholicism in general, I cite this passage—as I do a range of texts that fall under this category—because it directs attention to the gendered politics of confession and to the particular vulnerability of confessional women where the very act of narrating transgression itself occasions or unfolds other transgressions.

Anti-Catholic propaganda, circulated in the middle of the nineteenth century in England, propels into print descriptions of invidious patriarchal power, something that often goes down in silence, swept into the obscurity of domestic privacy as a so-called family matter. Drawing broadly on Benjamin's observation, I do not mean to suggest that such partial representations are truthful accounts of the practice of Roman Catholic priests or the religious sacrament of confession. What I maintain, however, is that such "document[s] of civilization" do embed a kind of "barbarism"—or, as I prefer to term it, a ferocity of power—that is more widespread than such nationalistic, extremist texts might imply. It is precisely because of the cultural context of this discriminatory, inflammatory discourse intended to discredit the Roman Catholic church, its agents, and its adherents, that these tracts inadvertently yield a glimpse of a pernicious domination, one based on patriarchal privilege, that structures the Victorian family.

While this chapter focuses on mid-nineteenth-century representations of Catholic confession, the frequently sexualized power dynamic of such professional intimacy also characterizes other institutions of confession including, as Chapter 1 discusses, Freudian psychoanalysis. In the following excerpt from an early-nineteenth-century text, *Considerations on the Moral Management of Insane Persons*, medical discourse defensively wards off any speculations about the consequences of immodesty when female patients divulge their sexual secrets: "It ought to be fully understood that the education, character, and established habits of medical men, entitle them to the confidence of their patients: the most virtuous women unreservedly communicate to them their feelings and complaints, when they would shudder at imparting their disorders to a male of any other profession; or even to their own husbands. Medical science, associated with decorous manners, has generated this confidence, and rendered the practitioner the friend of the afflicted, and the depositary of their secrets."[2] The justification expressed in the passage even implies the precarious nature of this sanctioned seclusion of medical man and female patient whereby "the most virtuous women unreservedly communicate to them their feelings and complaints." Yet any potential danger is checked both by the individual doctor's professional credentials—"the education, character, and established habits of medical men"—and by the status of the institution itself of "medical science, associated with decorous manners." As a result, "the most virtuous women" can confess the disorderly secrets of their bodies with greater impunity to a doctor than "to a male of any other profession; or even to their own husbands."

This question of the benefits of confession alters, however, in the context of an unauthorized institution in Victorian England, namely the Roman Catholic church. Richard Blakeney's 1852 monograph, *Popery in Its Social Aspects*, for instance, emphasizes the unwholesome impact of confession on both listener and speaker: "The confessional is contaminating alike to confessor and penitent. The great ornament of the female is modesty and purity. But when a female is taught, that *shame in the confession* is a soul-destroying sin, and required to unfold all, even her secret thoughts to a man in private, can it be imagined, that modesty and purity do not suffer by such a system."[3] The "contaminating" influence of religious confession here seems to be predicated on the condition of a woman "required to unfold all, even her secret thoughts to a man in private," an obligation that also structures the relationship between the female patient and her medical man. Why should divulging "secret thoughts" to a father confessor pose such dangers for a female penitent whereas the doctor for his female patients is "the friend of the afflicted, and the depositary of their secrets"? Put differently, why does one text demonize an act of confession while the other condones and encourages such confidences?

These positions on confession are complementary in the sense that each one illuminates from different vantage points a ferocity of power, a dubious domination that is gendered and sexualized, in relation to the disclosure of female confessional subjects. At the same time, these documents make evident conflicted and contradictory attitudes toward women as confessional subjects in Victorian culture inasmuch as to a medical man virtuous women can "unreservedly communicate" with impunity while to even enter the edifice of confession in a Catholic church bodes ill for every woman. This paradox exemplifies Foucault's "repressive hypothesis" whereby talking and documenting sex may be prohibited in one discursive sphere while mandated and extorted in another. The anti-Catholic fictions that this chapter largely pursues have at least one transparent agenda in disparaging the practice of church confession: to undermine a powerful religious institution in nineteenth-century Europe from making any inroads on domestic—British and familial—authority. In one arena, the father confessor is repeatedly construed as the interloper in would-be domestic affairs, the enemy of the father and the state who violates their precious possession of women. In a different discourse, the medical man is a "friend" who treats and heals afflicted female patients. This disparity suggests that a woman's confidence in a man of considerable power is only treacherous when the man's institutional alliance does not square with the existing structures of power in the culture.

I examine the rhetoric of power in Victorian anti-Catholic documents, tracts that condemn confession as an abusive practice and father confessors as sexual violators, because such representations provide suggestive material about cultural configurations of gendered domination and subordination. In doing so, I make no claims about the truth-value of history over fiction, of impartiality over propaganda, since any description is shaped by social positioning, by the vested interests of ideologies, whether explicitly articulated or obliquely inferred. Where Bakhtin questions the boundary between fiction and nonfiction, I likewise juxtapose these anti-Catholic essays and lectures from mid-century alongside a contemporary Victorian novel, Brontë's *Villette*, and its treatment of Roman Catholic confession. Jenny Franchot's *Roads to Rome*, a remarkable study of anti-Catholicism in the United States during roughly the same period, comprehensively explores anti-Catholic rhetoric in a manner similar to mine, that is, as "an imaginative category of discourse through which antebellum American writers of popular and elite fictional and historical texts indirectly voiced the tensions and limitations of mainstream Protestant culture."[4] My project differs from Franchot's not only because I focus on England but also because anti-Catholicism furnishes merely a suggestive starting point, and not a sustained concern, for Victorian constructions of women as confessional subjects. For I am less interested here in deciphering arguments over English encounters with Catholicism at mid-century than I am in offering a historical context for my analyses of literary representations of confession.[5] By the same token, I am especially interested in whatever limited potential these confessional narratives bear as testimony of transgressions attributable to figures of patriarchal authority. I read these acts of witnessing and constructions of confession to explore the way gendered power relations bolster Victorian ideals of family and domesticity.

Domesticating Confession: From Catholic Rome to English Homes

In order to appreciate the significance of Catholic confession in the cultural imagination of Protestant Victorians, I briefly outline its history as well as that of Catholicism in nineteenth-century England. With the establishment of the Anglican church in 1563, the sacrament of confession, along with Roman Catholicism, ceased as a regular and far-reaching practice in Great Britain.[6] But after Catholic emancipation in 1829, interest revived in religious confession in conjunction with the Oxford movement (1833–1845). Led by a group of Oxford theologians, including John Henry Newman and William Pusey, the Tractarians of the Oxford movement advocated "romanizing" the Anglican church by returning to pre-Reformation rituals. In an age of declining church attendance along with a correlated anxiety about morality, Tractarians revived not only private confession, a practice that spread during their influence in the 1840s among Anglican parishes, but also installed monasteries and nunneries, the religious houses hitherto affiliated exclusively with the Catholic church.

The overall consequence of the Oxford movement was twofold. First, in 1850 Pope Pius IX reestablished a Catholic hierarchy of bishops and cardinals in England. Rather than bringing the Anglican church into a closer affiliation with Catholicism through various religious sacraments and practices, the Oxford movement only amplified distinctions between the two religious institutions and gave the impression of a more secure foothold of the Roman church on English soil.[7] For example, many former notable Tractarians, such as Newman, who eventually became a Roman Catholic cardinal, converted to Catholicism. Second, religious antagonisms between Anglicans and Anglo-Catholics accelerated. With this increasing presence of Catholicism in England came an agitated reaction to the supposed infiltration of agents of the Roman Catholic church in the guise of priests, bishops, and cardinals. Regarded by Catholics as an indication of a "second spring" of the Church of Rome, the restoration of the Catholic hierarchy provoked a wave of anti-Catholic sentiment in England.

Yet it was not only the legitimization of the Catholic hierarchy that spawned what became known as the "antipapist excitement" of the 1850s. This fear of what was commonly referred to as "papal aggression" offered a rationale for English discrimination against Irish Catholic mass immigration, heightened by the potato famine of the 1840s. Charlotte Elizabeth Tonna's *The Rockite*, published in 1829, the year of Catholic emancipation, views Irish social unrest as a dire consequence of Catholic influence rather than contingent on material circumstances.[8] Given Tonna's devotion to many social problems including slavery, factory conditions, child labor, and women's labor, her position on Catholicism—in Ireland and in England—seems both contradictory and a sign of a larger cultural anxiety about foreign incursions from Rome on the domestic scene.[9] British opponents of Catholicism tended to the conviction that political nationalism and the Irish Roman Catholic church were inextricably linked together.[10]

Anti-Catholic enthusiasm gradually constituted a trope for xenophobia and social unrest, for popular and broadly supported beliefs that England was being overrun by foreign, hostile, or radical elements, whose imagined massive power was condensed into the figurehead of the Roman Catholic church and the derogatory locution of "popery." Indeed, much anti-Catholic material—in the forms of lectures and pamphlets circulated through numerous Protestant societies—aligned Catholicism with radical politics. Even before the reemergence of the Catholic hierarchy in England, E. Bickersteth's *The Divine Warning to the Church* (1842) associated Chartism and the Anti-Corn Law League with "popery." At the same time, "anarchic tendencies" were ascribed to Irish Catholicism, while both were identified with absolutism on the European continent.[11] This climate of anti-Catholic paranoia, one that also characterized other European nations at the time, occasions a remark Queen Victoria's eldest daughter made in a letter home while in Berlin: "People will have it here that the Catholic religion is making rapid progress in England, that the aristocracy are going over to the Church of Rome—that there are new conversions every day."[12] The prevalent impression that papal power was making inroads on even the British monarchy is encoded in the title of a pamphlet issued by the Protestant Evangelical Mission: *From Windsor to Rome through Anglican Sisterhoods*.[13]

This notion of conversions to Catholicism as quotidian events in mid-century England fosters the image of a nation under covert attack by a multinational power. And the confessional box figured as a primary site for this incursion of the Church of Rome into English domestic life, into the private sphere of the individual home as well as the public realm of the national home office. For example, in an 1848 issue of *Fraser's Magazine*, an article entitled "Why Should We Fear the Romish Priests?" explicitly concocts "priestcraft" as the enemy of domesticity on the levels of family and nation: "The real history of England . . . is the history of a struggle, issuing in the complete victory over the laity, the anti-national and hierarchic spirit gradually absorbed by the national lay spirit, which asserts the rights of the citizen, the husband, the individual conscience."[14] The passage constructs a dichotomy between Catholicism or "the anti-national and hierarchic spirit," on the one hand, and Englishness or "the national lay spirit," on the other hand; by doing so, it obscures the fundamental hierarchy of male power or "the rights of the citizen, the husband" on which the family is predicated.[15]

In the array of propaganda against satellites of the pope, nowhere is the fear of the Catholic church's power more pronounced than in speculations about the command father confessors hold over their female penitents. In the anti-Catholic Victorian imagination, confession epitomizes this proliferating foreign power that extends from family to nation. For the excitement over papal aggression envisioned confession as a menace to English domestic authority where church fathers usurp the privilege of domination over women usually awarded to familial patriarchs. Brockman's *Letter to the Women of England* locates a prelapsarian history to this insidious use of paternal power in the confessional: "Be not startled when I tell you that this institution was first established nearly 6,000 years ago in PARADISE! That the person who first confessed was a woman—Eve. That the being to whom she confessed was that old serpent, the *devil*! And the consequences were, ruin to herself, ruin, through her influence, to her consort, Adam, and ruin through them both to their *whole posterity*!"[16] This rendition of the first female fall suggests that Eve's confession leading to her disobedience began the cycle of "ruin" that continues. The passage excoriates both the first biblical confessor and his confessional subject, again in keeping with anti-Catholic discourse.

Repeatedly, diverse texts of this mid-century anti-Catholic discourse delineate a contest for power between spiritual father and domestic father or husband, with women as the spoils of this struggle. In *Philip Paternoster*, an 1858 novel that dwells on this anxiety about the untoward influence priests might exert, Charles Maurice Davies articulates a perilous analogy between the confessional booth and the home: "It would be a fatal day for England if ever England's wives and daughters were led to deem the confessional a more sacred place than the home."[17] Davies's observation locates the foundation of national security within the English family, and most especially with "England's wives and daughters." By sexualizing this ferocious power associated with the Roman Catholic church, such discourse transposes the intimacy of the confessional box into the threat of state insurrection from within. These formulations imply that for father confessors, who are agents of the Church of Rome, Englishwomen are pillage along the way to the real object of domination, the entire English nation.

The Victorian anti-Catholic position centered its critique on the authority that father confessors wielded in the private—that is, sexual—lives of its English penitents. That the priest through the act of confession was believed to encourage, demand, and explore the sexual practices of its confessants signified a breach of the privacy of marital relationships and the "sacred place" of home. Moreover, the nature of this intrusion endangered the typically unquestioned sexual and economic domination husbands maintained over their wives. As John Wolffe notes in *The Protestant Crusade in Great Britain 1829–1860*, "Fears for sexual purity blended with concern that the authority of husbands and fathers should not be intruded upon by priests."[18] Not only does the peculiar seclusion of the confessional pose a danger to the "sexual purity" of English wives and daughters, but it also renders the father confessor, as spiritual advisor to these women, a counterforce to the power of the husbands and fathers in the home and, by extension, to the rule of the British nation.

Adversaries of Catholicism believed that confessing sex, that is, discussing private subjects that belonged within the home, was an inherently corrupting activity that more often than not led to female sexual and moral depravity. Such perversion made manifest the ascendancy of religious fathers over domestic ones. Anti-Catholic documents linked the spiritual, social, and political sway of the Roman Catholic church in England with "infidelity," a blanket term for various dangers Catholicism represented in the Protestant imagination, a word that collapses these threats of sexual, familial, and national disloyalties. This infidelity earmarked a perception of a swelling social and moral decadence in English society, something again linked back to the volatile practice of talking sex in the confessional.

A popular anti-Catholic pamphlet, circulated from 1836 through the 1860s, "The Confessional Unmasked," contained juicy excerpts on various erotic activities from a theological manual for father confessors. The quoted passages came from Peter Dens's *Theologia Moralis et Dogmatica*, a text first published in Dublin in 1832 which included material on confessing sexual transgressions. According to a review published in the *Times*, this guidebook to sexual sin entailed "three pages of more systematic and disgusting obscenity than ever the Society for the Suppression of Vice had to deal with in their war against the filthy panders of this metropolis."[19] The stated intention of this popular anti-Catholic tract swiftly draws together the evils of confessing sex with the susceptible Englishwoman: "To expose . . . the blasphemous and corrupt practices of the 'confessional,' and to warn Englishmen of the lewd conduct of the Confessors with their wives, daughters, sisters, and sweethearts if allowed to frequent them."[20] In order to conserve English patriarchal domination from the detrimental power of confessors, the text warns "Englishmen" against confession, particularly for female family members. Confession becomes synonymous with an imperious inquisition, one that defiles the sanctity of domestic affairs.

Suspicious of "priestcraft" that supposedly promulgated such smut, this propaganda regarded monasteries and nunneries as dens infested with unbridled sexual promiscuity and as cells of the kidnapped with underground graveyards littered with the corpses of illegitimate babies.[21] While I do not delve into the prolific propaganda in mid-century England against the Catholic conventual system, I will mention by way of illustration one text discussed at greater length below. In Blakeney's *Popery in Its Social Aspects*, an entire chapter is devoted to this subject. Blakeney offers testimony from former nuns and monks on the practice of "nuns by compulsion," as well as the prevalence of "monastic immorality." In one section, the writer concludes: "Bound by an unnatural law of celibacy,—placed in circumstances in which their animal passions naturally become ascendant,—with females in the confessional, and nuns in the cloister at their disposal,—is it not likely that immorality will ensue?"[22] The structural isolation of the confessional box and its inhabitants nourish this fantasy of rampant degeneracy so that stories flourish about the sexual atrocities father confessors perpetrate on young women whose conversion into harlots originates with the primary scene of confession. The confessor is clearly the violator in these narratives, unusual instances where male authority is cast in the role of sexual villain. As such, this anti-Catholic material rivets attention on the abuses of patriarchal power. While such depictions of confession are fictional, highly wrought as propaganda to outlaw in England Catholicism, along with its practices and disciples, at the same time they provide a discursive site for locating contradictions surrounding paternal authority, female desire, and the Victorian family system. Although religious confession assumed this menacing aspect in the context of the anti-Catholic fervor, criminal confessions enjoyed varied appearances in nineteenth-century print culture.

Popularizing Confessions

This anti-Catholic position on confession circulated in mid-century through lectures and sermons, through numerous tracts sponsored by evangelical Protestant societies, and through an assortment of novels. In a different register, cheap broadside presses popularized an appetite for another kind of confession in Victorian culture. James Catnach's confession factory transposed newspaper accounts of horrid murders into posters that sold rapidly on the London streets. Appropriating from gory police and courtroom evidence a narrative of transgression, these broadside confessions became a staple in the popular print industry; such items are included in Richard Altick's list of nineteenth-century English best-sellers.[23] For instance, in 1828 Catnach sold over a million copies of the "Last Dying Speech and Confession" of William Corder, the murderer of Maria Marten; in 1837 he topped his previous record with over a million and a half copies of the joint confessions of James Greenacre and his lover Sarah Gale for the murder of Hannah Brown. Granted that these "last dying speeches" were often sheer fabrication, Catnach's success witnesses the commodification of confession as a lucrative business. By the 1860s, broadsheet and ballad confessions had declined as they were gradually displaced by reports of crime and punishment in the widely circulated sensational writings of the day appearing in newspapers, cheap magazines, and, increasingly, in railway-stall novels. The mid-century saw the eruption of a "murder industry" where the confessions of criminals in broadside and newspaper publications in the popular presses gave way to a spate of sensation novels and to the establishment of detective fiction.[24] Despite diatribes against the Catholic sacrament, the considerable popularity of these print confessions qualifies the wholesale condemnation of confession in Victorian culture.[25] This ambivalent treatment of confessional discourse provides a crucial backdrop to novels, such as *Villette* (1853), that seem to denounce Catholic confession, yet alternatively promote a secular, if recondite, confession as the representation of female interiority and as testimony of patriarchal oppression.

Religious confession is also a popular feature of anti-Catholic novels of the same historical period. As the staple of Victorian antipapist fiction, conversion plots chronicle the seduction and abduction of young women by Catholic priests. Through the enclosed space of the confessional, for example, the father confessor converts an Englishwoman from a life of innocence to one of sin. Or the conversion plot functions through an inversion of this narrative. Instead of inducting a woman of unprotected sexual virtue into service as a prostitute, the tyrant priest coerces a young woman of unprotected material wealth to assume the vocation of virginal sisterhood where she is imprisoned in a convent so that the church can claim as its property all her worldly goods. In Frances Trollope's *Father Eustace, A Tale of the Jesuits* (1847), written in the aftermath of Newman's would-be defection to the Church of Rome, father confessors mastermind intrigues of power by routinely excelling in spiritual, sexual, and material seduction. Under orders from his Jesuit general, Father Eustace must convert to Catholicism an affluent young woman. He does so without revealing his identity as a Catholic priest in order to trick the woman into the transgression of "falling" in love with a man who turns out to be her spiritual father. Afterwards, as a "fallen" woman, her only option is to surrender both herself to a nunnery and her family fortune to the church.[26]

In either case, the conversion plot deploys two divergent consequences of the confessional: the inauguration of illicit sensuality and the ambivalent enforcement of sexual repression. According to Foucault's repressive hypothesis, the selective channeling of the discourse of sex functions as a mechanism of power. Rather than the utter repression of talking sex in Victorian culture, Foucault maintains that various discourses both harness and proliferate this scrutiny.[27] Such contradictions are evidenced by the sensation of confession in public culture in the form of propaganda lectures against Catholicism. Of particular note was William Murphy, a circuit lecturer across England in the 1860s. His widely advertised lecture on the evils of the confessional booth was billed as the most spectacular event in a given program. Often this performance behaved as the ultimate showstopper where members of the audience could purchase their own copy of his oration, "The Confessional Unmasked," for private delectation. The *Times* reported that six thousand tickets for this infamous lecture were sold for a hall with half the capacity. As historian Walter Arnstein observes in his study of the "No Popery" movement in post-Emancipation England, Murphy's lecture on confession "confirmed in the minds of many a Victorian paterfamilias a very genuine fear that the Roman Catholic 'father' would serve as a rival household head and assert an alternative authority over his wife and daughters."[28] Despite Arnstein's dubious insistence that the threat papal aggression posed to English fathers was "very genuine," his comment stresses the issue of domestic power in these anti-Catholic lectures, a matter that converged around the question of patriarchal authority in the family. In the 1867 Birmingham riots, a repercussion in part from Murphy's incendiary lectures, his defenders actually identified with the American abolitionist movement by singing "John Brown's Body" and "Glory, Glory Hallelujah."[29] This popular Victorian fantasy imagined father confessors as slavemasters exercising unsanctioned, immoderate, and immoral power whose effects were most noxious to vulnerable, dependent women.

One of the most publicized controversies over Catholic confession as priestly transgression was the June 1852 Newman-Achilli case tried at the Queen's Bench in London. In his 1851 *Lectures* John Henry Newman denounced Giacinto Achilli, an Italian former priest and self-proclaimed Protestant convert engaged in "No Popery" tours throughout Great Britain. Newman contended that Achilli was notoriously promiscuous while in holy orders. Although Achilli had been defrocked and condemned by the Roman Inquisition for his manifold acts of sexually violating girls and women through his office as father confessor, he maintained that he was the victim of unfounded slander, that the real malefactor was the Roman Catholic church.

Newman's position in his lecture "The Present Position of Catholics" amounted to a paradox: as a Catholic, he condemned the scurrilous propaganda exposing father confessors as sex offenders; but in his attack on Achilli he actually uncovered precisely such a profligate career of a one-time Catholic priest. In this lecture Newman adopts the structure of confession by appropriating Achilli's voice: "I am that Achilli, who in the diocese of Viterbo in February, 1831, robbed of her honour a young woman of eighteen; who in September, 1833, was found guilty of a second such crime . . . and who perpetrated a third in July, 1834. . . . I am he, who afterwards was found guilty of sins, similar or worse, in other towns and neighborhoods . . . known to have repeated the offence in Capua, in 1834 or 1835; at Naples again, in 1840, in the case of a child of fifteen."[30] At the trial, Newman was able to produce a few of Achilli's victims; these women testified before an overcrowded room that Achilli as their father confessor had deflowered and otherwise sexually assaulted them. Converting the courtroom into a replay of the confessional booth, the trial conflated and sensationalized religious and criminal confession in Victorian culture. Given the pervasive anti-Catholic sentiment, the judge and jury ultimately ruled against Newman, one of the most renowned Anglo-Catholics of the day. Nevertheless, the celebrated case called direct attention to the sexual violation of women by a man in a position of power, even if bigotry clearly compromised the status of this power.

"The Master Key":
Father Confessors and the Hazards of Paternal Power

The mid-nineteenth century witnessed an upsurge in anti-Catholic propaganda in Western Europe and in North America. Yet some pamphlets reissued in the 1850s had been circulating for well over a century. For instance, Anthony Gavin's *The Great Red Dragon; or the Master-Key to Popery* enjoyed numerous printings in England and in the United States from its initial

British publication in the eighteenth century.[31] Of a piece with the sensationalism of Murphy's lecture series on the Catholic confessional, with the featured profile of the father confessor as a lecherous menace to familial and national domesticity, Gavin's book was reissued several times, particularly in the 1840s and 1850s. Viewing Roman Catholicism as an immoral system, *The Great Red Dragon* collected a series of narratives about wanton priests who use vows of celibacy as a disguise for their ferocious sexual power, which they exercise repeatedly in the confessional box. The "Master-Key" in the title refers specifically to the power of judicial rights accorded to the Catholic hierarchy to control penance and absolution. As Mike Hepworth and Bryan Turner illuminate in their sociological study of confession, this "Master-Key" gradually expanded over the centuries so that so-called voluntary confession of the early Roman Catholic church becomes by the nineteenth century "a bureaucratically controlled system of penance in which confession had become private, frequent, and obligatory."[32] "The Great Red Dragon," however, refers to Roman Catholicism and (not unlike the century-later "Red Menace" of anti-Communist discourse in the United States) its encroachment on domestic or British free enterprise structured through the separate spheres of family and state.[33] In this representative anti-Catholic document, confession is billed as a threat to the stability of the middle-class family. Accordingly, this risk is most drastic through the exclusive intimacy of the confessional and the priest's ready access to confessing women.

As an ex-Catholic priest, the author of *The Great Red Dragon* provides detailed dialogues direct from the confessional where, in one instance, a young woman confesses to eight years of committing "all sorts of lewdness, only with ecclesiastical persons," and a priest admits that he "spared no woman of any parish, whom I had a fancy for." Similar to Freud's stipulation that the patient must tell all, these father confessors begin to ply their several powers by commanding young female penitents to divulge "your sinful thoughts, words, actions, nay, your very dreams" about fornication.[34]

In an interpolated narrative that circulates through the ears of various holy fathers, Leonore first confesses to a Dominican friar about a Franciscan friar. As her dying parents' spiritual advisor, this confessor inherits their goods and money to settle on the daughter at his discretion, which he determines is contingent on her obedience to his arrangements for satisfying the sexual desires of assorted johns, both secular and religious. The transgressor in these sensational stories of the confession booth is the father confessor who behaves as blackmailer, rapist, and pimp. Of course, in anti-Catholic discourse the ultimate transgressor is the Church of Rome, otherwise known as "the Whore of Babylon" with its penchant for sexual promiscuity occasioned through the very act of confession.[35]

Gavin's case histories of women who fall prey to the sexual and economic iniquities of the Roman Catholic church characterize the sacrament of confession, due to the father confessor's influence over daughters and wives, as an unchecked affront to bourgeois domesticity and the authority of the familial father. Concealing ulterior designs, suggests this propaganda, priests exploit the office of religious confession as a strategy to promote sexual slavery. Admits one reformed priest: "Our method has been, to persuade husbands and fathers not to hinder them [the handsomest women in the parish] any spiritual comfort; and to the ladies to persuade them to be subject to our advice and will; and that in doing so, they should have liberty at any time to go out on pretence of communicating some spiritual business to the priest."[36] Gavin's confessing cleric goes on to explain that the "spiritual business" of confession provides a serviceable alibi for the profane business of a prostitution ring in which religious fathers routinely deceive familial "husbands and fathers" for the illicit sexual use of their female property. In these accounts, the sacrament of confession itself surfaces as duplicity, a mockery through which the priest secures his manifold powers.

In contrast to the way power works in Foucault's or Freud's theories, here domination is writ large; yet this command likewise takes hold by accumulating degrees. The Catholic hierarchy assumes control over the secular family; priests and friars "are such officious and insinuating persons in families, that by their importunities and assiduity of visits, they become at last *masters of families and goods*."[37] The series of firsthand, part-confessional, part-testimonial anecdotes of the evils of "popery" construe the father confessor's untoward influence as a furtive encroachment on the family and on secular paternal, even national, authority. Making inroads on the domestic sphere, from the individual family to the nation at large, these secret agents of the Church of Rome seize their "goods" in the form of women and material possessions. Eventually the religious father displaces the household father and appropriates the physical luxuries, including the bodies of wives and daughters, that once belonged to the familial man.

These tendentious scenes from the confessional reverse the bias of Victorian gender politics because "fathers" rather than women are blamed for the transgressions. Such propaganda pits Roman ecclesiastical power against British domestic authority; by doing so, it contributes to the privatization of the family, to be protected in this case from religious—signifying foreign state—intervention. Notwithstanding, the slippage around "father" exposes patriarchal control as a peril for domestic security because of the potential for vulnerable women, defenseless by virtue of Victorian social conditions, to submit to nefarious men. The Catholic scare refutes a prevalent notion that all fathers are beneficent; instead, this literature emphasizes that there are sinister as well as benevolent ones. The consequent ambivalence about paternal power revises women's confessions as testimonies of the iniquities brought about by menacing fathers—whether men of the cloth or men of the family—who possess boundless and intimate authority. Interestingly, an article on confession published in 1851 in *The Christian Observer* contemplates reforming the practice of confession so that women penitents confess to "some discreet and pious female—a wife, a sister, or else some kind and experienced Christian woman."[38] This alteration recognizes the gender politics in which women are particularly embattled as confessional subjects.

Anti-Catholic propaganda warns against father confessors who threaten to overthrow the rule of domestic fathers; this discourse also worries about how priestly power shores up female resistance within the family. In *The Foreign Quarterly Review*, a journal issued in England and in the United States in the nineteenth century, a review assessing Jules Michelet's 1845 *Du Prêtre, de la Femme, et la Famille* accentuates and extends this danger of a proliferating, alien domination the Church of Rome supposedly maintains all over the Western world. Once more, the origins of this process of subjugation begin in the confessional box, something that the review essay's title, "Michelet on Auricular Confession and Direction," reinforces. While this mid-nineteenth-century prejudice against "popery" extends across Western Europe and North America, France's own history with Catholicism specifies the cultural context of this intolerance. For Michelet writes out of the eighteenth- and nineteenth-century conflict between Jansenists and Jesuits, a controversy centering on confession, much like the English anti-Catholic rhetoric. An anticlerical party, the Jansenists viewed confession as the institution at the local level, family and village alike, of papal power. Hepworth and Turner elaborate on the French anticlerical party position: "In particular, they saw confession as a threat to family life since the priest came between husband and wife thereby undermining the authority of the head of the family. . . . the confessor corrupted the innocent by suggesting sins to confessants of which they would otherwise be ignorant."[39] According to this perspective on confession held by Jansenists, the priest's "direction" also spurs women's disgruntlement with the power structure in the home.

Like the testimonies in *The Great Red Dragon*, the article, quoting generously from the French text under review, centers on the implication of confession in Michelet's study, which pinpoints the father confessor's would-be "spiritual" guidance that encourages wives, daughters, and mothers to challenge patriarchal order in the family.[40] Ultimately portending anarchy, religious confession, in Michelet's estimation, fans the flames of a woman's dissatisfaction; accordingly, the holy father figures as chief adversary or "invisible enemy" to male domestic authority: "There exists in the bosom of society—in the family circle—a serious dissension, nay, the most serious of all dissensions."[41] Appealing to domestic fathers, Michelet offers up a vignette of middle-class family life insidiously and invisibly divided by priestly intrusion:

Take the instant when you would fain find yourself united with your family in one common feeling, in the repose of the evening, round the family table; there, in your home, at your own hearth, venture to utter a word on these matters [on the soul]; your mother sadly shakes her head, your wife contradicts you, your daughter although silent disapproves. They are on one side of the table, you on the other, alone.

It would seem as if in the midst of them, opposite you, sat an invisible man to contradict what you say.[42]

The threat of female insurrection in the family is persistently tethered to "the dangerous powers given to the priest by confession and direction";[43] the supreme risk is not to women, but to the absolute jurisdiction of father, husband, or son in the household. Instead, "an invisible man" intrudes upon the intimate domestic relationship between a patriarch and his female dependents. While these representations do not actually question the disempowerment of women, they do dispute patriarchal might over women by asking whose power—religious or domestic, priestly or familial—should prevail.[44]

Since Catholicism is more widespread in France than in England, the reviewer consequently distinguishes between the discontented French wife, more susceptible to priestly blandishments, and the English wife, whose domestic dissatisfaction, unprovoked by outside influences, is often offset by a resigned devotion to family life, taken as a "refuge" from marital miseries. Yet this consolation of gender, a mainstay of Victorian domestic ideology that exhorts wretched wives to cling to marital and maternal duties for solace, begins to crumble once a father confessor hovers on the edges of the familial scene. For the French Catholic housewife, the priest becomes an agitator for domestic strife, aiding and abetting *la femme incomprise*, the misunderstood wife whose husband's will is displaced by her spiritual director's wiles. Although the "Master-Key" of the confessional circumscribes female resistance to the master of her home, nevertheless Michelet's partial depiction does introduce the possibility of an opposition to paternal power.

Once again, this domination assumes an explicitly sexual significance. Michelet's description of domestic insubordination is figured as a kind of adultery; the wife's love for the priest goads her noncompliance with her husband's rule. Here the reviewer cites a sweeping conviction in English culture, based on French romances, that married women in France frequently take paramours: "Indeed, to believe the novelists, love seems only possible when it is adulterous." However, this fictional perception is accorded the status of fact grounded in Michelet's so-called historical testimony: "Adultery does exist in France to a frightful extent."[45] This supposed fact of adultery, that is, a wife's disloyalty, is the direct consequence of the Catholic practice of confession:

To confess a woman! imagine what that is. At the end of the church a species of closet or sentry-box is erected against the wall, where the priest, wise and pious as I have known some, but yet a man, and young (they are almost all so), awaits in the evening, after vespers, his young penitent whom he loves, and who knows it. . . . They talk, or rather murmur, in a low voice, and their lips approach each other, and their breaths mingle. This lasts for an hour or more, and is often renewed.

Do not think I invent. This scene takes place such as I describe it, and through all France.[46]

Invoking the rhetoric of realism, Michelet claims his elaboration represents life in France, not a fabrication. But this assertion follows in the wake of a sensational scene where private conversation leads to sexual passion. In other words, this illicit love is structured through the unchecked intimacy of the confessional box so that "Parler l'amour c'est faire l'amour, is a profound truth."[47] Sign and event, word and referent, collapse so that speaking sex is equivalent to having sex: "To confess a woman!" signifies a scandalous act perpetrated by lecherous priests on women easily accessible through a religious sacrament.

The *Foreign Quarterly Review* essay on Michelet's text dwells on the character of confession to promote the father confessor's sway over his female spiritual wards. Describing what Freud a half-century later calls "transference," the reviewer delineates the psychological power of the priest based on his knowledge of a woman's most intimate—read sexual—thoughts extracted through the act of confession: "The priest, as confessor, possesses the secret of a woman's soul; he knows every half-formed hope, every dim desire, every thwarted feeling. The priest, as spiritual director, animates that woman with his own ideas, moves her with his own will, fashions her according to his own fancy." Consistent with Foucault's assertion that knowledge is power, the father confessor's access to "the secret of a woman's soul" jeopardizes a husband's prerogative over his wife: "You are made the repository of all her secrets, of thoughts which neither her mother nor her husband ever know; you are reverenced as a superior being; your word is law; your menace terrible." In this anti-Catholic rendition, the church father's "word" and "law" are dreadful precisely because they usurp the ascendancy of male domination within the home. The priest is figured as an interloper on the family; this domestic disturbance develops from his psychological, and, by implication, sexual possession of his female subjects through the process of confession. Thus the reviewer concludes: "M. Michelet says, that the priest is the cause of social disunion. . . . he is the cause, because he possesses the wife: possesses her soul as a confessor, directs it as a director. He is the real master of the house."[48] This undercover "real master of the house" makes evident that the family and its sovereign are vulnerable to outside influence; at the same time, this foreign force of the father confessor constitutes a dangerous instance of paternal power.

The French anti-Catholic perspective on patriarchal perverts who haunt the confessional in the guise of religious fathers also qualifies texts initially produced and circulated in the "No Popery" excitement of 1850s England. First published in 1852, Richard Blakeney's *Popery in Its Social Aspects* centers on the social injustices of the Roman Catholic church. Blakeney was very active during the 1840s and 1850s in the British Reformation Society, an Anglican Evangelical organization formed in 1827 to protest the imminence of Anglo-Catholic emancipation. Originally an Anglo-Irishman, Blakeney's antipapist stance was fueled by a commonly held, anxious belief that the Roman Catholic church determined and directed Irish politicians and government policy.[49]

Endorsed by the Reformation Society, *Popery in Its Social Aspects* provides catechisms to argue against Roman Catholicism. Blakeney's preface announces that the purpose of this text, a companion to his earlier *The Manual of the Romish Conspiracy*, is to pursue "the political question" of Catholicism, which he treats as a "politico-religious system." In this regard, he urges, "Popery should be combated, not only with spiritual but with political weapons—not only by the Church, but also by the State." Invoking lofty liberal abstractions, Blakeney claims that Catholicism thwarts social progress by obstructing peace, morality, and truth. While he finds sufficiently threatening clandestine "underground" intrigues of Jesuits against both the Protestant church and the British monarchy, Blakeney especially deplores the Catholic ritual of confession as the office that amplifies the power of priest and dispenses sexual depravity.

One chapter, "The Influence and Power of the Confessional," investigates the consequences of auricular confession on priest, penitent, and nation. In this section of the text, Blakeney underscores the nature of unchecked power attributed to Catholic priests as the root of all crime, domestic and state alike. Arranged in succinct textbites for ready consumption and rehearsal, the chapter is broken into a series of headlines, each followed by enumerated elaboration. The first, "ON THE SEAL OF THE CONFESSIONAL," argues that the privacy of confession secures the holy father's power over penitents. If any controversy were to arise, the absence of a third party guarantees that "the word of the priest is to be received rather than that of the penitent!"[50]

The next portion, entitled "THE IMMORAL AND UNCHASTE INFLUENCE OF THE CONFESSIONAL BOTH UPON THE PRIEST AND THE PENITENT," argues that sin as the very topic of confession necessarily corrupts both participants. Offering the customary equation between speaking and doing sex, Blakeney contends that transgression is a contagious disease that migrates from within the confessional booth to the general population: "Is it any wonder that immorality and degradation should characterize countries where Popery is dominant?" Originating in the practice of confession, this epidemic depravity is measured through national surveys on illegitimate births and murders under the heading "STATISTICS OF CRIME IN PROTESTANT AND ROMISH COUNTRIES."[51] The correlation between a supposed high incidence of illegitimate births and cover-up infanticides in Catholic or "Romish" nations and fewer such births and deaths in Protestant countries, namely England and Wales, supports the biased assertion that associates national social unrest with Catholicism.[52] Where Blakeney traces this rampant and sexualized immorality back to the priest's intimate license in the confessional, he assiduously dissects the nature of this power of the father confessor. The longest section of the chapter, "THE POWER WHICH THE CONFESSIONAL GIVES TO THE PRIEST," devotes its attention to the problem of priestly power in the confession booth, a force that is most prominent in two realms, "the domestic circle" and the political domain. Reading like a page from Foucault, here Blakeney cautions, "Knowledge is power." Because of the knowledge to which a confessor is privy, "he learns the state of the heart, and knows his victim." And because his penitents view him as "Physician, Counsellor, Father, and Judge,—in fact, as God in the confessional," he can execute his power by both advice and threat. Rather than assigning blame entirely to the confessing woman whose spiritual director means her own moral and social downfall, Blakeney acknowledges the problem of investing a patriarchal institution with such vast authority. Quite in keeping with the anti-Catholic ideology of his time, Blakeney uses such representations of the confessional to declare that the heads of the household and the state are subject to be dethroned from their positions of power. Finally, Blakeney asseverates that confession is "a widespread conspiracy against the liberties of nations. . . . a system of impurity. . . . it perpetuates a knowledge of sin, and sinks both priest and penitent deeper in the pit of moral pollution."[53]

Fictions of Catholic Confession

I took a fancy to change myself into a Catholic and go and make a real confession to see what it was like.—Charlotte Brontë to Emily Brontë, letter dated 2 September 1843

. . . As to my confession . . . I suppose you will think me mad for taking such a step, but I could not help it . . . I cannot put the case into words, but, my days and nights were grown intolerable; a cruel sense of desolation pained my mind . . . I wanted companionship, I wanted friendship, I wanted counsel. I could find none of these in closet, or chamber, so I went and sought them in church and confessional.
—Charlotte Brontë, *Villette* (1853)

Blakeney construes the Church of Rome as a decided hazard to English domesticity. In a similar vein, highly embellished representations of popery, the confessional, and conventual life understand Catholicism as an alien force posing particular dangers for young women. Like Gavin's sensational narratives of confessional violations, these anti-Catholic versions of confession not only migrated between France and England, but also between North America and England in the mid-nineteenth century. One of the most renowned of these documents, *Awful Disclosures of the Hotel Dieu Nunnery* (1836) by Maria Monk, was circulated in England in 1851.[54] The story of a Canadian woman sexually violated in a convent both as a novice and a nun, *Awful Disclosures* was the subject of considerable public controversy in the United States with various character testimonies and character assaults around the credibility of Maria Monk's tales.[55]

Since the reappearance of *Awful Disclosures* in England coincided with the anti-Catholic fervor in general and with the Newman-Achilli case in particular, it is hardly surprising that Newman should mention Maria Monk in a memo he composed for the lawyers preparing his defense against Achilli's libel charge. Newman specifies this text as an example of the "calumnies" against Catholicism that his lectures were intended to expose: "And lately new editions had been issued of the notorious work of Maria Monk, against a Convent in Mon[t]real in Canada, which, though again and again shown to be an impudent imposture was largely circulated in Birmingham making people believe that all priests and nuns were profligates."[56]

Awful Disclosures constituted a conflation of the sensational confessions of criminals that populated the cheap presses and the more erudite and subdued anti-Catholic propaganda that found its way into mainstream novels, such as those by Charlotte Elizabeth Tonna. Like its English counterparts, Maria Monk's narrative underscores the domestic dangers for young women that confession heralds in the form of clandestine patriarchal power. Thus Maria Monk describes her education through the would-be spiritual guidance of father confessors as ideological laundering in which "they always blinded my mind." Repeatedly urged to surrender the contents of her thoughts, Monk portrays the confessional as insidious indoctrination: "While at confession, I was urged to hide nothing from the priest, and have been told by them, that they already knew what was in my heart, but would not tell, because it was necessary for me to confess it." Through elaborate scenes of psychological torture, sexual exploitation, and physical hardship, *Awful Disclosures* chronicles events of domestic violence in religious houses resounding with "the shrieks of helpless females in the hands of atrocious men."[57] Illuminating the supposed sexual promiscuity ingrained in the conventual system and in the confessional sacrament, the plot itself revolves around Maria Monk's flight while pregnant with a priest's baby.

Newman dismisses the contents of Maria Monk's book as slanderous absurdity, yet historians of this era of so-called papal aggression appreciate the text for its resemblance to other Victorian genres including pornography and the increasingly popular appetite for mysteries of violent crime.[58] On the one hand, these outlandish depictions of villainous Catholic clerics are patent propaganda designed to discredit Roman Catholics from gaining any serious political leverage. On the other, this anti-Catholic figuration of the abusive powers of father confessors offers a screen discourse, an uncontroversial vehicle for a more mundane "awful disclosure," that is, the unsanctioned subject of the sexual disempowerment of women prevalent in Victorian culture. By "screen discourse," I am drawing on the notion that language both directs and deflects, that meanings can be constructed through indirect and contradictory associations. In a related vein, Franchot mentions that anti-Catholic rhetoric provided American women with a licit opportunity to speak about sexual intimacy, while Susan Griffin locates "an undercurrent of dissent" in escaped nuns' stories, a perspective that challenges ideals of femininity in orthodox domestic novels.[59]

Consistent with other popular tracts of its ilk, *Awful Disclosures* identifies the sacrament of confession as the golden occasion for church fathers to corrupt their nubile female penitents. Relaying the story of a thirteen-year-old girl, Maria Monk accentuates the horrors of unchecked paternal power issuing through the confessional booth: "She told me one day of the conduct of a priest with her at confession . . . It was so criminal, I could hardly believe it, and yet I had so much confidence that she spoke the truth that I could not discredit it. She was partly persuaded by the priest to believe he could not sin, because he was a priest, and that anything he did to her would sanctify her . . . A priest she had been told by him is a holy man, and appointed to a holy office, and therefore what would be wicked in other men would not be so in him."[60] In Maria Monk's account, this religious father invokes his elevated status to exonerate himself from the moral codes used to judge the actions of "other men." In other words, masculine and religious might makes sexual right. Clearly, this diatribe is leveled against priests as agents of the Roman Catholic church and not at domestic—that is, English, Protestant, familial—fathers. Yet this propaganda does generate representations of violent, sexist, and sexual exploitation which call into question patriarchal power.

Charlotte Brontë's British novel works as a provocative counterpart to Monk's North American story. Although *Awful Disclosures* was published as an autobiographical account, the various public reckonings of its fabrications recommend more clearly than other anti-Catholic documents its status as fiction. Moreover, as an extended tale written and narrated by a woman, *Awful Disclosures* differs from many of the English tracts that only incorporate piecemeal anecdotes from the confessional booth by female penitents. Like the array of anti-Catholic publications circulating in England at mid-century, Brontë's *Villette* provides an illuminating illustration of the contradictory tropes attached to Victorian representational uses of Catholicism. Like Monk's narrative, *Villette* encompasses many caricatures drawn from the antipapist arsenal: visions of Catholic intrigue, depravity, and ruthless authority; the panoptic surveillance of Madame Beck and her satellites; the dubious father confessor, Père Silas; tales of sensual indulgence at the cost of spiritual and intellectual sustenance; the stock-in-trade nun's story of passionate love buried to death in the convent. Written in 1851–52 and published in 1853, *Villette* coincides with the anti-Catholic agitation of the early 1850s. Yet Brontë's novel has a decidedly different disposition than most English fiction of the mid-century Anglo-Catholic backlash.

Lucy Snowe's narration deploys the Roman Catholic church as a tyrannical institution to launch and to disguise a general critique of male domination and female subordination intrinsic to the structure of English Victorian society.[61] Rather than sustaining a stark distinction between Catholic and Protestant cultures, between the foreign training of girls in Labassecour and English conventions of feminine conduct, *Villette* repeatedly intertwines the oppressions of patriarchal Catholic authority with English doctrines that reinforce female repression and self-denial. For Lucy's psychological trauma—her "cruel sense of desolation"—is most potent as she struggles to "put the case in words," to confess her miseries, a partial consequence of Victorian gender ideology that dictates women "suffer and be still."[62] Critics of Brontë's last novel have noted the paired veiling of Lucy's anguish and the source of her torment.[63] If the precise nature of Lucy's distress appears to be enigmatic, at least the Catholic church appears as a visible villain against which an unsupported Englishwoman can protest with impunity. The foreign setting of the Catholic country of Labassecour—"this land of convents and confessionals"—provides a screen discourse, a signifying disguise, for the novel's implicit objections to the insufferable isolation and self-constraint imposed on Victorian unmarried and unmonied women.[64]

Nowhere is this curious juxtaposition of foreign Catholic and familiar English cultures more apparent than in the novel's meticulous attention to the power relations in narrative acts of self-revelation and in the ecclesiastical act of confession. As many readers have observed, Lucy Snowe's narration traces an ambivalence between self-display and self-concealment, between resolute articulation and a wavering reticence.[65] The novel imparts an intricate sense of the contradictions of the gendered conventions of confession as autobiography or self-expression. For Lucy's story is alive to the ideological disabilities of women who violate the convention of modesty; at the same time, the narrative recognizes the varied costs of silence and self-censorship. Through conniving characters like Père Silas or Madame Beck, and through

HISTORIES AND FICTIONS

the act of church confession, the symbolic work of Catholicism stipulates that silence is not necessarily a sign of modesty, nor does silence necessarily harbor decided advantages.

Villette contains many of the clichés of anti-Catholic propaganda but with its own peculiar twists calibrated to the distress that punctuates Lucy's self-narration. As the assortment of documents quoted above makes manifest, Catholicism in the Victorian Anglo-Protestant imagination insinuates both unseemly public displays of self-expression, like confession, and the excesses of self-indulgence, including physical ease and sexual gratification. In the context of the novel, of course, the binary around religious identity organizes an opposition around national identity, between foreignness and Englishness; my use of "Catholic" and "Protestant" here should be understood in this sense.[66] The Protestant profile that the Catholic tropes work against include such qualities as introspection, reserve, internalized self-censorship, an obsession with self-correction. Yet in *Villette* the would-be Catholic spectacle of affect—pain and suffering as well as joy and erotic pleasure—offsets the Protestant convention of self-denial and feminine submission. Although ostensibly disparaging of such Catholic traits, the novel also implicitly draws a comparison between Catholic and Protestant cultures of gendered tyranny. These parallels are encapsulated in Lucy's church confession and the way this particular scene and its aftermath affiliate the Catholic father, Père Silas, with the English paterfamilias, Doctor John. Following this pattern, the institutionalized surveillance and patriarchal authority embedded in the Catholic act of confession condenses the more subtle, more pernicious because less discernible, internalized control promulgated by Anglo-Protestant doctrine.

Early in the novel, when Lucy is shipbound from England to her employment in a Catholic country, she first meets Ginevra Fanshawe, who parodies the uncertain distinction between Catholic and Protestant identity that the narrative later exploits. Thus Ginevra tells Lucy: "I have quite forgotten my religion; they call me Protestant, you know, but really I am not sure whether I am one or not; I don't well know the difference between Romanism and Protestantism. However, I don't in the least care for that. I was a Lutheran once at Bonn . . . where there were so many handsome students."[67] For Ginevra, religion is determined by national culture and personal opportunism, not spiritual belief; as a traveler throughout Europe, she assumes various religious identities much as one dons the latest dress fashions. Despite Lucy's critical regard of Ginevra's indulgent lifestyle, Ginevra also functions as an intriguing foil to Lucy's vexed stance, tooled by an ideology of female repression and denial, on her own passions. Of all the female characters, Ginevra is most articulate, forthright, and successful about stipulating and gratifying her own desires; remarkably, it is the derogatory image of a Catholic spectacle of pleasure this character enacts to her own advantage.[68] Yet Lucy's narration wields anti-Catholicism to vent her own emotional existence, shaped by social circumstances, as an exhibition of pain.

Although repeated anti-Catholic tropes pepper the novel, many passages underline the ways in which zealous rhetoric misconstrues identities all over the map. By pointing out "crafty Jesuit-slanders" of Protestants that strikingly resemble anti-Catholic propaganda, the narrative suggests that such stereotyped differences of identity are slippery at best. Notwithstanding his indoctrination by these "crafty Jesuit-slanders," Paul Emanuel characterizes Lucy's national and religious profile in a manner that mimics anti-Catholic discourse on the indulgent and excessive abandon of Catholic church fathers and their charges. Thus, Paul asks, "What limits are there to the wild, careless daring of your country and sect?" and Lucy endeavors to undo this reverse propaganda by persuading him that "Protestants were not necessarily the irreverent Pagans his director had insinuated." In this scene, Lucy assumes the role of confessor and from this posture reveals how emotional, spiritual, and ideological direction are packaged together. Mirroring the work of anti-Catholic dogma, the text describes the workings of anti-Protestantism: "I found that Père Silas (himself, I must repeat, not a bad man, though the advocate of a bad cause), had darkly stigmatized Protestants in general, and myself by inference, with strange names, had ascribed to us strange 'isms.' "[69] Neither Père Silas nor Paul is "a bad man"; their failings are attributed to the cultural networks that underlie their beliefs, actions, and identities.

Lucy's narration suggests much the same about Englishmen. For here the Catholic church provides a cover for a critique of ideology that permeates various arenas of society: "Poverty was fed and clothed, and sheltered, to bind it by obligation to 'the Church'; orphanage was reared and educated that it might grow up in the fold of 'the Church'; sickness was tended that it might die after the formula and in the ordinance of 'the Church'; and men were overwrought, and women most murderously sacrificed . . . that they might serve Rome, prove her sanctity, confirm her power, and spread the reign of her tyrant 'Church.' "[70] In this passage that aptly describes, despite its anti-Catholic tones, the operations of indoctrination, "the Church" becomes a feasible foe against which Lucy can inveigh for social injustices where women are "most murderously sacrificed."

In particular, Lucy repeatedly transposes the horrors of her own subdued life into the garish atrocities attributed to the Church of Rome. In the "lecture pieuse" at Madame Beck's school for young girls, for instance, Lucy overhears a lesson rife with anti-Catholic mythology of "monkish extravagances" and "priestcraft": "The ears burned on each side of my head as I listened, perforce, to tales of moral martyrdom inflicted by Rome; the dread boasts of confessors, who had wickedly abused their office, trampling to deep degradation highborn ladies, making of countesses and princesses the most tormented slaves under the sun. Stories like that of Conrad and Elizabeth of Hungary, recurred again and again, with all its dreadful viciousness, sickening tyranny and black impiety: tales that were nightmares of oppression, privation, and agony."[71] These lavish transgressions inflicted on "high-born ladies . . . countesses and princesses" approximate the ineffable affliction to which Lucy testifies through her own autobiographical revelations amounting to "tales that were nightmares of oppression, privation, and agony." To directly confess her own sufferings would constitute a transgression of the proper feminine decorum of English middle-class reserve. But through the hyperbolic rhetoric of anti-Catholic fables, Lucy obliquely airs her grievances over a domestic, that is, English, social system that reduces the life of an unattached woman to abject isolation and alienation.

Apparently Brontë knew the story of Elizabeth through Charles Kingsley's verse drama, *The Saint's Tragedy:, or, the True Story of Elizabeth of Hungary* (1848), which portrayed yet another wily Catholic father confessor, a monk named Conrad, whose object was to commit Elizabeth to a life of self-denial and seclusion in a convent.[72] This familiar anti-Catholic theme of a young woman's conflict between her secular, worldly lover and her enforced devotion to her spiritual director is recycled in *Villette* through its diverse uses of the nun's story. Like the narrative's enactment of religious confession, the figure of the young Catholic nun assumes alloyed and contradictory meanings. Lucy hears from her would-be father confessor, Père Silas, the story of Justine Marie, the unrequited love of Paul who died as a novitiate in a convent. This spiritual father embarks on such a narrative precisely to dissuade Lucy from any amorous designs on Paul, his ward under the auspices of the Church of Rome; nonetheless, a distinct analogy emerges between Lucy's present situation and that of Justine Marie, whose socially unsanctioned love dooms her to a life of self-denial, one of figurative and literal burial inside a cloister. Of course, this threat of a young woman's untimely death due to thwarted passions and a social system indifferent or inimical to unmarried and unsupported women is a narrative motif of Brontë's female characters from Jane Eyre and Caroline Helstone to Lucy Snowe. Brontë lambastes in *Villette* "the self-denying and self-sacrificing part of the Catholic religion," the very gendered conventions of repression and renunciation that hamper those English heroines of previous novels who reside not in a foreign Catholic country but in England, and who are not religious sisters but isolated Englishwomen.[73]

The figure of the nun in the convent also functions in Victorian culture as an index of mysterious and illicit practices, or more precisely, as a marker for concealed but excessive female sexuality. This version of nuns and the conventual system generously populates anti-Catholic texts of the mid-nineteenth century. Besides *Awful Disclosures of the Hotel Dieu Nunnery*, such tracts issued by the Protestant Evangelical Society as *Convent Education and Nun-*

nery Victims, Plea for the Inspection and Suppression of Nunneries, and *From Windsor to Rome through Anglican Sisterhoods* all help to publicize the idea that Catholic holy houses for women were actually no more than dens of assorted sexual iniquities. In *From Windsor to Rome,* a newspaper item cites the discovery of "literally hundreds upon hundreds of skeletons of infants" at "the site of a suppressed or abandonned Nunnery."[74]

Pre-Raphaelite art also participated in this mythology with such paintings as John Everett Millais's *The Vale of Rest* (1858), which depicts two mysterious young women dressed as nuns and positioned within the walled-in space of a cemetery, the spire of a convent in the background. While one woman gazes directly, with an expression that mingles defiance with contemplativeness, toward the spectator, the other woman assumes the incongruous activity of a gravedigger with her sleeves and skirt rolled up. Sensuality is often encoded in Victorian depictions of women's exposed limbs and flexed muscles. For instance, Arthur Munby's photographs of working-class women engaged in manual labor were objects of titillation for this English gentleman who wrote about them in his diaries.[75] Millais's image conjoins such eroticism with the anti-Catholic mythology of nuns as disguised whores. To spotlight the narrative theme of mysterious burial in *The Vale of Rest,* just above the church steeple in the distance hovers a dark cloud whose oblong shape resembles a coffin. This scene, which intimates some kind of illicit conduct, capitalizes on the anti-Catholic trope of not just nuns as prostitutes but even the Church of Rome as "the Great Whore," rhetoric lifted from Revelations.[76]

Brontë makes use of this representational scheme of religious sister as cover for profligate woman in *Villette* with the ruse in which Ginevra's lover impersonates the legendary nun of the attic in order to facilitate their forbidden liaisons within the walls of a Catholic girls school, an institution and domicile that Brontë explicitly associates with convents by stipulating that "the queerest little dormitories" of the Rue Fossette "had once been nun's cells." As for the legend of the nun that haunts the premises of Madame Beck's school, the narrative sympathetically unfolds the story of a nun's unsanctioned passions for which she is brutally punished. "The legend went, unconfirmed and unaccredited, but still propagated, that this was the portal of a vault, emprisoning deep beneath that ground, on whose surface grass grew and flowers bloomed, the bones of a girl whom a monkish conclave of the drear middle ages had here buried alive, for some sin against her vow."[77] The conflicting anecdotes of a nun "buried alive" either for passions expressed or— in the case of Justine Marie—for passions denied does more than rehearse scenes from the tracts of anti-Catholic imagery. For such depictions complicate Brontë's own position on female sexuality where neither extreme of denial nor indulgence, repression nor expression, is wholly tenable. The narrative even identifies Lucy herself with the legend and figure of the nun. Only here Brontë substitutes the buried letters of a lonely woman for the corpses of illegitimate babies so popular in anti-Catholic lore, two very different conceptions of the products of passion. Lucy's act of burying her letters from Doctor John signifies a ritual of self-denial just as much as it is a strategy to evade the panoptic and Catholic surveillance of Madame Beck.[78] Then Lucy finds in her bed one night the effigy of the legendary nun that Ginevra and her paramour have devised, a symbolic token of the unsteady contrivance of Lucy's own attempts at renunciation.

However, it is Lucy's act of ecclesiastical confession that signifies the novel's most salient correlation of anti-Catholic tropes with a critique of untoward repression of the passions that hamper Lucy's narrative career of self-revelation. For this exceptional act in which an English Protestant woman enters the confessional booth of a French Catholic priest also constitutes a kind of protest; both what compels Lucy to confess and the confession's aftermath serve as narrative testimony of the social, affective, and material afflictions that plague her. Desperately unhappy from her isolation exacerbated by the school vacation, Lucy divulges obtusely in her narration that she suffers from "miserable longings" and "a despairing resignation" in which her life appears "a hopeless desert." At this point, Lucy acknowledges and rebukes her reader's implicit position as confessor who sits in judgment of her rather cryptic revelations by invoking not only a "Religious reader" but also a reader who is alternately "moralist," "stern sage," "stoic," or "cynic."[79] Yet the novel's ambivalence toward representations of Catholicism emerges as Lucy seeks solace in the religious sacrament of confession, an activity that at least assures her some human interaction, if only through a formulaic dialogue.

At the same time, the narration of the scene of confession testifies to the pitch of her anguish. Lucy's transgression is not the usual confessional fare of sex crimes or murder, but rather her expression of loathsome misery.[80] The pageantry of ritual, the excesses of conduct that form the foundation of anti-Catholic fictions also furnish a suggestive antithesis to Lucy's "extremity of want." From her Anglo-Protestant perspective Lucy is suspicious of the supposed extravagances of Catholics—"the Pomp of Rome" with its associations of theatricality and hypocrisy. Yet during the school fête before the holiday, Lucy admits: "A keen relish for dramatic expression had revealed itself as part of my nature."[81] However, she is equally dubious about a gendered doctrine of denial and self-effacement regulating her very existence. Although the inverse of exhibitionism and "the Pomp of Rome," this attitude is also attributed to Catholicism, again providing a benign vehicle for a critique of self-repression.

That Lucy's confession embeds a furtive criticism of conditions about which she is not licensed to speak is implied by her first words in the confessional booth to the father confessor: "Mon père, je suis Protestante." Using a foreign tongue, a foreign setting, a foreign culture, Lucy can assume this posture of *protest* precisely as a "Protestante"—that is, a Protestant woman— in a Catholic country. Here the very act of confession is transgressive as a kind of remonstrance against her own vulnerable domestic circumstances, against the plight of unmarried Englishwomen. When the priest inquires why Lucy, as a Protestant, has entered the confessional, she continues her skewed complaint: "I said, I was perishing for a word of advice or an accent of comfort. I had been living for some weeks quite alone; I had been ill; I had a pressure of affliction on my mind of which it would hardly any longer endure the weight." The foreclosure of any specific content to her confession here is of a piece with Lucy's narration about her "unutterable sense of despair" in which "indescribably was I torn, racked and oppressed in mind."[82] Clearly Lucy's confession of a different religious faith deviates from an admission of sin customary to the Catholic confessional box. Still, by confessing the "unutterable" and the indescribable, Lucy does transgress in the sense that she voices a discontent rather than accept her meager lot and stifle her affliction, the proper path according to Victorian gender ideology. At the same time, this confession signifies a testimony to the plight of solitary women whose keen passions, resentment, and anger fall outside the bounds of sanctioned feminine feeling. Whether or not Lucy does confess a sin, her confession itself is a twofold transgression: both her participation in this foreign, secret, and suspect religious ritual and her expression, no matter how oblique, of protest against social conditions that undergird her own private agony.

While the episode does not elaborate on Lucy's mental torment, it does explore the power relations between a father confessor and an irregular female penitent, between the institutionalized obligation to confess and conflicting psychological and cultural compulsions to reveal and to conceal at the same time. The relief Lucy experiences from her confession approximates something like what Freud terms as "abreaction" some decades later; Lucy acknowledges "the mere pouring out of some portion of long accumulating, long pent-up pain into a vessel whence it could not be again diffused—had done me good." But unlike the prescribed relationship between authorized confessor and submissive patient or penitent that frames psychoanalytic or Catholic confession, Lucy does not comply with the priest's directive that she "return to [him] again," even if she does encounter Père Silas toward the end of the novel.[83]

Lucy's explanation for her refusal veers toward the stockpile of anti-Catholic clichés; yet she also appreciates her own susceptibility to the power of paternal attention:

> Did I, do you suppose, reader, contemplate venturing again within
> that worthy priest's reach? As soon should I have thought of walking

into a Babylonish furnace. That priest had arms which could influence me; he was naturally kind, with a sentimental French kindness, to whose softness I knew myself not wholly impervious . . . . Had I gone to him, he would have shown me all that was tender, and comforting, and gentle, in the honest popish superstition. Then he would have tried to kindle, blow and stir up in me the zeal of good works. I know not how it would all have ended . . . I might just now, instead of writing this heretic narrative, be counting my beads in the cell of a certain Carmelite convent.[84]

The passage insinuates that confession's force of intimacy, in this case the priestly arms of influence, ultimately leads to monotonous incarceration and dull servitude. Recent feminist criticism tends to read the confession scene as a parable for Lucy's resistance to the convention of feminine passivity in marriage.[85] Here the description accents the hazards of tenderness as an instrument of manipulation for a single woman. Rather than accenting the moral turpitude of Catholic clerics, Lucy focuses on her pliability in the face of "all that was tender, and comforting, and gentle." If this narration explicitly highlights the blandishments of the confessional, it implicitly highlights the ideological persuasions that accompany any ritualized act that results in spiritual, psychological, even material imprisonment. As if to accentuate her unconventionality, at this postconfession juncture Brontë dubs Lucy's story a "heretic narrative," a circuitous story protesting female subjugation and male might masked as kindness.

The novel's ambivalence toward patriarchal power is evident by virtue of the repeated qualifications of Père Silas as a "good" or "benign" man underneath his Catholic trappings and by virtue of the ways in which the narrative links Père Silas to Doctor John Graham Bretton through Lucy's body. For it is Père Silas who commits "a perfectly unconscious, perfectly bloodless, and nearly cold" Lucy to Doctor John's care. Of the Catholic father confessor, Lucy observes: "There was something of Fénelon about that benign old priest; and whatever most of his brethren may be, and whatever I may think of his Church and creed (and I like neither), of himself I must ever retain a grateful recollection. He was kind when I needed kindness; he did me good. May Heaven bless him!"[86] By invoking the image of Fénelon, a seventeenth-century archbishop whose generosity and gentleness won many converts to Catholicism, Brontë again recognizes the surreptitious and insurmountable mechanisms of any ideological conversion. The anti-Catholic response to the would-be papal aggression in England of this period insistently locates the origins of this power in the intimacy of the confessional booth. Remarks the author of *From Windsor to Rome*, "The almost complete destruction of the moral sense in women, through the debasing and contaminating influence of the Confessional is one of the chief reasons why few of Rome's *female* victims can be induced to abandon so vile a system."[87] While Brontë is not promoting this image of unmitigated corruption issuing from the confessional box, her depiction features the more subtle and complicated operations of patriarchal authority.

If the novel's position on paternal powers is inconsistent, its stance on confession—whether the Catholic ritual or the act of self-expression—is equally uncertain. Where the immediate consequences of Lucy's confession are daunting as she "seemed to pitch headlong down an abyss" from which she does not recover for weeks, the more deterring outcome is her deliverance to another paterfamilias, Doctor John, who manages her recuperation and indifferently acquires her urgent affections. That the narrative structures this analogy between Roman Catholic confessor and English medical and familial man is clear at several turns. On one hand, Père Silas is a "benign old priest" at heart despite his devotions to a suspect church; on the other hand, Doctor John Bretton's youthful kindheartedness disintegrates into the superficial charms of a misguided and rather shallow and representative Englishman or "incipient John Bull," as his mother calls him.[88] And John surely makes a bid for Lucy's confidences, which she avoids as assiduously as she has already with Père Silas in the confessional booth. Says Doctor John, "You may trust me as implicitly as you did Père Silas. Indeed, the doctor is perhaps the safer confessor of the two, though he has not gray hair."[89] During Lucy's recovery at La Terrasse from her postconfession fainting fit, the narrative elaborates upon this parallel between religious and familial, foreign and domestic male confessors.

In both cases, Lucy refuses to submit herself to the power of confession; she also shirks from an articulate recital of her own affliction. When Lucy reports to Dr. John that a "cruel sense of desolation" drove her to confess to a Catholic priest, she ambiguously qualifies the confession: "As to what I said, it was no confidence, no narrative. I have done nothing wrong: my life has not been active enough for any dark deed, either of romance or reality: all I poured out was a dreary, desperate complaint." The transgression that Lucy laments is the imposed passivity that makes "any dark deed, of romance or reality" improbable, a gendered disempowerment that outlaws the act of narrative itself. As for the remedies Père Silas and Doctor John prescribe for Lucy's disorder, one that she characterizes as "a cruel sense of desolation" for which she "wanted companionship," Père Silas offers more intimate contacts at his house whereas Doctor John recommends her departure through the travel cure "for a change of air—change of scene."[90] Clearly, neither alternative is acceptable to Lucy, although Père Silas at least acknowledges her craving for close friendship, a capacity of which Doctor John appears incapable.

Entering the confessional constitutes for Lucy a transgression, a daring escapade in which a Protestant Englishwoman trespasses on the foreign and forbidden domain of the Roman Catholic church. That this act can be construed as a defiance, no matter how roundabout or limited, of patriarchal domination emerges in a 1843 letter Brontë wrote to her sister Emily in which she describes her own foray into the confession booth while living in Brussels.

> I was obliged to begin, and yet I did not know a word of the formula with which they always commence their confessions. It was a funny position. I felt precisely as I did when alone on the Thames at midnight. I commenced with saying I was a foreigner and had been brought up a Protestant . . . I actually did confess—a real confession. When I had done he [the priest] told me his address, and said that every morning I was to go to the rue du Parc—to his house—and he would reason with me and try to convince me of the error and enormity of being a Protestant!!! I promised faithfully to go. Of course, however, the adventure stops there, and I hope I shall never see the priest again. I think you had better not tell papa of this. He will not understand that it was only a freak, and will perhaps think I am going to turn Catholic.[91]

Unlike the episode of the church confession in *Villette*, here Brontë suggests some substance to her disclosure to the priest as she claims "I actually did confess—a real confession." In a curious book first published in 1914 and entitled *The Secret of Charlotte Brontë*, the author, once a student at the same pensionnat in Brussels that Brontë attended, devotes a chapter, "The Confessions at St. Gudule," to this foreclosed transgression and speculates that the "real confession" must be her secret, unrequited love for Monsieur Héger, the historical person with whom many readers have identified Paul.[92] Deferring the truth-value of this speculation on Brontë's excised confession, more notable is her negotiation of patriarchal authority again, as in *Villette*. For this incident occasions Brontë's circumvention of the command of both ecclesiastical and domestic fathers. If she prevaricates to escape the threatened domination of the Catholic confessor, she likewise withholds confession of her own transgressive confession from her father, a notoriously dogmatic Anglican curate. For Brontë, the "adventure" of a young Englishwoman confessing to a French Catholic priest elicits a peculiar sensation—like being "alone on the Thames at midnight," another boldly independent action likewise undertaken by Lucy in the narrative when she commences her journey from London to Labassecour.

In *Villette*, Lucy Snowe's confessional endeavors complicate the possibilities of self-expression and at the same time implicate a critique of male domination and female subordination throughout a range of cultural locations from the Catholic church to Victorian domesticity. The novel's outlook on Catholicism in general and the confessional in particular has a more mosaic composition than the scornful depictions in the array of anti-Catholic documents of mid-century England. Even so, these textual rebukes of the religious rite of confession all underline the institutional subordination of women to patriarchal rule. By extension, these fictions also embed a cautious commentary on a gender ideology that mandates female submission to the father's will, no matter how benign this familial authority and his convictions may appear. What I suggest here is that such anti-Catholic representations of the father confessor's psychological, material, and sexual powers offer a discourse for exploring the contours of gendered disempowerment in Victorian culture. These paranoid visions of confessional women and the Catholic church also position and legitimize female rebellion from paternal domination. At the same time, they demonstrate the enormous difficulties of eluding power that is so deeply entrenched, so widely reinforced.

In other Victorian novels following the tumult of the 1850s over Catholicism in England, women's confessions are most frequently secularized and domesticated, unfastened from the virulent moorings of anti-Catholic rhetoric. Yet as a discourse in which a woman discloses a narrative of transgression, confession still provides a space for unwrapping the ideological constructions of gendered power and for testifying about material and psychological consequences of male sexual, economic, and social privilege. Rather than the would-be tyranny of the Catholic sacrament, fictional confessions are reorganized around marriage and family. Nevertheless, these domestic scenes of confession expose an endangered intimacy with hazards for women not unlike the perils of the confessional booth and father confessor promulgated by anti-Catholic rhetoric. The ominous figure of the father or husband—or some other male relation—as confessor, and as source of the miseries and privations the confession unfolds, dominates the confession scenes in *Lady Audley's Secret*, *Daniel Deronda*, and *Tess of the d'Urbervilles*. Although these three novels collectively span the last four decades of the nineteenth century, years in the wake of the antipapist turbulence of the 1840s and 1850s, it is useful to read such fictive and secularized confessions against this background of the treachery of paternal power suggested by the concerted backlash of the early 1850s against Roman Catholicism. For these antipapist tracts open up a potential for Victorian narratives to speculate about women's oppression by patriarchal institutions at home in England and at home within the seemingly sacred and protected realm of the family. Despite an evident distance from Catholic powers infiltrating the minds, souls, and bodies of Englishwomen in the domesticated representations of confession examined in the next chapters, the sheer spectacle of such anti-Catholic themes continues to cast shadows, however faint, on these scenes of domestic confessions. For instance, Chapter 3 extrapolates from figurative uses of the nun whose anti-Catholic valence suggests that the self-denying virgin is but a masquerade for an insatiable prostitute. In Braddon's *Lady Audley's Secret*, the title character's confession enlarges upon this idea that differences between a degenerate woman and a virtuous lady are difficult to detect. Indeed, the problem of readability, attached as it is to questions of what may be expressed or represented, typifies each confession from Lucy Snowe's cryptic identity assertion to Tess Durbeyfield's textually blank disclosure. In addition to the complexities of reading transgressive women and their transgressive narratives, these confessions also expose varied contradictions in Victorian medical and sociological discourses on aberrant femininity, just as the anti-Catholic depictions suggest the incongruities of paternal authority.

THAT NARROW BOUNDARY LINE

Figures of Female Degeneracy
and *Lady Audley's Secret*

I killed him because I AM MAD! because my intellect is a little way upon the wrong side of
that narrow boundary-line between sanity and insanity.
—Mary Elizabeth Braddon, *Lady Audley's Secret*

For one woman who thus, of deliberate choice, sells herself to a lover, ten sell themselves
to a husband. Let not the world cry shame upon us for the juxtaposition.
—William Rathbone Greg, "Prostitution"

From the title, through an elaborate plot of detection, to the confession scene itself, Mary Elizabeth Braddon's sensation novel, *Lady Audley's Secret*, advertises the spectacular value of uncovering hidden transgressions. As a popular Victorian genre that trades on the power of the secret and frequently sexualized sins of its heroines, sensation fiction provides a resourceful perspective on the contradictions that frame these villainous victims who are simultaneously diseased, depraved, and socially and economically oppressed. Unlike Lucy Snowe's cryptic and condensed church confession of one sentence, Lady Audley's protracted confession—virtually her autobiography—occupies an entire chapter; unlike Lucy's confession again, Lady Audley clearly admits to the criminal acts of bigamy and of murdering her first husband and to a specific pathological condition of inherited madness. My reading of confession in *Lady Audley's Secret* explores the ensemble of cultural discourses that mediate the construction and interpretation of this narrative of wayward female passions. Whereas the previous chapter addresses the symbolic uses of the power of father confessors in anti-Catholic accounts of confession, this chapter focuses on the symbolic uses of the transgressive female figure, along with wider questions about how Victorian culture defines and understands deviancy in women. For in order to appreciate the dynamics of gendered power arrangements in these Victorian scenes of female characters as confessional subjects, it is crucial to examine the prevailing pictures of sinful, or in the Victorian and biblical vernacular, "fallen" women. In particular, I am interested in the figure of the prostitute, an image that haunts Lady Audley's own confession about selling herself twice on the marriage market for upward mobility. As in this sensation-fiction account, Victorian definitions of female depravity are persistently sexualized, with aberrant behaviors often pathologized in terms of reproductive processes.

Indeed, the prostitute has a distinctive place in the cultural semiotics of Victorian England; with the development of modern sociology, the prostitute—along with the related condition of "fallenness"—functions as a new social identity, one used to define not only deviance in women but also larger social problems from contagious diseases to urban poverty. I will argue that Braddon's sensation novel rehearses in the confession scene and its consequences the salient debates surrounding the syphilitic prostitute, an assimilation of assorted cultural notions about female degeneracy from madwomen to malcontent wives. For prostitution was a hot topic at mid-century; from a range of vantage points including medicine, law, economics, and the evolving discourse of urban sociology, essays circulated throughout mainstream newspapers and periodicals on the causes and management of prostitution in England.[1] Henry Mayhew's columns in the *Morning Chronicle* brought first-person narratives of common London prostitutes into the homes of middle-class readers during 1849–50.[2] These compelling stories disseminated the issue into other publications such as economist William Rathbone Greg's 1850 essay in the *Westminster Review* on prostitution in which he generously incorporates Mayhew's tales of streetwalkers.[3] Then, in 1861–62, the years that Braddon's novel also first appeared in serial form, Mayhew published *London Labour and the London Poor*, in which the fourth volume is primarily a monumental treatment of prostitution.[4]

This energetic discourse on prostitution reveals the contradictory ways in which Victorians regarded aberrant femininity, a cultural ambivalence that surfaces as well in the conflicting explanations Braddon's novel offers for Lady Audley's depravity. As the following pages investigate, theories on the origins of prostitution deploy biological accounts and moral judgments to contain, displace, or disguise the material circumstances that contribute to this etiology. In the space of one essay, Greg variously axiomatizes prostitution as a "hideous gangrene of English society," as "one of the sorest evils," and as "the great social vice."[5] Mirroring these arguments on prostitution and venereal disease, Lady Audley's secular confessors construe vague biological explanations of her inherited madness to mediate and mask their own vested interests in her diagnosis and treatment. However, in the confession itself, Lady Audley uses the biological condition of madness to expose economic and social circumstances that so restrict her that she becomes, in a sense, "mad." Given my larger interest in how confession scenes reveal and participate in paradigms of gender and power, this attention to contradictory constructions of female perversion is critical.

At her most sensational pitch, Lady Audley confesses her crimes as a consequence of her madness, yet she also emphasizes "that narrow boundary-line between sanity and insanity." My approach to Braddon's confessional subject likewise attends to the "narrow boundary-line" between the figure of the madwoman in *Lady Audley's Secret* and the ever-present prostitute in Victorian culture, between biological and social understandings for these images of female degeneracy, and between criminality and insanity, villainy and victimage, agency and passivity. At the same time, my reading attends to another "narrow boundary-line" that these various divisions expose, namely, a distinction between confession and testimony, between imputing wrongdoings to discrete individuals and attributing deleterious acts to the larger responsibility of many individuals who collectively reap the advantages of a social structure predicated on privilege to some, deprivation to others. This double emphasis on confession and testimony is not intended to replay a "containment versus subversion" argument in which a historically positioned text both reproduces and contests dominant ideology. For my part, I am less interested in assigning a specific political value to the confession or to the novel's depiction of transgressive femininity than I am to the ways in which Braddon's mixed portrayal represents complexities of causality not unlike those that arise in contemporary accounts of prostitution.

Since the figure of the prostitute looms large in the Victorian cultural imagination, it is no surprise that this image of female degeneracy lurks behind sensation heroines, transgressive by definition.[6] Braddon's first popular sensation novels—*Lady Audley's Secret* and *Aurora Floyd*—star heroines who commit bigamy, itself a limited variant of prostitution, whereas the sensational transgression of *East Lynne* is Isabel Vane's adultery. Deviant femininity is even encoded in the names of two sensation heroines—Magdalen Vanstone in *No Name* and Lydia Gwilt in *Armadale*.[7] My point in mapping out Lady Audley's confession through other discursive treatments of anomalous female identity is to show that, rather than constructing a sexual "truth" of the subject, such confessional narratives delineate truths of a culture where prevailing metaphors encode ideological arrangements of power.

From the Whore of Babylon to the Lady of Audley Court:
Anti-Catholicism, Sensation Fiction, and Prostitution

First, I want to explore another boundary line that forms a significant context for confession in *Lady Audley's Secret*, that is, a transition from religious to secular notions of confession. In contrast to the scene of Catholic confession in *Villette*, here confession moves from church to home, from the foreign setting of a Catholic country to England. With this secularization and domestication of confession and transgression, Lady Audley's team of interlocutors include her second husband, an attorney who is also her nephew, and a medical man. These domestic and secular confessors regard her transgressions as the consequences of a pathological body rather than a sinful soul. Despite this evident shift from the religious to the secular, vestiges of the anti-Catholic tropes of the 1850s cast irregular and fleeting shadows on the setting of Braddon's novel as well as on accounts of the evolution of prostitution in nineteenth-century England. As *Villette* demonstrates and as the Pre-Raphaelite painting *The Vale of Rest* insinuates, the prostitute and the nun are intertwined figures of sexual duplicity in mid-century anti-Catholic depictions; so too does Braddon utilize this cultural correlation for framing the sensational story of a multiply transgressive female character.[8]

Although neither Lady Audley nor any other character is identified as Catholic in *Lady Audley's Secret*, traces of anti-Catholic mythology contribute to an impression of illicit mystery that the setting of the novel unfolds. Like Gothic fiction a half-century earlier, *Lady Audley's Secret* relies on the lure of hidden violations circulating in Victorian culture, offenses frequently associated with the sacrament of Catholic confession and with the activities of religious houses. This initial depiction of Audley Court, where much of the novel and Lady Audley's confession and transgressions occur, exploits this cultural lore: "To the left there was a broad gravelled walk, down which, years ago, when the place had been a convent, the quiet nuns had walked hand in hand." Once a Catholic convent, the house itself presents a maze of concealed chambers, including "a hiding-place so small," wedged between floor and ceiling, "that he who hid there must have crouched on his hands and knees or lain full length and yet large enough to contain a quaint old carved oak chest half filled with priests' vestments."[9] Although this priest hole alludes to clandestine violations of earlier anti-Catholic laws that forbade harboring priests and holding mass, its location in what was once a convent also capitalizes on the popular propaganda in Victorian culture that likened religious cloisters to dens of sexual intrigue.

The narrative's investigation of such secret spaces and relics of an illicit Catholicism within the home parallels the scrutiny of Lady Audley's body for traces of her own transgressive history. Like the seeming disparity between a chaste nun and a tainted prostitute, the novel registers this discontinuity between appearance and an ulterior "truth," between the benign surfaces of home and femininity and a recondite story of violations and degradation. In addition, this juxtaposition of priest holes with Lady Audley's clandestine and criminal activities underlines the secularization and domestication of the surveillance of illicit behavior, suggesting that, in the words of Braddon's narrator, "physicians and lawyers are the confessors of this prosaic nineteenth century."[10]

If Braddon uses anti-Catholic motifs to frame her sensation heroine's submerged transgressions, contemporary debates use anti-Catholic motifs to frame the violation of contracting sex for money. For these delineations of prostitution cite the Roman Catholic church as an institution that implicitly supports such sex trafficking. Like Braddon's sensational portrait of Lady Audley as angelic wife and demonic criminal, these depictions contribute to the mythology that the semblance of piety and devotion among Catholic priests, monks, and nuns is but a clever front for scandalous sex rings. The metaphoric significance of this association between prostitutes and religious sisters is encoded in the pejorative nickname for Roman Catholicism, "the Whore of Babylon," that circulated through Victorian anti-Catholic rhetoric. Jenny Franchot describes the ideological work of this elocution in relation to sanctioned ideas of femininity, the domestic ideal of "true womanhood," in the antebellum United States: "Protestants created in Romanism an imaginary container whose alluring multifaceted surface disguised a violent, even devouring, interior, images drawn from the sexually fearful and punitive rhetoric of the Book of Revelation. Rome, as the Scarlet Woman and the Whore of Babylon, had 'polluted' female recesses and an alluring female surface. Protestant womanhood, undergoing its own strenuous purification through the 'cult of true womanhood,' was thought especially vulnerable to Rome's unbridled female sensualism."[11] In a similar manner the detective plot leading to the confession scene constructs Lady Audley as this combination of "alluring female surface" disguising her "'polluted' female recesses." Compared to two Italian Catholic villainesses, Lucretia Borgia and Catherine de'Medici, Lady Audley is represented in the exaggerated modifiers that comprise this vilifying personification of Catholicism as a sexually debauched woman.[12] Thus the "Lady" of Audley Court signifies an updated, Anglicized version of the Whore of Babylon.

In *London Labour and the London Poor*, prostitution is offered up as evidence that duplicity and profligacy thrive under Roman Catholicism. A segment on prostitution in modern Rome begins with this pronouncement: "Mortification of the flesh is one of the first principles of the Romish faith, and a stranger would expect to find any laxity of morals amongst the inhabitants of the eternal city severely punished; but in point of fact prostitution is tolerated and regulated in Rome."[13] Although Catholicism is routinely indicted for the toleration of prostitution in various European countries, the public health lobby in England actually supported precisely the legalization and regulation of prostitution along the lines of the so-called continental model that Greg recommends in his 1850 article. In keeping with this anti-Catholic rhetoric, Mayhew and co-author Bracebridge Hemyng enumerate five different forms of clandestine prostitution practiced in Rome by prostitutes, driven by their "brutal cravings and bestial desires," who frequent both public streets and private homes. This rendition primitivizes prostitution as the base action of mere animals, a characterization corresponding with reams of images of lascivious father confessors, monks, and nuns whose sexual appetites know no bounds.

In an article published in the *Westminster Review*, editor John Chapman lambastes Catholicism for its policy of repression; exemplifying Foucault's repressive hypothesis, Chapman claims that the refusal and denial of illicit sexuality contributes to the proliferation of prostitution in Catholic cultures, particularly Rome. Chapman's 1870 essay is designed to champion the embattled Contagious Diseases Acts of the 1860s that instituted government surveillance of prostitution.[14] Consequently, he maintains that because prostitution is legally neglected, it flourishes everywhere: "Alas, evil is not annihilated by our refusal to see it; and though prostitutes are legally unknown at Rome, they are none the less abundant in the Holy City. Just as because the Church declares marriage a sacrament and indissoluble, the people of Catholic countries have adopted the practice of divorcing themselves and remarrying under the name of concubinage to an extent unknown in the Protestant parts of Christendom; so, precisely because the Church legally ignores prostitution, it prevails in Rome, not merely among the lower classes, but in almost all classes of society. And not only so, but the feeling of its 'sinfulness' is so feeble, that a very slight temptation suffices to induce its practice."[15] The impossibility of securing divorce under the jurisdiction of the Roman Catholic church weighs in Chapman's assessment of this supposed epidemic of prostitution in Catholic countries. This rationale links the impossibility of sanctioned divorce with condoned promiscuity and pinpoints how different arrangements of cohabitation and domesticity, particularly for women without viable alternatives to men as sexual partners (in or outside matrimony) for material support, tend to get subsumed under the rubric "prostitution" throughout a range of Victorian texts.

Insisting that prostitution thrives well in Catholic countries laboring under this doctrine of repression, which in Chapman's estimation amounts to harmful neglect, the essay goes on to illustrate the way this reprehensible state of affairs exposes the depraved hypocrisy of a religion that supports the ideal of celibacy: "Rome, and indeed the whole of Italy, which has been almost equally dominated by the Roman Catholic creed and Papal influence, have long been notable for that peculiar form of sexual license called cicisbeism, which has been justly defined as domestic prostitution *assise au cheval conjugal*, and tolerated by the husband." In this passage, the evident ignominy of cicisbeism, where the husband tolerates the wife's paramour in the Italian household, bolsters English ideals of domesticity and gender through the inversion of the practice of husbands with numerous mistresses. Chapman's position here suggests a contest over power; domination at the level of the state is correlated with domestic rule. The power of the Church of Rome vitiates not only government but also familial authority, so a husband even stomachs his wife trading sex for money within his own home. By the same token, secrecy and undetectability typify this rendition of a middle-class home converted into a brothel, a wife into a madam, again recycling anti-Catholic visions of religious houses as lairs of lechery. Taken together, these portrayals stimulate an anxiety that a paterfamilias may well not rule his roost, but instead he might, wittingly or not, harbor concealed menaces to his very supremacy. Chapman's assertion that "domestic prostitution forms a large feature in the general licentiousness of Roman life" also complements a tendency in Victorian culture to sexualize and criminalize any semblance of female power.[16]

The idea of domestic harlotry in Catholic Rome has its analogue in definitions of prostitution applied to conjugal arrangements in England. Greg's idea of prostitution encompasses the primacy of money in a woman's contract to marry, although he uses this correspondence to argue against the rigid condemnation of prostitutes that embodies prevalent social attitudes: "For one woman who thus, of deliberate choice, sells herself to a lover, ten sell themselves to a husband. Let not the world cry shame upon us for this juxtaposition. The barter is as naked and as cold in the one case as in the other; the thing bartered is the same; the difference between the two transactions lies in the price that is paid down." Despite this recognition that marriage and prostitution are twin "transactions," Greg nevertheless understands the financial remuneration under any circumstances as "the worst and lowest form of sexual irregularity" in women.[17] Greg's stance on this subject reveals the ways in which notions of degenerate femininity might implicate material circumstances of want, but inevitably foster explanations of intrinsic and immoral perversity.

Braddon's depiction of Lady Audley's own marital matches reproduces this split perspective, although the novel's rendering is careful to problematize what Greg considers a woman's "deliberate choice." Following the opening pages of *Lady Audley's Secret* with its setting of an abandoned Catholic convent converted into a private, privileged-class home, the narrative unfolds the particulars of the Audley marriage. When Sir Michael Audley proposes to this mysterious governess, it becomes immediately clear that for this woman the offer signifies a marriage of purely material advantages. Yet her suitor resists this motivation: "I scarcely think that there is a greater sin, Lucy . . . than that of the woman who marries a man she does not love. . . . nothing but misery can result from a marriage dictated by any motive but truth and love." Dropping on her knees at Sir Michael's feet, the same fallen position she takes in the confession scene much later on, Lucy delivers an impassioned speech about how preposterous is Sir Michael's—and by association, Greg's—pronouncement against marrying for money when a woman is so tempted by this promise of material security: "You ask too much of *me*! Remember what my life has been; only remember that. From my very babyhood I have never seen anything but poverty. . . . Poverty, poverty, trials, vexations, humiliations, deprivations! *You* cannot tell; you, who are amongst those for whom life is so smooth and easy; you can never guess what is endured by such as we. Do not ask too much of me, then. I *cannot* be disinterested; I cannot be blind to the advantages of such an alliance. I cannot, I cannot!"[18] Here, in the trajectory of the narrative, Lady Audley commits her first transgression, one that repeats and forecasts similar failings, vices that can also be construed as attempts to protect "the advantages" she acquires upon marrying a wealthy, entitled man. For the novel makes patently clear from the beginning that her interests in marriage are material, and in this sense Lady Audley assumes the station of a prostitute.

Frames of Fallenness:
Female Degeneracy as Madness and Prostitution

The steadfastness of the trope of prostitution for degenerate femininity endures beyond these dubious constructions of Catholicism as well as Lady Audley's marriage of convenience. Clearly, the figure of the prostitute has a symbolic stranglehold on Victorian visions of the illicit and dangerous, which are repeatedly gendered and excessively sexualized. Writing about insanity in 1854, Alfred Beaumont Maddock showcases the "morbid conditions of the generative apparatus" in the etiology of women's mental and moral disorders.[19] Writing on prostitution in 1869, John Chapman pathologizes the most blatant cultural image of unsanctioned female sexuality as he distinguishes prostitution itself as the "worst" malady "with which humanity is afflicted," with its physical, social, and moral repercussions.[20] My intention here is to delineate the ways in which diagnoses and judgments—the counterparts to secular confessions—expose vested interests in defining and treating transgressive women. I would now like to investigate associations between madwomen and prostitutes, between the ideas of moral insanity and venereal disease as transmittable conditions, since this contiguity is crucial in Lady Audley's confession of her own madness as an "inherited taint."

Although the text never explicitly labels Lady Audley a prostitute, elements of Lady Audley's "story of my life" overlap with representations of prostitution and coordinate with a cultural fascination over transmitted degeneracy. For Lady Audley's crimes are referenced repeatedly to sexuality. Without knowledge of her first husband's death, she commits bigamy by marrying Sir Michael Audley, an act she carefully chronicles in her confession. In pleading insanity to charges of bigamy, arson, and murder, Lady Audley asserts that this madness is a consequence of sexual reproduction, that is, its initial expression coincides with the birth of her child. Yet Lady Audley's narrative also links this "inherited taint in [her] blood" with fears of material privation. Along with the confession of inherited madness, Lady Audley furnishes her occupational history; this career ranges from marriage and motherhood to governessing and marriage again, with an intermediary and elusively cast education in London from which she emerges with her proper name altered from "Mrs. George Talboys" to "Lucy Graham" and her social identity adjusted from a deserted wife and a mother to a young working woman of obscure origins. The resemblance between Lady Audley's confession and accounts of prostitution that most interests me here hinges on the idea of a circulating disorder, whether construed as inherited madness or sexually transmitted disease.

Often described as "pollution" and "contamination," prostitution itself is frequently coupled with venereal disease in Victorian discussions to the extent that even the streetwalker herself comes to figure the scourge of syphilis. Citing "the deplorable extent and virulence of disease which prostitution is the means of spreading throughout the community," Greg reiterates this fear that prostitution facilitates the transmission of infectious disease. Yet working-class women, rather than their male and often middle-class sex partners, become the object of detecting, diagnosing, and treating this unregulated sexuality as a medical and social disorder. Invoking the terror of this "mischief of syphilis," Greg urges government involvement in the surveillance of prostitutes: "Let us, therefore, weigh dispassionately the objections commonly urged against any attempt to check and eradicate the spread of syphilitic poison through our population, by such regulation and supervision of prostitutes as shall prevent them from practising their *métier* when diseased."[21] Here the status of the common prostitute as an object of exchange in the sphere of trade is refurbished, perhaps with a tinge of sarcasm, through the French "métier." Nevertheless, this preoccupation with syphilitic women rather than their presumably afflicted sex partners radiates out in Victorian culture to sensation fiction's fascination with irregular female characters.

An emphasis on the swift and often imperceptible transmission of disease likewise pervades speculations about insanity in women. Where insanity is regarded as a consequent condition of syphilis itself, this pathology undergirds the symbolic constellation of prostitution, contagion, and inherited madness. Victorian psychologist John Pritchard cites hereditary traits as predisposing causes of moral insanity that could be latent, emerge gradually in later years, or flare up through environmental aggravation.[22] If prostitution and syphilis are difficult to decipher, moral insanity is difficult to discern. This problem of readability provides justification for intensifying vigilance directed at women, whether policing working-class women on the streets or medically treating privileged women whose behavior seems suspect.

This concept of moral insanity betrays how physiological and psychological explanations mediate social standards. For moral insanity in females signifies a departure from conduct deemed appropriate such as self-control and moderation.[23] If a woman behaved outside these middle-class norms of femininity, then she suffered from moral insanity; by these terms, the common prostitute's conduct rendered her morally insane as well. Rather than a loss of reasoning capacities, moral insanity meant "a morbid perversion of the natural feelings, affections, inclinations, temper, habits, moral dispositions, and natural impulses, without any remarkable disorder or defect of the intellect."[24] Most significant about Pritchard's construction of insanity is the prominence of "inherited taint" that subsumes other explanations such as "environmental aggravation." This reiterated rhetoric of "inherited taint" indicates not only a cultural obsession with transmission but also how an emphasis on genetic degeneration attempts to minimize and mystify material conditions and social circumstances. In this discourse, pathology becomes another way of talking about morality, about what is sanctioned as proper behavior; lower-class conditions and the "temper, habits, moral dispositions" such limited circumstances might shape are translated into a lower or lesser moral consciousness. In turn, the concept of moral degeneracy, tethered in Victorian debates on both prostitution and madness, naturalizes the political and civil disadvantages of impoverished women, something Lady Audley's confession illuminates.[25]

Both inherited madness and prostitution play up the Victorian concept of degeneracy whereby social, physical, and moral anomalies result from a weakening genetic stock; degenerationists related this enervation to the moral fall of Adam and Eve, herself an allegorical ancestor of the modern-day prostitute.[26] The most contested theory of prostitution in fact coincides with this prevalent idea of the escalating degeneracy of the human race heralded by the biblical Fall. This "downward-path scenario" views the prostitute's physical, social, and moral conditions as increasingly disintegrating with no hope of reversal or restitution. Amanda Anderson's study about the Victorian rhetoric of fallenness and prostitution offers an inventory, drawn from contemporary theories on the subject, of this downward-path trajectory: "Wretchedness, misery, destitution, loss of the affections, deadening of the mind (or, in some alternative formulations, insupportable mental anguish), disease, decay, death (often by suicide)."[27] As in depictions of moral insanity, here the material circumstances of "destitution" are assimilated into a litany of both physiological and psychological conditions. Like theories of moral insanity, this doctrine of irretrievability from such varied forms of deprivation renders prostitution a condition of progressive, inherited degeneracy that vindicates the ineffective social measures of reclamation known as rescue work. Greg sums up this narrative profile of the prostitute's plummeting course: "The career of these women is a brief one; their downward path a marked and inevitable one; and they know this well. They are almost never rescued; escape themselves they cannot."[28] The general cohesiveness of this viewpoint throughout Victorian culture explains in part the unfortunate closure of a miserable death doled out to various female characters in mid-century novels who are associated with prostitution.[29]

Yet there were alternatives to this governing narrative. William Acton, a medical doctor in England who endorsed a perspective held by Alexandre Parent-Duchâtelet in France, asserted that rather than following this regrettable one-way street, prostitutes were capable of rescuing themselves and assimilating into mainstream, even middle-class society: "Prostitution is a transitory state through which an untold number of British women are ever on their passage."[30] As Acton's words suggest, the idea of transience condenses a cultural anxiety about the visibility and readability of degenerate women, here "an untold number" who pass imperceptibly from this temporary falling of a streetwalker into the securely sanctioned calling of a lawful wife. Interestingly, *Lady Audley's Secret* structures its sensation heroine's history through both narratives of prostitution. On one hand, the abandoned and destitute wife quite capably refurbishes herself into marriage material for a lord; on the other, Lady Audley's inherited madness seemingly leads to death in an asylum.

The downward-path and transience narratives represent the span of cultural stories about prostitutes' lives. Explanations for the causes of prostitution also tend to privilege fundamental, biological factors that dismiss or disguise social considerations. The standard line on the biological causality of prostitution revolves around the notion of an inherent weakness, a trait connected in various discourses to class, gender, and Victorian ideas of race.[31] For example, Greg maintains that women's intrinsic sexual passivity contributes to their induction into prostitution; women do not experience sexual feelings until they experience sex, and at that point they tend to lose all self-control: "In men, in general, the sexual desire is inherent and spontaneous, and belongs to the condition of puberty. In the other sex, the desire is dormant, if not non-existent, till excited; always till excited by intercourse. Those feelings which coarse and licentious minds are so ready to attribute to girls, are most invariably *consequences*. Women whose position and education have protected them from exciting causes, constantly pass through life without ever being cognizant of the promptings of the senses."[32] For men, carnal desire is strong and basic, while their concomitant moral weakness is excused by virtue of this essential sexual agency. Yet women prostitutes are not granted this dispensation for their intrinsically passive or "dormant" natures. While the gist of the passage focuses on what is constructed as a biological difference, Greg also implies that class position and material circumstances determine sexual knowledge.

Elsewhere Greg does allow that social conditions beget prostitution—"that hard necessity—that grinding poverty approaching to actual want—which, by unanimous *testimony*, is declared to be the most prolific source of prostitution, in this and in all other countries." Greg's use of "testimony" underscores that, in the accounts of poor women compelled to take up prostitution, the burden of the transgression lies with economic and social circumstances rather than individual shortcomings. Despite this clear determination of "grinding poverty" as "the most prolific source of prostitution," at other points in Greg's account these very same material conditions take on a decided moral cast: "Some, too, there are for whom no plea can be offered—who voluntarily and deliberately sell themselves to shame, and barter in a cold spirit of bargain, chastity and reputation for carriages, jewels, and a luxurious table."[33] Although "hard necessity" might dictate prostitution, this "actual want" suddenly evaporates if a woman appears to act with deliberation. By the same token, Greg's shift from viewing prostitutes as passive victims to calculating agents of their own demise seems predicated on a perception of which and how many material comforts are acceptable for an impoverished woman to desire and to procure. Another aspect of this kind of reasoning surfaces in Greg's assertion that "the snares of vanity" drive lower-class women into prostitution.[34] As with his remarks about bargaining for luxuries, this attitude suggests that poor people should not mingle socially with those who are more financially secure, nor should they avail themselves of material items that are deemed above their station.

These contradictory attitudes about the poor—"deserving," but only to the degree that they ultimately maintain their class status—characterize Henry Mayhew's documentation of urban poverty. Mayhew's prodigious and diverse examinations of prostitutes and prostitution commence with his observations about the London poor in the *Morning Chronicle* in the weekly number of November 13, 1849, on slopworkers and needlewomen.[35] Inasmuch as Mayhew introduced his general, middle-class audience to the details of streetwalkers' lives, these letters delivered a sensation in journalism.[36] Presumably, Mayhew's readers had little occasion to hear first-person descriptions of prostitution, no matter how edited and otherwise constructed these stories were. Using what he termed "street biographies," Mayhew strung together his interviews with London women whose impoverishment was so extreme that they were "driven to the street." As the following discussion reveals, Mayhew tends to be more sympathetic to and more complicated about the subject of prostitution when he is recounting for his *Morning Chronicle* audience his interviews with women on the streets of London than when he treats the subject from a greater distance, and with Bracebridge Hemyng, in the voluminous exposé on prostitution a decade later in *London Labour and the London Poor*.[37]

This four-volume study classifying the urban poor compresses the spectrum of economic problems of poverty into deviant female sexuality. Invoking the biological clichés of the era, Mayhew and Hemyng utilize the prostitute as an extended metaphor for all criminality and social misfortunes befalling not only Victorian England but also other cultures throughout history.[38] Consequently, the text offers capacious definitions of prostitution that include perjury and bribery: "Literally construed, prostitution is the putting of anything to vile use." If Greg equates marriage with prostitution, Mayhew equates wives with prostitutes so that any use of a woman's body in exchange for money, whether in prostitution or a marriage of convenience, is more a function of sexual misconduct rather than one of economic need. Prostitution thus demarcated in the fourth volume, titled "Those Who Will Not Work," does not constitute work at all but rather "a means of subsistence without labour."[39] In this analysis, women acting in their own economic interests are outlawed as social and sexual misfits, while prostitution itself figures as both symptom and cause of urban disorder.

Yet the initial representations of prostitution over a decade earlier in the *Morning Chronicle* yield an altogether different impression, one that highlights material conditions over moral degeneracy. In these anecdotes, Mayhew stresses substantive privation as the most conspicuous cause of prostitution, and he introduces the first narrative account accordingly: "During the course of my investigation into the condition of those who are dependent upon their needle for their support, I had been so repeatedly assured that the young girls were mostly compelled to resort to prostitution to eke out their subsistence, that I was anxious to test the truth of the statement. I had seen much want, but I had no idea of the intensity of the privations suffered by the needlewomen of London until I came to inquire into this part of the subject. But the poor creatures shall speak for themselves."[40] Mayhew's ethnographic chronicle replicates a structure of secularized confession inasmuch as he elicits narratives from these "poor creatures," women who transgress through prostitution. Despite the pretext that his confessional subjects "speak for themselves," it is clear that his social identity as a middle-class literate man and as self-appointed investigator of the urban poor renders Mayhew the power enabling the execution and the legitimation of these stories of illegitimacy. One of Mayhew's subjects even alludes to the privilege of speaking her story which, in effect, constitutes a testimony to conditions that compel her into a life of sin: "If I was never allowed to speak no more, it was the little money I got by my labour that led me to go wrong. Could I have honestly earnt enough to have subsisted upon, to find me in proper food and clothing, such as is necessary, I should not have gone astray; no, never—As it was I fought against it as long as I could—that I did—to the last."[41] This testimony from one of Mayhew's subjects also reveals the power dynamics that frame confessional discourse: she recognizes that her interlocutors license her to speak about her "wrong," something that undercuts Mayhew's assertion that his streetwalkers are "speaking for themselves."

If the political arrangements of transgressive speaker and authorized audience replicate the structure of confessional discourse here, the process of gathering these stories also replicates the structure of the confessional booth. After Mayhew broaches the sensational topic of prostitution in the newspaper, he orchestrates an unprecedented meeting of twenty-five needlewomen claiming that low wages had driven them to the streets.[42] Calling this gathering a "test" in order to confirm the veracity of the individual tales of prostitution previously collected, Mayhew reviews the precautions he and his fellow investigator take to assure the confidentiality of the disclosures: "It was arranged that the gentleman and myself should be the only male persons visible on the occasion, and that the place of meeting should be as dimly lighted as possible, so that they could scarcely see or be seen by one another or by us."[43] As in the structure of the Catholic ritual, here the very emphasis placed on limited, even deceptive, visibility in this scene suggests the transgressive and unspeakable nature of these revelations.

Mayhew goes on to describe a surveillance device, a forerunner of the one-way mirror: "Behind a screen, removed from sight, so at [*sic*] not to wound the modesty of the women—who were nevertheless aware of their presence—sat two reporters from this Journal, to take down *verbatim* the confessions and declarations of those assembled."[44] Whereas the women become the exclusive objects of visual and auricular examination, this arrangement ensures the panoptic gaze of this team of secularized confessors by maximizing their visual advantage through "*verbatim*" transcription under the pretext of "modesty" accorded by middle-class spectators to these fallen working-class women.[45] Mayhew's words signify these collected narratives of transgression as both "confessions and declarations"; Mayhew's syntax signifies that the speakers are first and foremost confessional subjects with witnessing merely of secondary importance.

Similar to the vision Greg's essay provides, Mayhew's divided treatment of prostitution characterizes his subjects' confessions of streetwalking as testimony to the social problem of penury in his *Morning Chronicle* letters, but in *London Labour* Mayhew and Hemyng dilute this materialist perspective by representing prostitutes as intrinsically depraved. Thus the demands of material necessity in the earlier Mayhew shade into craven selfishness in subsequent depictions. *Lady Audley's Secret* likewise exhibits this range of attitudes about deviant femininity in the novel's conflicted treatment of Lady Audley's transgressions that stem from the desire to improve her lot by marrying up the social ladder. The confession itself threads these strands of testimony about the politics of impoverishment into Lady Audley's revelations of moral and biological fallenness. Her confessors, however, emphasize her pathology of an "inherited taint in her blood" to disguise their vested interests in maintaining this diagnosis and managing her accordingly. This split stance manifests a cultural ambivalence about transgressive femininity—whether the madwoman, the bigamist, or the prostitute—that both pathologizes and demonizes the subject of its attention. For Lady Audley's confession interacts suggestively with other representational systems of deviant female sexual identity. Like the literature on prostitution, the novel stresses a series of tenuous boundary lines besides the one between sanity and madness that informs a reading of Lady Audley's "secret." In all these accounts, the borders between the violator and the violated, between criminality and pathology, between the social, the biological, and the moral, are hazy indeed.

From Madwoman to Madame

The confession scene inaugurates the fulfillment of Robert Audley's detective work to uncover the secret history of his uncle's mysterious wife. It is also the incomplete resolution toward which the narration has directed its assiduous attention as this nephew-turned-attorney searches for clues to Lady Audley's fraudulent identities and criminal activities. In this sense, the narrative reproduces a cultural obsession with recognizing and classifying depraved femininity, a preoccupation exemplified in the debates on prostitution. Before reading the role of power in the confession itself, I concentrate on how Lady Audley's lengthy revelations about her origins and about the origins of her "secret" disease resonate with different representations of the prostitute, prostitution, and venereal disease. My object here is to demonstrate how Lady Audley's narrative of "the secret of my life" works as both confession of individual pathology and as an act of witnessing larger social inequities.

The organization of Lady Audley's confession, contained within one lengthy chapter, renders an appearance of an integral and full narrative; yet the "secret" of the confession, and its manifestations elsewhere in the novel, works against this formal coherence. At the outset of the scene, Lady Audley's words about struggle and conquest suggest the power dynamics that structure the very act of confession. Yet this opposition between the confessor's domination or "triumph" and the confessional subject's subordination also falters. Although Robert demands the confession upon threat of criminal prosecution, Lady Audley's mocking disclosure affords her a provisional position of power by claiming inherited insanity, a diagnosis that Robert's compulsive detective work has failed to uncover: "I will confess anything—everything! What do I care? God knows I have struggled hard enough against you, and fought the battle patiently enough; but you have conquered, Mr. Robert Audley. It is a great triumph, is it not? a wonderful victory! You have used your cool, calculating, frigid, luminous intellect to a noble purpose. You have conquered—a MADWOMAN!"[46] The correlation of "anything" with "everything" sets the substance of this revelation on shaky ground, stressing the way power and not a secret "truth" defines the content of the confession. This confessing "MADWOMAN" orthographically overpowers the "cool, calculating, frigid, luminous intellect" of her confessor; Lady Audley's secret challenges the value of rational detection on which Robert has staked his accusation and his professional reclamation. Instead, madness becomes the trope for a contagious indeterminacy that the novel exploits. For in this novel, culminating with the confession, insanity functions as rhetorical, biological, and social conditions that circulate among characters, narrator, and reader. Lady Audley confesses that when her material welfare is threatened, her mind periodically loses its balance; she consequently commits crimes of passion—including bigamy, murder, and arson—that also attempt to secure her prosperity. Prior to the confession scene, Robert and Lady Audley engage in a semiotic struggle over competing definitions of madness as each endeavors to label the other insane as a way to protect one's position in the family. Yet in the act of confessing, Lady Audley invokes this self-diagnosis to ridicule Robert's mastery; by extension the notions of "power" and "truth" assume relative and unsteady significance.

Titled "My Lady Tells the Truth," this confessional chapter multiplies the meanings of both truth and madness, while the larger narrative underscores both the mediated character of determining truth and the vested interests in diagnosing madness. In Lady Audley's own lexicon, "lie" and "truth" are qualitative distinctions whose contiguity resembles another slippery demarcation: "When you say that I killed George Talboys, you say the truth. When you say that I murdered him treacherously and foully, you lie. I killed him because I AM MAD! because my intellect is a little way upon the wrong side of that narrow boundary-line between sanity and insanity."[47] "Say[ing] the truth" is not so simple a matter, as the plot works out, since George Talboys survives Lady Audley's push down the well. She "kills" her estranged husband in her recitation, but does not kill him in the plot; neither does she "murder" him in her confessional reconstruction of this event because her violence resulted from a fit of insanity rather than a premeditated act.

Elsewhere the narrator invokes this "narrow boundary-line" in the minds of others within and beyond the text: "There is nothing so delicate, so fragile, as that invisible balance upon which the mind is always trembling. Mad to-day and sane tomorrow. . . . Who has not been, or is not to be, mad in some lonely hour of life? Who is quite safe from the trembling of the balance?"[48] This epidemic of madness that is invisible precisely because it is everywhere re-plays a cultural fear about the supposed ubiquity of prostitution and sexually transmitted disease, "a pestilence whose march is so secret, and whose attacks are so insidious, that none can be certain of escape."[49] The problem of detect-ing infected prostitutes condenses an anxiety about social assimilation, a worry that lower-class, degenerate women invisibly infiltrate the higher ech-elons of English society. The madness that the narrative explores, and the confession consolidates, intimates a confusion over categories of identity rooted in class-specific gender distinctions—a "narrow boundary-line" be-tween a working woman and a lady, a prostitute and a wife—that are in-creasingly difficult to discern.[50] Passages liberally punctuating the novel asso-ciate this proliferation of insanity with faulty policing devices, with the failure to perceive the signs of deviance as it becomes more widespread, more du-plicitous. Lady Audley's intermittent and inherited insanity metaphorizes this fear of inadequate surveillance at the same time that it questions the ideologi-cal meanings of disease and degeneration. The idea of transmission provides this link between the madwoman and the prostitute, the explicit and implicit figures of female depravity that undergird Lady Audley's transgressions. This association of transmission of madness with transferable identity in *Lady Audley's Secret* develops in the context of a historical moment that fo-cuses social disorder through gendered and sexualized notions of contagion and dangerous circulation. Lady Audley's confession suggestively calibrates the idea of circulated insanity to the traffic in female sexual slavery, whether marriage or prostitution.

At the start of her confession, Lady Audley reveals herself a "MADWOMAN"; as a consequence of her confession, Lady Audley's identity shifts again from "Lady Audley" to "Madame Taylor." In order to protect the patronym, Robert adjusts this proper name as he commits his aunt to a Belgian asylum. While "Taylor" is a skewed anagram of "Talboys," Lady Audley's initial married name, this ultimate designation of "Madame" also provides a key to another veiled and shocking identity, the figure of the prostitute, which invites a suggestive subtext and cultural reference point for Lady Audley's story of transmitted pathology.

The narrative's emphasis on Lady Audley's transferable, transgressive identities encodes this concern with deleterious transmission.[51] Indeed, words describing such sensation heroines invoke the idiom of pathological social contagion. Immediately preceding Lady Audley's confession of madness, Robert castigates her as the embodiment of contamination: "I look upon you henceforth as the demoniac incarnation of some evil principle. But you shall no longer pollute this place by your presence."[52] Lady Audley "pollutes" Audley Court's sanctified familial space much as Victorian discourses argue that prostitutes recycle venereal infections into middle-class domesticity. In a related way, Mrs. Oliphant qualifies Collins's sensation heroine: "The Magdalen of *No Name* does not go astray after the usual fashion of erring maidens in romance. Her pollution is decorous, and justified by law."[53] The image of the prostitute informs this fictive "Magdalen" as well as Oliphant's diction. Again invoking the language of a contagious pathology difficult to pinpoint, Oliphant's description betokens class anxieties whereby social subordinates— figured through a transgressive woman—imperceptibly trespass on the world of their superiors. Of course, this notion of the lowly encroaching upon the socially elevated conforms to Acton's theory that prostitution is a transient occupation facilitating a woman's social climb. Sensation fiction regularly features narratives that capitalize on this disquieting belief that a common magdalen might ascend to the rank and prosperity of a lady. The passage from the review of *No Name* implies this fear of undetected or uncorrected corruption, of "pollution" that is both dangerously refined and legitimate.

If *Lady Audley's Secret* condenses and encodes this cultural preoccupation with locating imperceptible disorder, Lady Audley's confession condenses and encodes a narrative of female depravity inflected by biological and social ideas of degeneration.[54] Lady Audley asserts that her secret madness is the consequence of an inborn disorder of matrilineal descent that encompasses three generations. Accordingly, Lady Audley describes her mother's condition for which she is locked up in "her prison-house" of an insane asylum: "Her madness was an hereditary disease transmitted to her from her mother, who had died mad. She, my mother, had been, or had appeared, sane up to the hour of my birth; but from that hour her intellect had decayed, until she had become what I saw her."[55] It is noteworthy that this "hereditary disease" is difficult to detect, just as Oliphant describes the "decorous" pollution of sensation heroines, and Chapman qualifies the "secret" onslaught of disease through prostitution. Framed as female sexual reproduction gone awry, this construction of madness as a "hereditary disease" passed on from mother to daughter insinuates a wry commentary on the domestic ideal of motherhood; here childbirth heralds not feminine fulfillment but the loss of reason.

In "Prostitution in Relation to the National Health," Chapman recasts marriage and motherhood as domestic scenes of abhorrent contamination: "Many a trusting maiden radiant with happiness, health, and beauty, who gives herself in marriage, speedily finds her joy turned to mourning, her health to disease, and, it may be, her beauty defaced by its loathsome poison; many a mother has to deplore the contamination, not only of her own constitution, but that of her child, to which, either before or after birth, in countless instances that poison proves fatal." In this report, the reproductive female body operates as origin and conduit of syphilitic infection that is ubiquitous: "It is in the midst of us; it pervades every rank of society; its traces may be discovered in almost every family; its Protean and ever-changing forms are too numerous to be computed, and often elude detection even by the most experienced eyes; it attacks by preference the young and vigorous; the strength of manhood in the prime of life it reduces to weakness; the healthy blood of blooming womanhood designed to nourish the coming generation into vigorous life, it converts to poison; it blights the infant in the womb, and contaminates the milk drawn by the child from its mother's breast."[56] Contraction and expression of this degenerative condition are clearly referenced to female sexuality, just as prostitutes in Mayhew's study provide the organizing trope for social discontent. Furthermore, Chapman underlines the duplicity of the disease and, by extension, of prostitution itself in Victorian culture.

Like this narrative of venereal disease, the madness, otherwise known as lactational insanity, that infects Lady Audley and her maternal forebears depends on sexual reproduction for its transmission and its manifestation.[57] For Lady Audley acknowledges lactation as a source of her inherited madness, "the hidden taint that I had sucked in with my mother's milk."[58] Besides asserting that her "hidden taint" is a transmitted disorder, Lady Audley's words underscore an ambiguous onset of pathology whereby her mother "had been, or had appeared, sane." Here the narrative begs the question of whether insanity is a matter of appearance or a verifiable and fixed fact, an uncertainty contained within the notion of "intermittent" madness. Of course, Lady Audley's sensational confession amplifies this inability to perceive periodic mental degeneracy; despite Robert Audley's best efforts at surveillance and detection, the duplicity of Lady Audley's condition outwits his "cool, calculating, frigid, luminous intellect." This description of Lady Audley's condition is also compatible with constructions of moral insanity in which reasoning capacities remain surprisingly intact.

Throughout the novel the narrator maximizes an uncertainty about visibility and readability and in this sense replicates the imbricated cultural anxiety over prostitution, syphilis, and class position. It is madness, however, that inhabits this dominant trope of undetectable, ever-present pathology: "Mad-houses are large and only too numerous; yet surely it is strange they are not larger, when we think of how many helpless wretches must beat their brains against this hopeless persistency of the orderly outward world, as compared with the storm and tempest, the riot and confusion within:—when we remember how many minds must tremble upon the narrow boundary between reason and unreason, mad to-day and sane to-morrow, mad yesterday and sane to-day."[59] Whereas Greg, Chapman, Mayhew, and Hemyng deploy female prostitution as an extended metaphor for social disease and discontent, in *Lady Audley's Secret* intermittent madness becomes the condition of everyday life. The "narrow boundary between reason and unreason" again suggests the difficulty of detecting degeneracy or disorder of any kind.

Lady Audley's inherited madness behaves like a sexually transmitted disease at the same time that her confession contextualizes this intermittent malady by relating the social circumstances from which it arises. As Greg and Mayhew both recognize, economic disadvantages compelled Victorian women, especially those with the responsibility of children, into prostitution. Also converting social considerations into a pathological condition, medical experts describe a defining symptom of puerperal insanity as a mother's repugnance for and refusal of her domestic life—"a total negligence of, and often very strong aversion to, her child and husband . . . explosions of anger occur, with vociferations and violent gesticulations."[60] For Lady Audley, poverty compounded by the "burden" of her child precipitates her episodes of insanity. Soon after her first husband's desertion, Lady Audley describes the initial manifestation of her madness: "People pitied me; and I hated them for their pity. I did not love the child; for he had been left a burden upon my hands. The hereditary taint that was in my blood had never until this time showed itself by any one sign or token; but at this time I became subject to fits of violence and despair. At this time I think my mind first lost its balance, and for the first time I crossed that invisible line which separates reason from madness."[61] The passage again capitalizes on the notion of an "invisible line" that barely distinguishes Lady Audley's "hereditary taint . . . in my blood" from her indignation over her predicament as a single, unsupported mother and her irritation with the gratuitous sympathy of onlookers, all occasioned by her husband's unaccountable disappearance. Much like the representations of prostitution and puerperal insanity, here biology is tailored to material position; Lady Audley's "fits of violence and despair" seem less a consequence of something "in my blood" than angry desperation over social and economic circumstances. Inasmuch as she confesses another transgression, a lack of love for her child, the text insinuates that maternal love in this instance is not a natural affect but a mediated effect of social conditions.

By the same token, Lady Audley's tale undercuts the ideal of romantic love by doggedly pursuing a marriage plot in which "love" is defined by material comfort and social status; she loves her second husband more than her first because he has provided Lady Audley with sustained wealth and the luxury of peerage: "Mr George Talboys was a cornet in a dragoon regiment. He was the only son of a rich country gentleman. He fell in love with me, and married me three months after my seventeenth birthday. I think I loved him as much as it was in my power to love anybody; not more than I have loved you, Sir Michael; not so much; for when you married me you elevated me to a position that he could never have given me."[62] Where Greg assesses pecuniary motives behind marriage and prostitution, Lady Audley's confession treats the Victorian marriage of convenience like a dignified version of sex trafficking. In a similar vein, Mayhew and Hemyng reinforce this realistic estimation of matrimony as a woman's most salient economic opportunity. Lady Audley is demonized for her exploitation of this structured prospect; Mayhew and Hemyng blame any woman who resorts to such limited resources for improving her lot in life. Thus *London Labour and the London Poor* specifies prostitution as "the using of her charms by a woman for immoral purposes," which "may be done either from mercenary or voluptuous motives" or may or may not be legitimized by marriage, distinctions that matter not at all. Mayhew and Hemyng even stipulate that some marriages of financial expedience (for women, that is) are intrinsically more suspect than others: "It is this moral offensiveness which often makes the licensed intercourse of the sexes, as in the marriage of a young girl to an old man, for the sake of his money, as much an act of prostitution as even the grossest libertinism."[63] With Lady Audley nearly four decades younger than Sir Michael and with Lady Audley's evident predilection for luxury, their marriage qualifies, in Mayhew's analysis, as "an act of prostitution."

This bifurcated explanation of money or lust propelling women into prostitution in *London Labour* also shapes Greg's understanding: "The sin that is induced by the intolerable anguish of a child's starvation, must be regarded, both in heaven and on earth, with a very different degree and kind of condemnation from that which is called forth by frailty arising out of the cravings of vanity, or the unbridled indulgence of animal desire."[64] Although Greg doesn't clarify to whom this "very different degree and kind of condemnation" should be directed, he does posit these divergent sources of "the sin" and "frailty" of prostitution. His stance exposes the ways in which material necessity of "a child's starvation" dissolves into sexual and moral failings. Braddon likewise offers a contradictory story of a deviant woman who marries for money, commits bigamy, and attempts murder, in part because she is bereft of money, in part because she is "mad" with excessive passions. Again, the equivocal meaning of inherited madness in Lady Audley's account consolidates these conflicting explanations about prostitution and, as such, her words constitute both confession and testimony.

With repeated attention to her sense of alienation, Lady Audley's "madness" takes on yet another permutation: forbidden feelings of rage and resentment toward her husband and over her limited circumstances. The narrative mapping of Lady Audley's initial outbreak of insanity follows the portion of her story in which she delineates her indignation over the impoverished conditions aggravated by her husband's disappearance: "I resented it bitterly —I resented it by hating the man who had left me with no protector but a weak, tipsy father, and with a child to support. I had to work hard for my living, and in every hour of labour—and what labour is more wearisome than the dull slavery of a governess?—I recognized a separate wrong done me by George Talboys. His father was rich; his sister was living in luxury and respectability; and I, his wife, and the mother of his son, was a slave allied for ever to beggary and obscurity."[65] Here Lady Audley commits another violation inasmuch as she has the audacity to express wrath over the social and financial advantages enjoyed by her in-laws. Again traversing a "narrow boundary-line," this social posture of a degraded woman forced to hire out as a governess converges with various images of female degeneracy such as Mayhew reports in the *Morning Chronicle* of low-paid needlewomen driven to the streets to sell sex for money.

For unsupported Victorian women with middle-class training, the most prevalent source of income, "the dull slavery of governessing," was barely a notch above the female sexual slavery of prostitution. As Mary Poovey persuasively maintains, the governess in Victorian culture was regarded much like a licensed prostitute due to her position as a salaried employee of ambivalent class status who labors in the intimate surroundings of her employer's domicile.[66] In the *London Labour* rendition, a wife who marries for money is a sanctioned prostitute. In Braddon's fiction, an abandoned wife and mother who independently pursues a livelihood in whatever fashion available is a mad fiend, with her resourcefulness an emblem of her mental pathology and her moral degeneracy. Whereas Lady Audley's inherited insanity seems comparable to the sexually transmitted disease afflicting prostitutes, her "labour" as governess participates in cultural tropes of degraded, degenerate femininity.

Lady Audley's "secret" insanity also refurbishes Acton's idea of prostitution as a transient career. Provoked by the threat of indigence, this intermittent madness acts as a temporary condition precipitating unfeminine behavior, including her separation from her child, her flight alone to London to seek dubious training as a governess, her salaried work as a governess through which she meets Sir Michael Audley, followed by her bigamous act of marriage to him, and her attempted murder of George Talboys.[67] Yet these transgressive and violent acts also procure or protect Lady Audley's material well-being consolidated in and dependent on her current marriage. As with any Victorian working woman, from streetwalkers to governesses, the ultimate objective of employment is retirement from the labor market through matrimony. In *London Labour*, one prostitute recounts, "We often do marry, and well too; why shouldn't we, we are pretty, we dress well, we can talk and insinuate ourselves into the hearts of men by appealing to their passions and their senses."[68] These words reveal the common course of events for women on the legitimate sex market known as marriage—or, as Lady Audley puts it, "the world's great lottery"—in contrast to romance plots of mainstream domestic fiction that mystify with affective love such transactions.

In other ways Lady Audley's history between her marriages supports the theory of transience. After George deserts her and the baby, Lady Audley modifies her "inherited" madness over her deplorable straits: "At last these fits of desperation resolved themselves into a desperate purpose. I determined to run away from this wretched home which my slavery supported . . . I determined to go to London, and lose myself in that great chaos of humanity."[69] There seems to be a method to her madness in this shift from "fits" to "purpose." As in the narratives of women driven to the streets that Mayhew captures, Lady Audley's depiction is remarkable for the sense of agency and deliberation, a tone undercutting an utter lack of control that madness typically implies. As part of her mysterious conversion in London where she determines to "lose" herself, Lady Audley sheds her restrictive proper name, "Mrs. Talboys," by changing her social position to the unmarried, unknown, and finally transitory "Lucy Graham." In the course of the plot, this sensation heroine possesses five different sets of proper names. Such alterations suggest the transient and tenuous social identity of women. So begins one prostitute's narrative in *London Labour*: "My name is Ellen, I have no other. Yes, I sometimes call myself by various names, but rarely keep to one longer than a month or two."[70] As in Lady Audley's story, assuming "various names" is a matter of social, economic, and legal expedience.

Moreover, the phrase "lose myself" also encodes the narrative of a fallen woman where unsanctioned sex means a loss of a legitimate social identity. Representations of Lady Audley play with this prevailing figure of deviant femininity where her flight to London to "lose myself in that great chaos of humanity" dovetails with profiles of prostitutes: young indigent women from the countryside in search of a better life but ignorant of the ways of the urban streets who arrive alone in the sprawling city and quickly become vulnerable to female sex trafficking. "Lose myself in that great chaos" also suggests the invisibility of prostitution, an assumption that bespeaks a middle-class anxiety of assimilation, or the inability to perceive degeneracy—or any discrete social identity—in the swollen urban masses.[71] Lady Audley's "secret" madness likewise exploits this class-specific worry. In fact, Mayhew condenses and reproduces this anxiety in his taxonomy of "clandestine prostitution," which encompasses assorted women laborers from factory operatives to maidservants. Of this widespread multiplication of prostitutes, to which Mayhew and Hemyng rhetorically contribute with their capacious definitions, they state that many "become comparatively respectable, and merge into the ocean of propriety."[72]

After Lady Audley declares her determination to "lose" herself in London, she eclipses the next segment of her history: "I had seen an advertisement in the *Times* while I was at Wildersnea, and I presented myself to Mrs. Vincent, the advertiser, under a feigned name. She accepted me, waiving all question as to my antecedents. You know the rest. I came here, and you made me an offer, the acceptance of which would lift me at once into the sphere to which my ambition had pointed ever since I was a school-girl, and heard for the first time that I was pretty."[73] By folding this portion of her confession into "You know the rest," Lady Audley avoids specifying the nature of her relationship "under a feigned name" and without benefit of "antecedents" with Mrs. Vincent. Lady Audley's words do little to elucidate the line of employment or training she embarks upon in London. Such ambiguity surrounds the histories of prostitutes in *London Labour* where "loose women generally throw a veil over their early life."[74] Furthermore, the juxtaposition of her acceptance at Mrs. Vincent's London establishment and her "acceptance" of Sir Michael's "offer" linguistically recommends a correlation between the two events. Rather than qualifying her marriage through the rhetoric of romantic love, Lady Audley designates it an "offer" that gratifies her "ambition," much like a business proposition, and much like definitions by Greg and by Mayhew and Hemyng of any marriage with monetary interest on a woman's part as a form of prostitution. Lady Audley's own representation of her ambition to marry well resonates with the "cravings of vanity" that discussions of prostitution offer up as a cause, an explanation that overrides material need. Nevertheless, her confession habitually translates Lady Audley's failings from vain "ambition" and from her bouts of inherited madness—those "fits of violence and despair"—into the desperate acts of a woman who pursues her desires for a financially secure and comfortable life.

While material scarcity generates her episodes of mad degeneracy, Lady Audley's confession conversely links together wealth with sanity and feminine propriety once she is elevated to "Lady" through her more prosperous second marriage: "I had been poor myself, and I was now rich . . . I took pleasure in acts of kindness and benevolence . . . I dispensed happiness on every side. I saw myself loved as well as admired; and I think I might have been a good woman for the rest of my life, if fate would have allowed me to be so . . . I believe that at this time my mind regained its just balance."[75] Similar to her perspective on romantic love and maternal devotion, Lady Audley insinuates that selflessness is also shaped by social circumstances. In other words, this confessional narrative of unwitting bigamy provides a skeptical and discriminating testimony on the profile of essential womanhood promulgated by domestic ideology. Lady Audley associates poverty with the disease of mental imbalance that transforms her into a socially aberrant or immoral woman, contrary to the "good woman" she becomes under prosperous conditions. In this case, the fallen woman is rehabilitated through her rise on the socioeconomic ladder, yet this advantageous marriage further contributes to her fallen status.[76] Although the larger narrative demonizes Lady Audley's concerted efforts to secure and safeguard such substantive ease, her confession accentuates how affluence guarantees the virtues of mental health and social benevolence. In this instance, Lady Audley's violent act retaliates against the more attenuated social, legal, and economic violence against women which enforces their material dependence and yet outlaws, sexualizes, or pathologizes attempts to improve their lot in life. Put differently, this sensation heroine's transgressions tacitly indict a class system whose rigidity and restrictions push the disempowered to such criminal extremes.

Lady Audley's confession manifests this connection between material need, on one hand, and desires as sexualized deviance, on the other. At the same time, she stresses that social circumstances shape how her confessors understand her transgressions: "I dare say I was very despicable. You and your nephew, Sir Michael, have been rich all your lives, and can very well afford to despise me; but I knew how far poverty can affect a life, and I looked forward with sick terror to a life so affected."[77] In the *Morning Chronicle*, Mayhew includes a passage in which a prostitute offers a similar commentary directed at those empowered with the luxury to condemn without an inkling of the dire deprivations that drive "young girls" to the streets: "I know how horrible all this is. It would have been much better for me to have subsisted upon a dry crust and water rather than be as I am now. But no one knows the temptations of us poor girls in want. Gentlefolks can never understand it. If I had been born a lady it wouldn't have been very hard to have acted like one. To be poor and to be honest, especially with young girls, is the hardest struggle of all."[78]

In both Mayhew's case stories and in Lady Audley's own defense, remorse is a complicated matter; this streetwalker knows her trade is "horrible," yet, like Lady Audley, she recognizes that class position and material security necessarily condition what is sanctioned, ladylike behavior. By virtue of disclosing these inequities, by daring to desire what their class position denies them, both women again commit transgressions in the very act of confessing. Repeatedly the confession scene in *Lady Audley's Secret* unfolds this offense of entitlement on the part of a woman of inferior class origins who refuses to keep to her place. For instance, Lady Audley delivers her confession devoid of affect: "Throughout her long confession her voice was never broken by a tear. What she had to tell she told in a cold, hard tone; very much the tone in which some criminal, dogged and sullen to the last, might have confessed to a gaol chaplain."[79] If the narration insinuates moral vacuity by comparing Lady Audley with a convict on the brink of execution, her "dogged and sullen" manner insinuates the determination of this fractious character who testifies that material destitution provoked, if not justified, such outrageous actions.

Similarly, Lady Audley's abject posture with her face "bent obstinately towards the floor" embodies a conflated image of subjection and power. This deportment reproduces the contradictions whereby confessions of moral and biological depravity contain women's testimonies of social, economic, and legal disempowerment in these accounts of female waywardness.

London Labour and the London Poor also exhibits this ambivalent tone, divided between its overall condemnation of prostitution as a degenerate moral and biological condition, and the adamant, even self-righteous testimonies of its case-study subjects. Yet unlike the initial emergence of these witnessing voices a decade earlier in the *Morning Chronicle*, here any pretense of prostitutes speaking "for themselves" fades behind the grammar of Mayhew's appropriation: "Another woman told us, she had been a prostitute for two years; she became so from necessity; she did not on the whole dislike her way of living; she didn't think about the sin of it; a poor girl must live; she wouldn't be a servant for anything; this was much better."[80] As Mayhew absorbs first-person testimony into a third-person report, this organization illuminates confession as a mediated disclosure. Like Lady Audley, the unrepentant prostitute exacerbates her transgression by claiming this preference for "much better" living conditions than what a "poor girl" can ordinarily attain. For Lady Audley and her prostitute counterpart uncover another unspeakable postulate of Victorian consumer culture where in order for a woman to have commodities she must become one herself.[81]

Disciplining Confession

Lady Audley's confession opens up spaces for an explanatory narrative of deviant femininity that implicitly accentuates material circumstances and political disempowerment alongside the explicit biological determination of the "hereditary taint in her blood," used variously as alibi and consequence, as symptom and as subterfuge. By the same token, the depictions of prostitution from Greg and Mayhew that haunt Braddon's sensation character also pit social factors against biological causes and pathological effects.[82] This recondite commentary on Lady Audley's economic straits renders the revelation of her "secret" madness a testimony to grievances against her rather than simply a confession of her own wrongdoings. Her narration of "the secret of my life" is sensational, in part, for Lady Audley's verbose account of her multiple transgressions, for the way in which she seems in control of her own narrative, two features that seldom distinguish women's confessions in Victorian novels. However, it would be misleading to attribute unqualified agency to Lady Audley's confessional construction of her history, just as it would be misleading to characterize the novel's dominant reading of her as a mistreated woman. For the vacillation that frames Lady Audley as both villain and victim consequently hems in her power to upbraid and to testify about broader inequities that compel a needy woman's deviancy. In a comparable way, the first-person accounts of London streetwalkers attesting to deplorable states of want are assimilated into larger arguments—from Mayhew's newspaper series on London poverty to Greg's essay recommending state regulation of prostitution—that take disparate stances on female depravity.

The text exposes the intricacies of domination through a series of contradictions that structure Lady Audley's deviance and the confession itself. First, there is a discrepancy between her assertion that the limited opportunities available to women to circumvent privation occasion her "mad" crimes and the larger narrative's tendency to privilege and pathologize the violent behavior that she claims results from her subordination. Second, a marked contrast is drawn between Lady Audley's narrative of empowerment during her confession and the curtailment of this authority by her male confessors who subsequently diagnose her degeneracy and who discipline her accordingly. Focusing on the dynamics of power and authority in these anecdotes of transgressive femininity delineates the pathways by which Lady Audley's provisional command at the start of her confession devolves into a position of subjugation. Once her confession is submitted for judgment and sentence, for diagnosis and treatment, biomedical explanations of an "inherited taint in her blood" channel a vested interest in establishing her as "dangerous," as an individualized social threat to reigning structures of power.

Where Lady Audley's autobiography offers competing and intertwined explanations of inherited degeneracy and material deprivation for her criminal acts, so does the equivocal diagnosis of madness by the medical man who examines Lady Audley after her confession. Needing an authority to confirm Lady Audley's confession of madness, Robert engages Doctor Mosgrave, whose position as secularized confessor is immediately established: "'The revelation made by the patient to the physician is I believe as sacred as the confession of a penitent to his priest?' asked Robert gravely." Another instance of the curtailment of Lady Audley's narrative power, Robert commandeers her confession, yet his rendition of the story to Doctor Mosgrave is excised from the text. In keeping with the novel's ambivalence about power, truth, and madness, Robert also proves an unwitting confessional subject as the doctor reads the motivation behind this interpolated confession:

"You would wish me to prove that this lady is mad, and therefore irresponsible for her actions, Mr. Audley?" said the physician.
Robert Audley stared wondering at the mad doctor. By what process had he so rapidly arrived at the young man's secret desire?[83]

Doctor Mosgrave anticipates the "mad" internal confessor of Freudian psychiatry, privy to what remains unspoken, to "the young man's secret desire."[84]

The narration has likewise noted that this medical confidence man appears to have "safely locked in his passionless breast, the secrets of a nation." These national secrets, in which Robert's "secret desire" figures, are the sanitized public facades of privileged-class families, pretenses to the advantage of their male members. Indeed, the phrase "secrets of a nation" echoes Lady Audley's confessional "secret of my life," a correspondence that invites a comparison between individual transgression and wider covert investments. For it becomes patently clear that Robert's motivated interest in purchasing Doctor Mosgrave's diagnosis of insanity for his aunt is to avoid a public scandal that would bring dishonor to the name of the patriarch: "I ask you to save our stainless name from degradation and shame."[85] Robert's apprehension manifests an anxiety of assimilation, just as Lady Audley's confession of her underclass origins and her incursions on upper-class homes rehearses a cultural fear of social degeneracy, of the threatened deterioration of a class system built on reputation, rank, and inherited wealth.

Like the contradictions between Lady Audley's history of her victimage and Robert's villainization of her, Doctor Mosgrave produces a divided reading of Lady Audley's transgressions. The first finds in her confessional narrative "no evidence of madness in anything that she has done"; the second, based on the additional information that Lady Audley is suspected of murdering her first husband, assembles the diagnosis of "latent insanity" based on "the hereditary taint in her blood." The doctor's initial conclusion coincides with Lady Audley's implicit argument that her depravity actually amounts to efforts to "better" her material circumstances: "She ran away from her home, because her home was not a pleasant one, and she left in hope of finding a better. There is no madness in that. She committed the crime of bigamy because by that crime she obtained fortune and position. There is no madness there. When she found herself in a desperate position, she did not grow desperate. She employed intelligent means, and she carried out a conspiracy which required coolness and deliberation in its execution. There is no madness in that."[86] This interpretation also highlights the "desperate position" of a woman where possibilities for advancement, opportunities to "obtain fortune and position," are so severely restricted that she must stoop to the base remedy of "crime." More than anything, Doctor Mosgrave's first evaluation delineates evidence of reason, or the absence of madness. Yet Victorian accounts of moral insanity posit affective aberrations—or glaringly unfeminine behavior—rather than "any remarkable disorder or defect of the intellect," to refer back to Pritchard's observations.[87] The contradiction between the two findings, where one is internally inconsistent as well, is further accentuated by the doctor's initial dismissal of her hereditary insanity: "Madness is not necessarily inherited from mother to daughter. I should be glad to help you if I could, Mr. Audley, but I do not think there is any proof of insanity in the story you have told me."[88]

Once Doctor Mosgrave learns that Robert suspects Lady Audley of murdering George, and once he has a ten-minute private interview with her, he reverses his medical findings: "There is latent insanity! Insanity which might never appear; or which might appear only once or twice in a life-time. . . . The lady is not mad; but she has the hereditary taint in her blood. She has the cunning of madness, with the prudence of intelligence. I will tell you what she is, Mr. Audley. She is dangerous!"[89] Foreclosed from the narrative, this crucial scene of confession seemingly determines the ultimate diagnosis and disciplinary action. This oblique process of assessment suggests that the degeneration of an "inherited madness" is also a motivated construction, a collusive conviction of medicine and the law, the doctor and the lawyer, the secular and the domestic confessors where the latter also doubles as the ascending Audley patriarch. Lady Audley's subsequent commitment to an insane asylum in Belgium exiles her from the domestic scenes of Audley Court and England and from immediate access to the family fortune, of which she has already managed to avail herself by means of her transgressive duplicity. Nevertheless, the abrupt and dubious nature of this medical judgment punctuates an anxiety over the hazards of imperceptible and violent encroachments by a lower-born woman "with the prudence of intelligence" on masculine and upper-class domains that Lady Audley's confession reveals. Much like Doctor Mosgrave's diagnostic dilemma, depictions of the vagaries of moral insanity outline the invisibility and unreadability of the disease. The concept of moral insanity nicely exposes how physiological and genetic explanations are defined and supplanted by social standards. In *Lady Audley's Secret*, the doctor's doublespeak implies that "latent insanity" and "inherited taint" are not absolute truths of biological conditions but rather manipulated justifications to incarcerate a woman who is labeled "dangerous."

The uncertainty of this medical conviction is repeated in the disciplinary actions, the medical treatment prescribed as a consequence of Lady Audley's confession. If nothing else, her confinement in a Belgian sanitarium also ensures Lady Audley's upper-class status, one she had attempted to secure through marriage. For she is committed neither to a squalid prison nor a lock hospital but to a "maison de santé" in which she is "buried alive" in "a stately suite of apartments" of "funereal splendour." Where this final resting place resembles the gloomy and unpredictable entrapments of a Gothic setting, it also parodies Victorian marriage for privileged-class women as domestic incarceration, an embellished version of a living death. Thus Lady Audley exclaims to Robert: "You have used your power basely and cruelly, and have brought me to a living grave." The narrative does make clear that Lady Audley had imagined a better outcome to her deportment: "Her heart sank when they left Brussels behind, for she had hoped that city might have been the end of her journey."[90] Her dashed desires highlight the meaning of Lady

Audley's enclosure in this caricature of home, represented as claustrophobic and maddening in the inaction and isolation it enforces on its inmates.

In the decade following the publication of Braddon's novel, a passage from Andrew Wynter's *The Borderlands of Insanity* draws a similar assessment of the debilitating "ennui" that results from such domestic circumstances: "Within these last twenty years the railway may be said to have driven female society farther and farther into the country. The man goes forth to his labour in the morning and returns in the evening, leaving his wife, during the whole of the day, to her own devices. Whilst our residences were in town, they always had that intensely feminine refreshment, *shopping*, to solace their ennui; but shops now being out of the question, what have our wives to do, especially the childless ones, under the present miserable views as regards their education?"[91] Indeed, the novel maximizes Audley Court's proximity to the railway lines that enable Lady Audley to dash to and from London as she advances her plot to conceal her various transgressions.[92] Rather than the belittling "solace" of shopping to cure a housewife's "ennui" that Wynter prescribes, this railway network facilitates Lady Audley's agency, her ability to move quickly and to effect critical events in her life. Lady Audley's preference for the city over a provincial retreat replicates the appeal of activity over passivity. The Belgian asylum, interestingly, is in the town of "Villbrumeuse" whose English translation of "foggy city" registers the obscurity that Lady Audley's banishment ultimately signifies. By the same token, Doctor Mosgrave assures Robert that in this establishment "her future life . . . will not be a very eventful one!"[93] In a related sense, this yearning for the city bespeaks an attraction to material luxuries of the marketplace and to the public sphere with its dangerous streets, temptations that signify an illicit, often sexualized passion like the "cravings of vanity" that Greg attributes to common prostitutes.

Disguising Lady Audley's ultimate discipline and punishment, the euphemistic "maison de santé" with its baroque appointments also suggests a garish brothel for which the heroine's title is suitably adjusted from "Lady" to "Madame." By a similar mechanism of masquerade or mystification, "madness" operates in Lady Audley's confession as a metaphor for a range of Victorian constructions of female depravity from wife as prostitute to unfeminine ingenuity and aggression. These ambiguous boundaries betoken the novel's preoccupation with distinctions between female criminality and pathology that frame a wider cultural interest in prostitution.

Foucault also explores the evolution of the category of madness in penal practice where insanity and guilt are relatively calibrated, but not effectively dissimilar, in compelling discipline. With regard to acts of violence, however, Foucault poses questions about the shifting meaning of murder: "How can we assign the causal process that produced it? Where did it originate in the author himself? Instinct, unconscious, environment, heredity?"[94] Such questions likewise underlie comparable constructions of female deviance, including theories of biological degeneration, psychological theories of inherited madness, and sociological treatments of prostitution. *Lady Audley's Secret* exhibits a similarly bifurcated position on its fallen heroine with her dubious social identity in which material conditions and wickedness, naturalized as an "inherited taint in her blood," explain and explain away Lady Audley's transgressions. The entire confession—both Lady Audley's narrative as well as her confessors' interpretations—offers a conflated representation by correlating moral degeneracy with genealogical erosion and with material deprivation. By the same token, Chapman qualifies the causes of prostitution and the sexually transmitted disease he identifies with this illicit practice as "at once social, moral, and physical" with enormous repercussions in which the "health and vigor" of an entire nation deteriorates by virtue of prostitutes "tainting their blood with an ineradicable poison."[95] In the debates on prostitution, the biological and moral aspects tend to absorb social components into the catastrophic sensation of such "tainting." Given the wider texts engulfing these already mediated disclosures from aberrant women, both the prostitutes' stories from the *Morning Chronicle* and Lady Audley's narrative expose how these confessions are coordinated discourses transposing into instances of female depravity any endeavor to testify to the violence and violation of gender and class disempowerment.

As the salient emblem of transgressive femininity, this Victorian figure of the banished prostitute continues to haunt confessional subjects of later nineteenth-century novels, namely *Daniel Deronda* and *Tess of the d'Urbervilles*. In Eliot's novel the selfish and vain woman and the ambitious stage artist constitute revamped renditions of the streetwalker with her inevitable "cravings of vanity" and her unsanctioned and sexualized passions that are again tethered to murderous rage. In concert with portrayals of prostitution in the 1850s and 1860s, Braddon's sensation fiction illuminates the ideological complications behind representations of deviant femininity in Victorian culture, conflicts which are less blatant in mainstream novels of the period. The emphasis on plot rather than character in sensation novels generally and in *Lady Audley's Secret* in particular accentuates material circumstances over the attention to psychological interiority characteristic of Eliot's realism. In this sense, Lady Audley's tales of transgressions—like the narratives of prostitutes in the *Morning Chronicle*—clarify the possibilities of confession as testimony. Yet the psychological realism of *Daniel Deronda* affords an excellent encounter with the rhetorical and symbolic operations of gendered domination and subordination manifested in its scenes of confession. In this novel, which encompasses a man's confession of Jewish faith and two women's secular confessions of domestic sins, we return to the intricate workings of paternal privilege to which the anti-Catholic representations of father confessors allude.

THE BONDS AND BONDAGE
OF GENDER AND RACE

Paternal Metaphors of Confession
in *Daniel Deronda*

Sometimes I thought he would kill *me* if I resisted his will. But now—his dead face is
there, and I cannot bear it.—George Eliot, *Daniel Deronda*

If this white-handed man with the perpendicular profile had been sent to govern a
difficult colony, he might have won reputation among his contemporaries.
—George Eliot, *Daniel Deronda*

Gwendolen Harleth repeatedly punctuates her confession to Daniel Deronda
with frightful allusions to "his dead face," that is, to the specter of her drowned
husband's gaze. In *Daniel Deronda* this haunting image highlights the spectacle of symbolic power that compels acts of confession from two female characters, both of whom have dared to trespass, whether imaginatively or materially, against the wills of their domestic masters. George Eliot's microscopic
interest in the rhetorical and psychological effects of surveillance as a sign
for unmitigated domination transforms the confessions of Gwendolen and
Leonora into scenes of torture. The varied occasions and structures of confession—from the anti-Catholic propaganda and the prostitution debates to *Villette* and *Lady Audley's Secret*—all register the meaning of surveillance as a
mechanism of power. As I have shown, anti-Catholic discourse transforms
father confessors into spies who secretly infiltrate the family and threaten the
dominion of domestic fathers; Lucy's portrait of Madame Beck, Père Silas, and

their respective satellites erects a complex scaffolding of pervasive scrutiny that targets Lucy; and Robert Audley's detective work persistently penetrates into the secret history of Lady Audley. *Daniel Deronda*, however, rivets its attention on the emotional control of such surveillance whereby patriarchs seem to orchestrate confessions from their very graves. If Chapter 3 investigates cultural figurations of female deviancy, this chapter investigates psychic figurations of paternal power.

Gwendolen confesses to murdering her husband Grandcourt, who has just drowned on a boat ride while she looked overboard; Leonora confesses that Daniel is her son whom she forsook years ago along with her Jewish heritage in order to avenge her despotic father. These twin confession scenes offer a consummate study in the gendered dynamics of psychological and linguistic power. Both Gwendolen and Leonora confess their respective marital and maternal transgressions to the novel's titular and entitled character Daniel, whose masculinity and patriarchal status are defined by his mother's confession and secured through his role as Gwendolen's confessor. Near the end of the novel, Daniel makes a confession to Mordecai of his newfound Jewish identity, a declaration that likewise appears under the spiritual management of a dead patriarch. The ambivalent complexities of Eliot's treatment of patriarchal figures are especially evident in that "Daniel Charisi" signifies the ancestor to whom both Leonora's and her son's confessions refer, yet the meanings of this paternal metaphor are strikingly divergent. While confession for the female characters replays the tyranny of husband and father, confession for and between male characters ratifies a different story of self-empowerment, a narrative bolstered by another discourse of patriarchal might, nationalism.

Notwithstanding its ennobling impact for Daniel, the consequences of his confession resemble the fate of both women. For the narrative's revelation of his foreign, unfamiliar identity propels Daniel's eventual banishment from England, and this exile of Jews that closes the novel replicates the expulsions of Gwendolen and Leonora from the marriage plot and from the novel. Despite these gendered distinctions, despite the reverence accorded Daniel's testimony of Jewish faith, confession in *Daniel Deronda* constitutes a way to refine a conservative and racialized notion of Englishness that upholds the authority of "white-handed" men by deporting self-interested women and self-affirming Jews. In terms of the gendered politics of the novel, the women are punished, whereas Daniel is validated; nonetheless, his Jewish nationalism—or Zionism—is ultimately subordinated to an English gentile nationalism that is Eliot's genuine concern here.[1] In the novel, therefore, paternal metaphors invoke the importance of loyalty to family and father writ large and metaphorically, but not necessarily Jewish. While the death of Henleigh Grandcourt might recommend a social realm purged of evil and "white-handed" patriarchs, the persistence of "his dead face" in Gwendolen's confession suggests the tenacity of such power.

Eliot's 1875 novel dramatizes the confessions of Gwendolen Harleth and Leonora Halm-Eberstein as narratives of domination and submission, domestic stories of sexism and power that radiate out to larger analogues of imperialism and racism. As Catherine Hall usefully observes, gender is one of several important axes of power.[2] On one level, Eliot deploys a binary logic between confession as disempowering for women and confession as empowering for and between men. Given that confession is a form of surveillance of the self, it is also crucial to consider the range of identity categories under its scrutiny. At several points Eliot draws parallels between the abusive powers of imperial masters at home and overseas as exemplified by the "empire of fear" that Gwendolen's husband—"this white-handed man"—holds over her.[3] With this recognition of the race and gender of empire, the novel records the punishment of a woman who presumes to possess such prerogatives: Gwendolen's belief in "her divine right to rule" her husband before marriage is converted into "a bitter sense of the irremediable" once she falls under the legal, domestic, and psychological jurisdiction of Grandcourt.[4] Yet Eliot's biting critique of the gendered privileges of empire, with a particular emphasis on the domestic ruler who governs his "difficult colony," is at odds with her vision of Zionist politics consistent with the traditions of patriarchy, racialism, and nationalism.[5] Although the scenes of women confessing expose and contest the brutal force of masculine power epitomized by both English and Jewish men, the scenes of Jewish confession, supported by various allusions to race and nation throughout the novel, also make clear that Eliot affirms a refined—that is, "white-handed" and English—patriarchy.

This chapter explores the ideological work of these confession scenes of domestic transgression in relation to a different kind of religious confession: the testimony of Jewish faith. Where masculine subjugation brands the confessions of both Gwendolen and Leonora, the figure of the Jewish grandfather legitimates the edifying bond of mutuality between Mordecai and Daniel, who both endorse and perpetuate the mission of this Zionist patriarch. Psychological and physical pain accentuate both women's confessions; Gwendolen's guilt is embodied as hysteria and Leonora's affliction with a fatal disease makes manifest a fear of her dead father's retribution. Their spectacular sufferings, however, displace a more muted cultural anxiety about widespread social and moral decay whose sources range from the unsanctioned and sexualized power of women resisting male domination to the assimilation of Jews into the English establishment.

Gwendolen's and Leonora's confessions testify to the psychological and material violence that results from domesticated masculine authority. In *Lady Audley's Secret* deviant femininity is sexualized through the capacious Victorian trope of the prostitute; in *Daniel Deronda* paternal privilege is likewise contoured in metaphors of male sexuality. Both Leonora's and Gwendolen's confessions to men and about male masters index a fear of rape, a dread of a perceived threat of masculine brutality in the domestic sphere. This horror of violent and punitive possession, a dominion both psychological and physical, operates as the engine of surveillance that compels these confessions and as the motivation behind the transgression in the first place. In other words, this fear of rape offers an explanatory narrative for the transgressive and the transgressed, for women whose violations are also retaliations against the debilitating privilege of patriarchs.

As many readers have commented, Eliot persistently qualifies Grandcourt's emotional tyranny over his wife through metaphors of physical torture. The effect of her husband's words on Gwendolen's nerves are likened to "the power of thumbscrews and the cold touch of the rack"; the force of his will signifies "a crab or a boa-constrictor which goes on pinching or crushing without alarm at thunder."[6] Gwendolen even imagines a gesture that condenses Grandcourt's ruthless ascendancy over her into an act of strangulation: "That white hand of his which was touching his whisker was capable, she fancied, of clinging round her neck and threatening to throttle her."[7] While none of these descriptions, as gruesome as they are, specify rape, the language of physical abuse bespeaks the terror of supreme patriarchal retribution encoded in "his dead face" that also coerces Gwendolen and Leonora to confess. For Gwendolen and Leonora confess precisely because they believe there is no longer any possibility of escaping—even through death—the omniscopic dominion of their masters.

In their introduction to the anthology *Rape and Representation*, Lynn Higgins and Brenda Silver point out that sexual violence against women is both obsessively inscribed and erased in Anglo-American cultural texts.[8] This equivocation betokens patriarchal perspectives that continue to dominate systems of representation; nevertheless, traces of "imperfect erasure" begin to divulge this unspeakable story of varying kinds of violations against women. In the context of Victorian culture, these textual signs of incomplete erasure assume different narrative shapes—from the hyphenated gaps in Gwendolen's confession to the framing of the blank space in Tess's confession. This fear of violent and violating power continues to undergird Gwendolen's terror of "his dead face" as it also motivates Leonora's confession. In order to examine the rhetorical operations of male domination over women as confessional subjects, I draw on Lacan's theory of signification and power, with special attention to the concept of the paternal metaphor. If the term "paternal metaphor" belongs to Lacan, the dynamics of power it outlines belongs to the work of Foucault. The idea behind the paternal metaphor is that domination works most effectively through figuration.

In *Daniel Deronda* the will that male masters assert from the unassailable realm of death underpins the very notion of "the dead face." Compelling Gwendolen's disclosures of transgressions, this dreadful vision embodies the terrors of panoptic surveillance—the incalculable scrutiny of the dead gaze that cannot be manipulated, evaded, or even ascertained. In this sense, the novel's depictions of the complexities of confession show how interpretation is organized by a mastering discourse or a male authority at some remove—in other words, by the paternal metaphor. According to Eliot's scheme, submission, also embedded in the notion of the paternal metaphor, leads to transcendence and salvation, but in the terms of the narrative these ideas are closely aligned with punishment and repudiation. Leonora's redemption seems precariously associated with her actual death; Gwendolen's meager salvation seems more in keeping with a punishment when she is left at the close of the novel to submit herself to the memory of another departed male face, namely Daniel's. The rehabilitation of Jews in England requires a radical transcendence—or disavowal—of their material or embodied ethnicity, which results in their departure altogether. At the end of the day, women and Jews, associated in Victorian culture as in Eliot's novel with prostitutes and usurers, are deemed mediums of transmission for the transcendence that belongs to the "dead face" of the "white-handed man."[9] For these confessions reveal the excruciating discipline exacted by a transcendent and panoptic male scrutiny. Although this subjugation is more expressly punitive for Leonora and Gwendolen than for Daniel, the outcome of all the confessions sanitizes the paternal metaphor encoded in British nationalism by containing or banishing the threatened pollutions of transgressive women and assimilating Jewish men.[10]

From "Father-in-Law" to Paternal Metaphor

As Gwendolen confesses to Daniel her involvement in Grandcourt's drowning, she recounts the sheer torture of her captivity on her husband's yacht. While Gwendolen describes the projective structure of Grandcourt's death as "I saw my wish outside me," this bondage aboard a boat inverts another earlier wish: "It came over me that when I was a child I used to fancy sailing away into a world where people were not forced to live with any one they did not like—I did not like my *father-in-law* to come home. And now, I thought, just the opposite had come to me. I had stept into a boat, and my life was a sailing and sailing away—gliding on and no help—always into solitude with *him*, away from deliverance."[11] This " 'father-in-law' " is Captain Davilow, or Gwendolen's mother's second husband who also, much to the child's dismay, substitutes for Gwendolen's dead father, just as *"him"*—or Gwendolen's unnamed husband—replaces "father-in-law" in this passage.

For Lacan, the paternal metaphor also performs an act of substitution, precisely the rhetorical function of metaphor and, indeed, of narrative itself, which organizes and represents absent events.[12] Typical of entries in the Lacanian lexicon, the term "paternal metaphor" takes up a series of overlapping meanings. In one sense, it refers to the symbolic order of culture: both the "name" and the "law-of-the-father," the father's prohibition, or the restrictions that shape social structures. This initial oedipal intervention of the "law-of-the-father" is encoded in Gwendolen's account through the linguistic resemblance of "father-in-law."[13] The correlation in the passage between this dubious stepfather and Grandcourt as "him" implicates a substitution of husband for father. At the same time, Gwendolen's statement, " 'I did not like my father-in-law to come home,' " suggests the status of the paternal metaphor as an undesirable and sinister intrusion, a painful condition that likewise plagues Eliot's rendition of the Grandcourt marriage.

Lacan stresses that the paternal metaphor refers to the place and function of the "Name-of-the Father" in the grammar and syntax of the unconscious, and not to an actual person, although the term does serve as a link between the material and the figurative. Moreover, the force of this patriarchal image derives from its association with the absent or dead father; as Jane Gallop states, "The Name-of-the-Father is bound by its legacy from the imaginary figure of the dead Father."[14] Neither Gwendolen's nor Leonora's father survives in the narrative time of the novel, and yet the imprint of the paternal metaphor molds the confessions of both women. These fathers in fact "exist" only through metaphor, only through the structure of allusions.

Surveillance, the act of categorizing meaning as the consequence of intense scrutiny, describes the field work of the paternal metaphor. In the lexicon of confession, the paternal metaphor signifies a metaphysical confessor, a probing force whose panoptic powers surpass the physical boundaries of a confessional booth. For each confessing woman, this paternal metaphor is an omniscopic dead face that functions as a placeholder for the oppressively powerful husband or father. As violent invasion, this phallic gaze enforces both women's confessions, their guilt, and their imagined penance. While a conventional psychoanalytic reading would locate an oedipal narrative of castration anxiety beneath this Medusan dead-face motif, I read the paternal metaphor otherwise when referenced to women. Rather than an anxiety of castration, a fear of rape or violence underwrites not only the "dead white face" torturing Gwendolen's conscience, but also the intense physical pain that compels Leonora to confess. With castration anxiety, only the dread of punishment, rather than its actual realization, shapes the male psychic landscape, according to Freud's conjectures. For women, fear of rape is a response to a gendered bondage, whether literalized through sexual force or actualized through social, economic, and rhetorical forms of possession.

Put differently, the paternal metaphor also constitutes an "imperfect erasure" of sexual violence perpetrated against women. Standing in for the drowned husband, the "dead face" figures the dread of violent and invisible scrutiny embedded in this sense of a fear of rape. Indeed, for Gwendolen this fear is evident long before the boating accident. In fact, the novel advances a signifying chain from "the picture of the dead face with the fleeing figure" that terrifies Gwendolen during the theatrical performance early in the narrative to the vision of "his dead face" from which Gwendolen is unable to escape in the confession scene.[15] This figure of the dead face stalking Gwendolen's imaginative life also surfaces in the account of her "father-in-law," whom she did not like "to come home" in her childhood, an earlier moment when she envisioned "a world where people were not forced to live with any one they did not like." Whether these words are imprecise traces of the unspeakable story of sexual violation, a submerged history of her stepfather's rape of her, as Judith Wilt has argued, they clearly register both a desire to escape the imprisonment of family and a fear of a father-in-law, that is, paternal power.[16]

My reading also explores what Robert Con Davis calls "the romance of paternal authority" or western idealizations of the father as the "natural" source of truth.[17] As I discussed in Chapter 2, Victorian anti-Catholic representations of confession unsettle the power of church fathers. In this chapter, I use the concept of the paternal metaphor to question the symbolic and cultural foundations authorizing domestic fathers. Since the status of paternity ultimately issues from the maternal word, the paternal metaphor also suggests how provisional and precarious patriarchal superiority is, given its dependence on figuration and surveillance. Lacan's scheme delineates "the paternal romance" of idealized authority that Davis addresses. The phallic power of the paternal metaphor can only function if veiled, if its vulnerability is disguised. In this sense, the confessions reveal an obsession with violent possession, which signals the urgency of the paternal metaphor to establish and fortify masculine power.

If the father of the law is subject to the word of the mother, the power of the maternal word is subject to the legal status that only the paternal metaphor can confer. In a related way, the paternal metaphor represents sexual identity as a categorical rule enforced on the subject whose entry into language and culture also means identifying with fathers or mothers. This regulatory function recalls the violence encoded in the paternal metaphor that executes the "law" of sexual identity for women. As Higgins and Silver observe, "Rape and rapability are central to the very construction of gender identity."[18] This theoretical algebra, therefore, links a dread of rape with the paternal metaphor. By invoking the paternal metaphor here, I am not suggesting that the fear of rape has no material counterpart; I use "fear" rather than "anxiety" precisely to distinguish between actual acts of violent physical possession dispersed throughout the history of the sexual suppression of women in contrast to an imagined threat of castration integral to various Freudian configurations of the psychic lives of men. Rather, my point in using the concept of the paternal metaphor to guide my reading of male authority in these scenes of confession is to illuminate how representations of patriarchal power frequently capitalize on the notion of rapability. The "dead face" of Gwendolen's confessional narrative metaphorizes her dread of Grandcourt's omnipotent gaze, itself a substitution for the "father-in-law" of her childhood. This obsessive figure in the text attests to the penetrating and menacing force of the paternal metaphor. Similarly, Daniel's mother submits to confessing her past under the shadow of the paternal metaphor, the vengeance of her dead father's "iron will" transposed into the punishment of her physical suffering.

The symbolic circulation of the paternal metaphor encourages another meaning: the status of paternity as only logically inferred but never indisputably ascertained. Where a fundamental indeterminacy disturbs the matter of paternity, the paternal metaphor disguises this uncertainty through the pretense of authority, hence the "no" and the "law" of the father. Expanding on this fictive nature of paternity, Judith Butler also allows that the structuralist rendering of a unified, universal, and unitary "paternal Law" again attempts to veil or discount the contradictions that frame this construction of power aligned with the father.[19] On the one hand, these inconsistencies again explain the very obstinacy of the paternal metaphor to guard assiduously a supremacy that resides in the mercurial powers of word and law. On the other, this recognition of variability opens room for representing the changing cultural and historical dimensions of patriarchal power. By definition the paternal metaphor functions in the sphere of language, yet power inevitably has material as well as symbolic significance.

While my reading of the paternal metaphor in scenes of confession favors Lacan's attention to psychic phenomena through linguistic processes, I also speculate on the social meanings of the paternal metaphor, that is, the ethnic and racial parameters of an historically specific sense of the Englishman— "this white-handed man"—that wields such terrific power in Eliot's novel.[20] For the construction of English patriarchal privilege in *Daniel Deronda*, referenced repeatedly to Empire and imperialism, depends upon the blatant exclusion and subjugation of women and Jews, whose subservient positions are in turn associated fleetingly with black Jamaicans. As the following discussion unfolds, the bonds and bondage of gender and race are crucial components in locating the historical and cultural operations of the paternal metaphor.[21]

Yet these traces of exclusion are often subtle and contradictory, a paradox that emerges in Eliot's portrayal of the Jewish patriarch. For the paternal metaphor also mediates Daniel's confession to Mordecai of his Jewish identity and as an avowal of his faith. In this instance between men, the paternal metaphor seemingly takes on a beneficent face where Daniel assumes the "name" and the "law" of the Jewish father in his professed commitment to furnish "a political existence to my people." Despite this gendered divergence, the paternal metaphor and sexualized exploitation in all three confessions supplement the novel's interest in the discourses of nationalism and imperialism.

"But Shadows Are Rising Round Me": Symbolic Patricide and the Father's Revenge

Leonora Halm-Eberstein's appearance in the novel entirely coincides with her confession to her son. In this sense, Leonora is the confessional character par excellence since her textual life is confined to this scene of transgressive disclosures. The language of oppression riddles the daughter's confession of her rebellion against her father, whom even in death she cannot evade. Again and again Leonora stresses that her revelation to Daniel is the consequence of sheer force exerted over her by "my dead father." She stipulates the coercive rather than consensual aspect of confession, a feature that defines this form of disclosure, as Foucault has argued, as an effect of power. Although the paternal metaphor operates on the level of symbol and rhetoric, Leonora's understanding of her body in pain signifies her fear of violent physical possession, a fear that reveals the enormous power accorded this dead father. For Leonora, the disease growing inside her body is a manifestation of patriarchal revenge; this pathological maternal body becomes the material site of the paternal metaphor in Leonora's account of trespassing against her father's will. Her compulsion to confess is part and parcel of the way she experiences her illness as physical torture; in this inversion of the conventional sequence of the religious ritual, confession follows penance.

Leonora comprehends her physical suffering as evidence of the avenging father who watches from death, much as the paternal metaphor can only function from a distance. While she steadfastly insists on her right to choose her own life, Leonora's resolve falters because of her terror of the father's punishment: "Do I seem now to be revoking everything?—Well, there are reasons. I feel many things that I can't understand. A fatal illness has been growing in me for a year. I shall very likely not live another year. I will not deny anything I have done. I will not pretend to love where I have no love. But shadows are rising round me. Sickness makes them. If I have wronged the dead—I have but little time to do what I have left undone." Leonora makes a distinction between reason and feeling, a division also enacted between a woman's willfulness and her vulnerable body. Leonora's "will" still reigns syntactically: "I will not deny anything. . . . I will not pretend." However, this "will," also embeds "ill"; the daughter's "will," or word, succumbs to the father's law. Ambushed by "shadows" that figure here the paternal metaphor, she can only speculate that perhaps the wronged "dead" in turn are responsible for the disease. This pathological occupation of her body by sickness—what she terms her dead father's "iron will"—rehearses a narrative of rape or malevolent intervention where "my father's threats eat into me with pain." Leonora describes the coercion behind her confession in terms of a fiercely embodied persecution: "What my father called 'right' may be a power that is laying hold of me—that is clutching me now."[22] This "right" of paternal authority doubles for the experience of pain seizing Leonora's body. If Gwendolen's anxious juxtaposition of her distasteful stepfather with the "dead face" of her sadistic husband insinuates a coded narrative of rape, Leonora's words here insinuate the daughter's corporeal subjection to the punitive power of the father.

In what conceivable way could the enormity of this imagined punishment fit the crime? Eliot's unforgiving attitude toward egoism in women renders her treatment of both Leonora and Gwendolen even more brutal than her ungenerous depictions of earlier selfish characters like Rosamond Vincy. In the context of this confession, self-aggrandizement is clearly a masculine prerogative; Leonora's efforts to usurp patriarchal privilege constitute a kind of symbolic patricide. Given the linguistic domain of the paternal metaphor, Leonora figuratively murders her father by erasing the name of the father in her son, changing Daniel's name from Charisi to Deronda, and by obliterating altogether the history of his origins. Leonora imagines the fatality of her disease as a slow form of execution enacting her dead father's retribution. The paternal metaphor reigns precisely because the father is dead; this daughter's racked body can therefore be attributed to his violent power rather than to an indifferent process of deterioration.

Lacan observes this affinity between the dead father and the symbolic father: "The appearance of the signifier of the Father, as author of the Law, with death, even to the murder of the Father—thus showing that if this murder is the fruitful moment of debt through which the subject binds himself for life to the Law, the symbolic Father is, in so far as he signifies this Law, the dead Father."[23] Lacan stipulates that "the murder of the Father" magnifies the force of the paternal metaphor as "the subject binds himself for life to the Law." Thus, the symbolic murder of the father through the displacement of "Charisi," the name or placeholder for the father, only intensifies Leonora's bond and bondage to the "Law" of her dead father's will.

Crucial is Leonora's interpretation of her illness as metaphor for the dead father's revenge over his symbolic murder. For the condition of Leonora's body manifests the power of the daughter's obligation to the father, that is, the inescapable nature of the familial bond. Although Lacan does not introduce the difference of gender into the presumed masculinity of the subject who "binds himself for life to the Law," the confession scene here illuminates this distinction through Leonora's identification of disease with punishment, a form of the father's will violently inhabiting her body. The sensations of pain peppering Leonora's narrative epitomize this fear of rape associated with patriarchal power: "I am forced to be withered, to feel pain, to be dying slowly. . . . I have been forced to obey my dead father."[24] Through the passive voice constructions, "I" is overwhelmed by the body in pain and by "my dead father." Echoing the idiom of rape, the repetition of Leonora's words, "I am forced. . . . I have been forced," indicate her fierce subjection to paternal power.

This rule of force also qualifies Leonora's depiction of marriage as a patriarchal plot: "I did not want to marry. I was forced into marrying your father—forced, I mean, by my father's wishes and commands; and besides, it was my best way of getting some freedom. I could rule my husband, but not my father. I had a right to be free. I had a right to seek my freedom from a bondage that I hated." Her father's "wishes and commands" that Leonora marry the man of his choice also signify an avenue to escape paternal "bondage." Yet the next passage elaborates upon this "bondage," which is not only a matter of the father's domination but also "the bondage of having been born a Jew." This ethnic overlay diffuses Leonora's assailment against the cruel hegemony of the law of the father by qualifying it specifically as the bondage of "the Jewish woman": "he only thought of fettering me into obedience. I was to be what he called 'the Jewish woman' under pain of his curse."[25] Leonora's confession enlarges upon her transgressions of the father's law inasmuch as she has endeavored to escape the bonds and bondage of her race, that is, her identity as a "Jewish woman."

Just as Brontë deploys anti-Catholicism to critique male power, Eliot conveniently relegates to Jewish men her most detailed unflattering portrayals of fathers. Besides the domestic despot that Leonora describes here, Mirah relates to Mrs. Meyrick the evils of her father, outfitted in all the clichés of anti-Semitism, who displays his daughter on the public stage in order to reap financial profits.[26] Leonora transposes the bonds of family into the "bondage" of a racialized gender—"the Jewish woman"—dictated by the father. Yet Daniel Deronda rehabilitates this domestic tyrant into the promise of a newly racialized patriarch whose very Jewishness is refined by Daniel's upbringing as an "English gentleman"—as his mother calls him—and diminished by this deferred revelation of his origins.[27] Thus gender seems to determine the difference between empowering and disabling bonds of identity. Leonora's confession reinforces the "fettering" of the disciplinary female subject controlled by constant paternal vigilance.

In pursuing her own career on the stage rather than complying with the prescribed role of mother within the home, Leonora also trespasses over the bounds of gender. Mimicking the power of the father, Leonora incorporates the paternal signifier Charisi into Alcharisi, her stage name, which "had magic wherever it was carried." In a way, the daughter appropriates the paternal metaphor and converts it, as an emblem of her celebrity status, into a commodity. Her stagewalking, therefore, also entails a prostitution of the patronym. Leonora highlights her resemblance to her father in word, will, and wits: she has both "a man's force of genius" and a "will . . . as strong as the man's who wants to govern her." Refusing to be "the Jewish woman," Leonora's shortcoming is this public act of self-determination, necessarily a masculinized trait that reinforces her identification with her father: "My father had no other child than his daughter, and she was like himself."[28]

By concealing the name and culture of the father in her act of renaming her son Deronda and entrusting his upbringing to Sir Hugo Mallinger, an English man of established rank, Leonora jettisons the perpetuation of the Charisi patriarchy. This threat to patrilineal descent again signifies the daughter's symbolic murder of and substitution for the father in which she favors her will over his: "My father had tyrannised over me—he cared more about a grandson to come than he did about me: I counted as nothing. You were to be such a Jew as he; you were to be what he wanted. But you were my son, and it was my turn to say what you should be. I said you should not know you were a Jew." Once again, Leonora's words here emphasize this symbolic patricide as she veils the father's legacy to his male descendants. Rather than conceding her body as merely a conduit for transmitting Jewish culture between men, Leonora refuses her gendered status as "nothing" and instead claims "my turn to say." However, Leonora's internalized anti-Semitism, her sustained emphasis on the ignominy of "the Jewish tatters and gibberish that make people nudge each other at sight of us," dilutes a critique against the bondage of gender.[29]

This unfeminine self-importance of "my turn" that runs against the grain of "the Jewish woman" ultimately reinforces the bonds of gender. Leonora's confession discloses the punishment accorded a woman who has the audacity to wrest from male authority the power to shape her life and to tamper with the paternal name.[30] The most serious transgression she has committed disrupts the male lineage that promotes and preserves paternal law: "If my acts were wrong—if it is God who is exacting from me that I should deliver up what I withheld—who is punishing me because I deceived my father . . . I have told everything."[31] Here the panoptic structure of the paternal metaphor gains potency through this convergence of "God" and "father," where the divine Hebrew father of her mortal father avenges the daughter who has defied this father's commands. Especially in death, the daughter cannot escape paternal surveillance and retribution.

Leonora's attempt to frustrate the rule of her father fails beneath the resurging pain of her body that she connects with patriarchal power: "It was my nature to resist, and say, 'I have a right to resist.' Well, I say so still when I have any strength in me. . . . But when my strength goes, some other right forces itself upon me like iron in an inexorable hand; and even when I am at ease, it is beginning to make ghosts upon the daylight."[32] Figuring the paternal metaphor in terms of the dead father, Leonora conjoins power in this passage with "ghosts." Psychological control managed through physical torture describes Leonora's sense of her infirmity. Where her "nature to resist" coincides with bodily "strength," her ability to defy paternal law collapses with the frailty of her body; when pain returns, resolve wavers. As in a narrative of rape, physical vulnerability occasions Leonora's subjection to "some other right" than her own will. The vision of "iron in an inexorable hand" figures patriarchal privilege as a transcendent and inescapable agency that compels Leonora's confession by tormenting her body.

Pain reinscribes the paternal metaphor at the level of bodily sensation; it also registers the mother's submission to the law of the father to be transmitted through her to his grandson. She tells Daniel, "Your mother is a shattered woman. My sense of life is little more than a sense of what was—except when the pain is present." Her physical torment only tightens the bonds and bondage of gender and Judaism that Leonora has struggled to evade. Despite Leonora's desire to separate herself from the paradigmatic "Jewish woman," to shed the domestic roles typically defining women's lives, she ultimately functions in the novel only as Daniel Deronda's mother. Leonora wryly recognizes her servitude to this procreative capacity: "I have after all been the instrument my father wanted—'I desire a grandson who shall have a true Jewish heart.'"[33] Besides her rank as reproducer of the father and his indomitable will, Leonora is also an "instrument" in a different sense. Rather than a sustained character, Leonora behaves in the narrative as a plot device both to explain Daniel's mysterious origins and to bestow on him an identity in which he discovers his "true Jewish heart," which furthers the patriarchal, nationalist, and imperialist plotting that the novel simultaneously controverts and endorses.

Gwendolen's Submission to the Dead Face

Like Leonora's narrative, Gwendolen's confession delineates the psychological operations of power where "his dead face" establishes the paternal metaphor as a trope of masculine fortitude. While the invisible eyes of the dead father elicit Leonora's confession, the image of "an upturned dead face" punctuates Gwendolen's psychic life from early in the novel to the confession scene where the metaphysics of death accentuates the durability of patriarchal omniscience. The paternal metaphor of the dead face also serves as an embodiment of abusive masculine domination over women. Leonora and Gwendolen dare to evade, thwart, or blind the mastering gaze of father or husband. Yet each confession represents the abiding force of this male scrutiny since both women's dread of the imagined power of the dead motivates their disclosures in the first place.

Because Gwendolen's narrative existence stretches across the novel, her fear of the power of male surveillance is documented well before her marriage, from the scene at Offendene where the "picture of the dead face and the fleeing figure" evinces Gwendolen's "susceptibility to terror."[34] But the specific masculine face that pervades Gwendolen's confession to Daniel encapsulates the horrors of marital bondage to a master of boundless powers. For Henleigh Grandcourt, that "consummate representation of the most detestable kind of Englishman," as Henry James puts it, offers male domination at its keenest and cruelest pitch.[35] As a marksman of psychological quarry, with Gwendolen as his especial target, Grandcourt is unparalleled. In keeping with the psychoanalytic notion of the paternal metaphor, inanimate qualities establish Grandcourt's very command even before he is dead. Cold and passionless with an unyielding will like "a fast-shut iron door," Grandcourt is depicted as inhuman; for a woman to petition Grandcourt means "crying in a dead ear and clinging to dead knees, only to see the immovable face and feel the rigid limbs." At the same time, his panoptic gaze effortlessly enforces subordination: "If Grandcourt cared to keep any one under his power he saw them out of the corners of his long narrow eyes."[36]

As her confession replays scenes from a marriage, Gwendolen's story offers a malicious vision of heterosexual relations; it is only possible to imagine sexual encounters between Grandcourt and Gwendolen as acts of violence whereby the wife is forced to submit to the husband's desire for a perfectly calculated possession. In this vein, "his dead face" personifies Gwendolen's fear of violent male intervention, something perilously akin to rape, as Grandcourt's imperial rule over her body and emotions during their marriage and over her imagination even after his death.

Clearly Gwendolen retreats from heterosexual encounters: she envisions beforehand that marriage is "a dreary state, in which a woman could not do what she liked"; she never evinces any sign of physical pleasure in relation to men. Her cryptic aversion for her own stepfather "to come home" also suggests, at the very least, a discomfort with familial men. By rendering Gwendolen fearful of sexual intimacy before her marriage and by emphasizing Grandcourt's psychological enslavement of his wife (matched only by his brutality toward his dog and his mistress), the narrative sexualizes Gwendolen's marital subjugation. As in Leonora's account of symbolic patricide, Gwendolen imagines herself a "murderess." Yet this transgressive desire to kill a genius at domestic tyranny represents a desperate means of preservation when Gwendolen finds herself forced to do "something dreadful, unalterable," essentially unspeakable. To counter violence with violence becomes a dire remedy in a gendered social system that renders Gwendolen nearly voiceless and unable to redress this sexually valenced crime of marital fascism. Marked by the syntax of her broken speech during the confession, her disempowerment reduces the confession of violent desires into the stuttering of guilty obsession: "His face will not be seen above the water again. . . . Not by any one else—only by me—a dead face—I shall never get away from it."[37] This menacing image of the dead face signifies not only the drowned husband, but also the paternal metaphor, the law of male license from which there seems no escape. The ubiquity of this authority enforces Gwendolen's guilt over her wish to depose such immeasurable power.

Complementing the nightmare of this "dead face," the garbled syntax of Gwendolen's confession illuminates her psychological oppression. Thus she embarks on her transgressive narrative "in a fragmentary way" that "seems to nullify the sense of time or of order in events": "All sorts of contrivances in my mind—but all so difficult. And I fought against them—I was terrified at them—I saw his dead face . . . ever so long ago I saw it; and I wished him to be dead. And yet it terrified me. I was like two creatures. I could not speak—I wanted to kill—it was as strong as thirst—and then directly—I felt beforehand I had done something dreadful, unalterable—that would make me like an evil spirit. And it came—it came."[38] The erotic undertones of Gwendolen's descriptions of her desire to and gestures toward murdering Grandcourt further point to the embodied, sexualized nature of her marital persecution. At the same time, this wish to kill corresponds to a dread of violent male possession: "I had done something then. I could not tell you that. It was the only thing I did towards carrying out my thoughts. . . . I did one act—and I never undid it—it is there still—as long ago as when we were at Ryelands. There it was—something my fingers longed for among the beautiful toys in the cabinet of my boudoir—small and sharp, like a long willow leaf in a silver sheath. I locked it in a drawer of my dressing case. I was continually haunted with it, and how I should use it. I fancied myself putting it under my pillow."[39] A kind of syntactical stammer, the dashes in both of these passages accentuate the rhetorical difficulties of representing sexualized and familial crime. Where "it" substitutes for a knife in Gwendolen's account, this unmentionable weapon is both object of desire and a sign of agency, "something my fingers longed for," a dream that makes its way to the nuptial bed. Gwendolen imagines the knife beneath her pillow in this fantasy of assaultive intimacy between husband and wife.[40]

While Leonora's illness means her body is occupied by a divine paternal judgment, Gwendolen describes a similar sadomasochistic arrangement: "I sometimes felt that everything I had done lay open without excuse—nothing was hidden—how could anything be known to me only?—it was not my own knowledge, it was God's that had entered into me, and even the stillness— everything held a punishment for me."[41] With Gwendolen's consuming guilt figured through the unbidden and painful penetration of a superior power, even God's knowledge of her murderous desires "entered into me." Gwendolen's marriage to Grandcourt becomes a punishment for her egoism, a discipline explicitly psychological, but implicitly sexual as well; so too does the paternal metaphor, construed here as God's knowledge, occasion this infliction of guilt that parallels sexual violation. Pictured as a divine takeover, Gwendolen's sense of her transgressions displaces the more troublesome impression of being transgressed against.

As Gwendolen approaches the moment of the ambiguous drowning, she tells Daniel of her fury over her enslavement to Grandcourt on his "plank-island" yacht: "I want to tell you what it was that came over me in that boat. I was full of rage at being obliged to go—full of rage—and I could do nothing but sit there like a galley-slave. And then we got away—out of the port—into the deep—and everything was still—and we never looked at each other, only he spoke to order me—and the very light about me seemed to hold me a prisoner and force me to sit as I did."[42] Stressed through repetition, her phrase "full of rage" conveys the dangerous threat of resistance to the power that enforces this domestic servitude of a husband who commands his wife "like a galley-slave." Associated with the divine realm of an hierarchical order, "the very light" surrounding this incarcerated woman constitutes the ultimate panopticon, the supreme mastery of the invisible gaze. With the language of bondage scattered throughout the passage, Gwendolen describes conditions foreboding a violent outcome of either insurrection or total suppression.

Yet if this passage portends acts "full of rage," her own splintered narrative compromises Gwendolen's power to oppose her husband's domination and Daniel's reading of the drowning deprives Gwendolen of any agency whatsoever. Although her own estimation clearly locates the desire to murder Grandcourt, her perspective falters on the precise sequence of acts that result in the death. Gwendolen confesses, "I knew no way of killing him there, but I did, I did kill him in my thoughts." This admission mitigates the power of Gwendolen's rage from the activity of material possibility to the passivity of a mental actuality. In Eliot's bleak design of social ordering, conscious desire approximates a form of commission, perhaps the only form available to the disempowered. The moment of the drowning also superimposes desire over external event: "I don't know how it was—he was turning the sail—there was a gust—he was struck—I know nothing—I only know that I saw my wish outside me."[43] The psychological logic of Gwendolen's words converts Grandcourt's fall along with her impulse to revolt into projected desire only, once again suggesting her ultimate powerlessness against the dominion of her husband. In terms of the imperialism that undergirds this scene of "galley-slave" and master, Eliot suggests that insurrection is inevitably futile, that the male might consolidated in Grandcourt's "dead face" ultimately rules. For in this scene, the transgressive commission is merely an act of omission; by holding the rope rather than hurling it toward her drowning husband, Gwendolen fancies she may have facilitated his death. This rope unextended from wife to husband breaks the chain of her servitude to Grandcourt in life, even if the memory of this act of omission strengthens Gwendolen's psychological surrender to the paternal metaphor represented through "his dead face." Inaction, or "I held my hand," constitutes her dubious agency as murderer.

Gwendolen's punishment for her questionable sins is executed on the level of narrative teleology; she is left alone after Daniel's marriage and in possession of only the scraps of Grandcourt's considerable estate. But in the confession scene itself, disciplining Gwendolen also takes the form of psychological torture, a consequence of her husband's reign of emotional terrorism that exerts its pressure after death. The harsh treatment of Gwendolen after Grandcourt's death is of a piece with her marital misery under his "empire of fear," for Eliot is resolute about reproving this heroine, "the spoiled child" whose egoism prompts her to fancy a "divine right to rule" when such imperial designs bespeak a specifically masculine prerogative. That Grandcourt is a despicable master seems almost besides the point since Eliot is bent on castigating Gwendolen for her dubious, misguided judgment on the marriage market. Despite such disciplinary actions, Eliot does open up possibilities for a feminist critique in her portrait of the Grandcourt union as a form of enslavement for Gwendolen. By the same token, the novel tentatively correlates sexism with imperialism and in doing so structures English masculinity.

Paternal Metaphors of Imperialism:
Domestic Transgressions and Current Events of Bondage

Like Gwendolen's depiction of herself as "galley-slave" under marital subjection, the rhetoric of slavery likewise accents Leonora's account of her father's mastery over her, much like other men "who turn their wives and daughters into slaves."[44] This painful subjugation and the idiom of enslavement punctuate both women's confessions and fortify the idea of the paternal metaphor, the symbolic power of male authority. Such tropes of bondage season Victorian descriptions of social problems from the plight of the working class to prostitution. John Stuart Mill's 1869 essay *The Subjection of Women* also invokes the figure of the slave in his condemnation of the immense powers of husbands over wives.[45] Eliot avails herself of the signifying potential of this rhetoric by implicitly comparing the Grandcourt marriage to a controversial event of 1865, the Jamaican uprising.

Although slavery was abolished throughout the British Empire in 1833, the inferior economic and social status of black inhabitants of the colony effectively perpetuated their servitude to colonial power. In October of 1865 a protest of a government fine by a group of black Jamaican peasants turned into a riot in which twenty people were killed. Because political tensions had already escalated on the island and colonial authorities feared a larger insurrection among Jamaica's 350,000 blacks against the 13,000 whites, Governor Edward John Eyre proclaimed martial law and deployed his troops to check the possibility of further violence. This rapid and brutal retaliation resulted in the murder of 439 and the flogging of 600 black and "coloured" men and women as well as the destruction of over 1,000 black homes.[46] These events provoked a great deal of debate in England about the question of unchecked imperial force. Public furor over the Governor Eyre controversy pitted the fundamental liberties of all people against the needs of empire to maintain domination. Only eight years earlier, the issue of imperial rule had arisen over the Indian mutiny of 1857. British representations of the Indian revolt justified violent measures of suppression largely through images of English women raped by Indian men despite the lack of evidence to verify such acts.[47] Citing sexual crimes of the colonized against the women of the colonizers was not a strategy used to vindicate Governor Eyre's harsh reprisal, but Eliot, like Mill before her, draws a pointed parallel between sexist and racist tyrannies by juxtaposing Gwendolen's marriage as an "empire of fear" under Grandcourt with the cruel domination of Governor Eyre.

Ann Cvetkovich argues that in many Victorian novels the domestic sphere signifies a sanctuary from the difficulties of political life but that *Daniel Deronda* inverts this scheme where the "public project" of Zionism supplants Gwendolen's dismal marriage.[48] Yet I would contend that this displacement is only partial. Supported by allusions elsewhere in the text to the dangers of colonialism, this reference to the Jamaican uprising in the section of the novel that first reveals the condition of the Grandcourt marriage actually correlates private and public forms of oppression. Figuring marital relations as martial subjugation offers a dire commentary on the possibilities of female emancipation or self-determination through a woman's supposed "choice" (the section of the novel in which this analogy appears is titled "Gwendolen Gets Her Choice") on the marriage market. Eliot's analogy here conflates the bondage of race and gender, but her critiques of imperialism and sexism are at odds with other aspects of the novel's double plotting. If Eliot emphasizes the horrors of imperial command at home and abroad, she also emphasizes an idealization of Jewish patriarchy, itself contingent on feminine submission, along with the promotion of colonization in an unqualified "East," supposedly available for reclamation.[49]

I read the implied comparison between Governor Eyre and Henleigh Grandcourt in order to particularize the paternal metaphors that orchestrate both women's confessions of domestic servitude. For the symbolic value of domination in Victorian culture is embedded in notions of empire and power that traverse a range of identities. Says Catherine Hall, "In the struggles which took place over the definitions of empire in the nineteenth century, English men and women were constructing identities which drew on, challenged and constituted hierarchies of power formed through the axes of gender, race, and class."[50] Eliot uses the figure of Jewish patriarchs both to idealize and vilify male domination, a subject on which she is scathingly critical in the context of Gwendolen's marriage. Yet in Eliot's notion of Zionism, patriarchy becomes a jurisdiction rooted in nationalism, that is, spiritual and moral obligations to a wider community that surpasses individual interests. For this reason, Eliot denounces Grandcourt's "empire of fear" not so much for his malevolent treatment of his wife but because his cosmopolitanism and his individualism take precedence over more elevated causes. In this light, the paternal metaphor of "his dead face" that haunts Gwendolen's confession is a sign of male power with no moral center, while the treatment of Leonora's father, threatening as his power seems in her confession, ultimately recommends the perseverance of this "iron will" devoted to a goal of national, racialized inheritance.[51] Regardless of this contradictory treatment of male domination, both confession scenes function as testimonies to the psychological despotism of men over women.

In the context of imperialism, moreover, Edward Said's "contrapuntal reading" offers a variation on what I construe as the dualism of confession and testimony. This reading practice recovers traces of resistance along with more overt signs of imperialism.[52] According to Said, the fact that the Jamaican uprising, or indeed Jamaica at all, is mentioned only briefly and only for its symbolic resonance with Gwendolen's marriage would constitute one such sign of imperialism, even as it does so by referring to a historical act of resistance. Reversing this logic, that *Daniel Deronda* affiliates an Englishwoman's marital oppression with the political conditions of black Jamaicans reveals the relative unimportance of Gwendolen's miseries in Eliot's grander, imperious scheme of things. Much like this allusion to opposition to imperial power abroad, the confession scenes punctuate the futility of resistance of subordinates. Within the novel itself, the intermittent use of colonial rule as a trope renders such cultural situations as commodities, interesting artifacts of history to be harnessed as an icon, in this case, for an English husband's dubious control over his wife.[53] My point here is to specify Eliot's use of paternal metaphors in relation to imperialism and in terms of what Gayatri Spivak has called "race-gendering," which hierarchizes different identities of subjection. At the same time, the portrait of British patriarchal authority that emerges from her scenes of imperialism advances Eliot's constructions of the nationality and race of gendered empowerment in her more abstract idealization of an "Invisible Power." For like the paternal metaphor, colonial rule signifies sovereignty from a distance.

The Jamaican revolt provides a salient historical framework for notions of mastery embedded in both women's confessions. Because Governor Eyre's suppression of black Jamaicans sparked much dissension about the powers of empire, a parliamentary investigation in England ensued, although the government ultimately did not prosecute Eyre. Nevertheless, committees formed supporting or opposing Governor Eyre; these positions on the debate also suggest opposing notions of masculinity underlying the changing sense of the middle-class Englishman.[54] Mill was a leader of the Jamaica Committee, which led the campaign to prosecute Eyre for murder; advocates of this position included working-class activists and evolutionists such as Charles Darwin and Herbert Spencer.[55] Advocating the right of imperial order, the literary establishment—led by Thomas Carlyle and supported by Matthew Arnold, John Ruskin, Alfred Lord Tennyson, Charles Kingsley, and Charles Dickens—championed Eyre's actions that reinforced the political polarity of empire and colony. Carlyle's defense of Eyre amounted to a reassertion of a natural inequality between whites and nonwhites, braced by similar views on the intrinsic superiority of men over women, of the upper classes over the serving and working class. For Carlyle advocated hierarchy over democracy, the cornerstone of conservative discourse where the privileged-class Englishman reigns as ultimate authority.[56]

Mill's liberal position urged individual freedom across races and before the law, much like his argument in *The Subjection of Women* in which he likens marriage to slavery. In this treatise, Mill maintains an analogy between the tyranny of husbands over wives and the rule of masters over slaves. Anticipating Eliot's portrait of Grandcourt, Mill offers a parable whereby the authority of husbands supersedes that of slaveowners: "Above all, a female slave has (in Christian countries) an admitted right, and is considered under a moral obligation, to refuse her master the least familiarity. Not so the wife: no matter how brutal a tyrant she may unfortunately be chained to—though she may know that he hates her, though she may feel it impossible not to loathe him—he can claim from her and enforce the lowest degradation of a human being, that of being made the instrument of an animal function, contrary to her inclinations."[57] Despite Mill's overall liberal position, the passage reveals not only his greater anxiety over the condition of English wives rather than colonized slaves, but also his rather romanticized view of the power of female slaves to resist rape or even "refuse her master the least familiarity." Ironically, Mill holds slave women responsible for their own sexual assault, at least "in Christian countries," but exonerates English wives of such accountability. Where Mill's stance against slavery abroad advances his interest in a restricted equality at home, Eliot uses British colonialism as an imperialist metaphor for domestic tyranny. Notwithstanding the implication from these depictions of domestic life that Eliot favors Mill's critique, in other ways the novel shores up a Carlylean version of masculinity through a different paternal metaphor, the transcendent image of the Jewish patriarch.

Within *Daniel Deronda* it is hardly surprising who approximates Carlyle's endorsement of Governor Eyre: "Grandcourt held that the Jamaican negro was a beastly sort of baptist Caliban." Here Grandcourt invokes the proper name of the Shakespeare character who represents a favorite western cliché for the colonized black man. In this primitivist assessment, "beastly" qualifies "baptist," a priority that exposes the Carlylean belief in the ultimately inferior position of nonwhites despite any civilizing efforts. Through this allusion to a founding father of the English literary tradition, the imperialism of the paternal metaphor prevails even in Grandcourt's discursive construction of current events. The passage continues to record other commentary on the subject of the uprising that takes place in the form of "polite pea-shooting," Eliot's expression for social chitchat: "Deronda said he had always felt a little with Caliban, who naturally had his own point of view and could sing a good song; Mrs. Davilow observed that her father had an estate in Barbadoes, but that she herself had never been to the West Indies; Mrs Torrington was sure she should never sleep in her bed if she lived among blacks; her husband corrected her by saying that the blacks would be manageable enough if it were not for the half-breeds; and Deronda remarked that the whites had to thank themselves for the half-breeds."[58]

With Caliban as imperialist metaphor for the demonized victim, the connection between the mythologized public event of the Jamaican rebellion and sexual politics is evident here. Capitalizing on the volatile image of white Englishwomen vulnerable to rape by such "beastly" nonwhites, an impression left over from British constructions of the Indian mutiny, the passage narrowly implicates "the whites" in this vision of sexual imperialism. Interestingly, Daniel's comment contradicts Mill's presumption that a female slave can "refuse" the sexual aggressions of a master. Given Daniel's "little" sympathy with Caliban, "who can sing a good song," he too resorts to racist stereotypes. By the same token, Mrs. Davilow's remark implicates Gwendolen's family in the history of British imperialism in the Caribbean. Taken together, the entire conversation condemns miscegenation, encoded in "half-breeds," an attitude indicative of the racialism of Eliot's culture. In keeping with this racist view, the subservient position of Jamaican blacks and the importance of British imperialist interests remain intact; the passage mildly questions only the use of the power of "the whites," while the right of colonial rule is not contested. At the same time, women are positioned as both subject and object of this racist imperialism.

Elsewhere Eliot amplifies the metaphoric capacity of this allusion to the Jamaican insurrection in order to take note of the male colonization of women. Yet this attention to such gendered imperialism only cautions against the degree and manner of the power wielded by domestic totalitarians. Although Leonora's and Gwendolen's confessions challenge political arrangements of gender, ultimately each woman's position of bondage to male authority is reinforced. This dichotomy is evident not only in Gwendolen's confession, but also in the representations of her marriage that precede it. With regard to Grandcourt's mastery as husband over Gwendolen, the narrator likens him to a colonialist of Governor Eyre's persuasion: "If this white-handed man with the perpendicular profile had been sent to govern a difficult colony, he might have won reputation among his contemporaries. He had certainly ability, would have understood that it was safer to exterminate than to cajole super-seded proprietors, and would not have flinched from making things safe in that way."[59] Grandcourt's "certain ability" to rule, even resorting to brutal measures, embodies the Carlylean concept of English masculinity given full license to "exterminate" any act of insubordination. In relation to Governor Eyre's militant measures, Carlyle extolled, "The English never loved anarchy; nor was wont to spend its sympathy on miserable mad seditions, especially of this inhuman and half-brutish type; but always loved order, and the prompt suppression of sedition."[60] Where Grandcourt's merciless control of Gwen-dolen is treated with some disdain, neither Leonora's nor Gwendolen's re-bellion is applauded. As "a difficult colony," Gwendolen challenges the su-premacy of her husband whose very "ability" to control is intimated by "this white-handed man," a phrase that conjoins the dominance of race and gender. Other rhetorical flourishes link the atrocities of imperial power to terrifying oppression within an English household. Grandcourt's treatment of his wife generates an "empire of fear" where marriage for Gwendolen becomes a form of incarceration and torture: "The walls had begun to be an imprisonment, and while there was breath in this man he would have the mastery over her. His words had the power of thumbscrews and the cold touch of the rack. To resist was to act like a stupid animal unable to measure results."[61] This meta-phoric equation of the very idea of resistance recalls the "beastly" Caliban and, by association, the Jamaican rebels; here opposition is not only futile but also undignified, performed by brutes devoid of reason.

The debate over the Jamaican uprising ultimately reinforced the illusion of democracy at home and the reality of tyranny abroad. Nevertheless, Eliot's extended deployment of this current event of rebellion reveals a different kind of domestic despotism. For both Gwendolen and Leonora, domestic relations mean servitude that unifies and reinforces a patriarchal hegemony. For Dan-iel, in contrast, his confession of faith secures his spiritual and cultural bond with Mordecai and with his Jewish forefathers. By submitting to the authority of the father, Daniel inherits the privileges of the father. These divergent consequences of confession, where familial bonds enslave each confessing woman and racialized religious bonds of a Jewish patriarchy empower the confessing man, underscore the gendered nationalistic project of the novel that separates the Jews from the English, and women from men.[62] Daniel embarks on his quest to found a homeland for the Jewish nation and Gwendolen returns to her mother's home; these movements ultimately promote the ascendancy of a racially pure British Empire as well as the primacy of male domination. This brief focus on British imperialism and the politics of persecution contextualizes the power dynamics of the paternal metaphor in relation to both women's confessions. For Leonora and Gwendolen, the paternal metaphor drives them to disclose their transgressions against patriarchal mastery. At the same time, these confessions both register and reinforce their surrender to this embattled masculine authority. Indeed, the urgency of submission characterizes not only the confessions of Leonora and Gwendolen but also Daniel's testimony of faith in his Jewish forefathers.[63]

Confession and the Making of Daniel's Masculinity

Catherine Gallagher's sardonic quip sums up the contradictory construction of Daniel's masculinity in the novel as he moves from a sympathetic affiliation with "wayward women" to an identification with his grandfather as the paternal metaphor for a Jewish nation: "A young man who thinks he has a mission to save wayward women turns out to have a mission to save a nation of usurers."[64] However, Daniel's encounters with both confessing women are pivotal to the making of his Jewish masculinity and his ascension to the role of grand-scale patriarch, an identity that is fortified later in his confession of faith to Mordecai. All three confessions shore up a metaphysical idea of masculine authority, one that replicates in different ways the psychoanalytic logic of the paternal metaphor. Leonora's and Gwendolen's revelations seal their submission to unkind fates, even as they record their subjection and resistance to unkind masters. Yet confession appears to have the opposite outcome for Daniel. Taken together, the three confession scenes enhance a gendered dynamics of power. Leonora and Gwendolen are punished for their attempted incursions into masculine prerogative; Daniel is rewarded for his assumption of patriarchal entitlement. As confessor to Leonora and Gwendolen, Daniel moves from a feminine to a masculine stance, from passive dependence to active authority.[65] Initially, as the ward of Sir Hugo, his nominal, economic, and social status are all uncertain; but as the grandson of Jewish patriarch Daniel Charisi, he manages to shoulder the paternal metaphor with a nationalist twist by spearheading a Zionist quest. While Daniel's own confession of faith certifies his remunerated submission to the name and law of biological and spiritual fathers, the construction of his masculinity begins with his role as confessor and privileged interpreter of Leonora and Gwendolen.

The rhetoric of Leonora's confession registers a shift from the mother to the father, from the ailing maternal body to the tradition and law of the Jewish patriarch. Once Daniel's mother becomes a speaking presence in the narrative, she loses psychological purchase on her son's imagination; instead, the name of the father, who is dead, is erected as the figurehead, or head figure, that reconstructs Daniel's identity. The mother's confession to the son also determines the son's confession, that is Daniel's subsequent testimony of faith in the traditions of his Jewish forefathers. By the same token, the mother's story is coterminus with and contained by her confession; after this disclosure, Leonora neither appears, nor does Daniel explicitly invoke her. Leonora functions as a plot device to facilitate a narrative of forefathers just as her story is contingent on the novel's larger interest in her son. Revealing the father's name, Leonora's confession secures Daniel's masculine and Jewish identity, and Daniel achieves differentiation from his assimilated Christian mother as he aligns himself with the Jewish patriarch.[66] By this affiliation with the paternal metaphor instead of the maternal body, Daniel also assumes the masculinized privileges of action and possession.

As confessor, this son comes around to represent the interests of the dead father and to chide Leonora for her duplicity and selfishness, for obscuring what is "truthful," ultimately for shirking paternal law: "I see no other way to get clearness than by being truthful—not by keeping back facts which may—which should carry obligation within them—which should make the only guidance towards duty. No wonder if such facts come to reveal themselves in spite of concealments. The effects prepared by generations are likely to triumph over a contrivance which would bend them all to the satisfaction of self. Your will was strong, but my grandfather's trust which you accepted and did not fulfill—what you call his yoke—is the expression of something stronger, with deeper, farther-spreading roots, knit into the foundations of sacredness for all men."[67] As power writ large and masculine, the paternal law permeates Daniel's speech through such words as "facts," "obligation," and "duty." When Daniel shifts to a verbal tense of command, from "which may—which should," this revision demonstrates his changed allegiance from the imaginary mother to the symbolic father. Confirming in effect Leonora's reading of her disease, Daniel construes that the patriarchal might of "generations" conquers her "satisfaction of self" and supplants it with "something stronger." Inasmuch as "something stronger" refers to a religious covenant, Eliot exploits a meaning of "yoke" in Jewish scripture as sacred obligations—that is, Judaism itself—to promote her ideal of a spiritually infused sense of dedication.

Thus this "something stronger, with deeper, farther-spreading roots" bespeaks Eliot's own commitment to the idea of national inheritance, a value supported through an ethos of self-abnegation and transmission. Bernard Semmel explains the weight Eliot placed on inheritance in terms of the cultural and historical traditions of a nation.[68] As an alternative to the liberal individualism and cosmopolitanism that Eliot deplored in English society, the "something stronger" of obligations to a national community, here also construed as a religious community, would transcend individual interests or "the satisfaction of self." Eliot's conservative idea of a homogeneous inheritance is informed by a belief in the importance of national and racial purity; this racialism of her times clearly opposed cultural diversity or heterogeneity of any kind. Accordingly, Eliot deploys the Jewish plot in *Daniel Deronda* as an exalted model of religious as national inheritance rather than as a particular endorsement of Jewish culture or religious life per se in England.[69] While Semmel disregards the role of gender in Eliot's belief in national inheritance, this passage from the confession scene points out that her paradigm tacitly privileges men over women. The conflict between a liberal position of self-fulfillment and the conservative tradition Eliot endorses of a "farther-spreading" social destiny has different implications for women, whose opportunities for empowerment are decidedly more limited in the first place.[70] Devotion to the transmission of a national culture signifies a version of self-fulfillment for Daniel, while a woman's role is to literalize this imperative to reproduce culture.

This gendered component behind Eliot's teleology of national inheritance emerges in the confession scene between mother and son. For the compulsion of a "stronger something" demands painful material submission from Leonora, whereas Daniel's submission to his racialized heritage bestows empowering compensations. The passage condenses the gendering of this mission where the desires of the masculine collective—"for all men"—prevails over the individual interests of one miserable woman. Eliot's conviction about national inheritance undergirds what I have been calling the paternal metaphor, mystified through the phrase "stronger something" and amplified by its repeated use: "But that stronger Something has determined that I shall be all the more the grandson whom also you willed to annihilate."[71] Clearly, Leonora has no everlasting place in this contract "for all men" as Daniel champions his grandfather's position and, "all the more the grandson," assumes his patriarchal birthright. The mother's attempts to jettison this legacy only bolster Daniel's resolve to entitlement, his reinscription in the symbolic order of paternal metaphors where even the title of the novel announces his name. As the medium of transmission, Leonora does become "a makeshift link" between her father and her son, the reproductive medium in this hegemony "for all men."

Earlier in the novel Mordecai offers an allegory for this gendered difference in Eliot's project of self-transcendence through the metaphysics of national inheritance: "A man is bound to thank God, as we do every Sabbath, that he was not made a woman; but a woman has to thank God that He has made her according to His will. And we all know what He has made of her—a child-bearing, tender-hearted thing is the woman of our people."[72] Leonora's confession testifies to her refusal of this defining script, which casts "a woman" in a subordinate and undesirable position, ultimately as "thing."

The closure of the interview between mother and son treats the evolution of Daniel's masculinity with reverence: "All his boyish yearnings and anxieties about his mother had vanished. He had gone through a tragic experience which must for ever solemnise his life, and deepen the significance of the acts by which he bound himself to others."[73] Although Leonora's confession constitutes the narrative of her entire life, this conclusion stresses the encounter as the confessor's "tragic experience," one that solidifies a different affiliation, the confession of the Jewish faith "by which he [will bind] himself to others." This parting commentary foreshadows the confession between Daniel and Mordecai, where this mutual devotion "for all men" replicates the "stronger Something" that likewise connects the living grandson and the dead grandfather over the dying body of his mother. At the end of the day, Daniel enjoys the advantage of masculinity, authorized by the ability to act and to possess, while Leonora fades away with the termination of her narrative. The confession releases Daniel from the ambiguity that has surrounded his identity. The mother's body, and her confession of his forefathers, is a means by which he secures his commitment to his newfound religious/national inheritance. Because of the heritage Leonora discloses, Daniel is also able to marry Mirah, a mirror of "the Jewish woman" his mother refused to be, and to reestablish traditionally gendered relationships structured by paternal authority and maternal submission.

Although masculine privilege elevates Daniel in contrast to Leonora and Gwendolen, a cultural context of anti-Semitism destabilizes the Jewish paternal metaphor. Unlike the readily understood "Cohen," the ethnically marked surname of the two Jewish characters Mirah and Mordecai who have endured enormous suffering as Jews, Daniel's ambiguous "Deronda" conceals his original identity from both of his people—his Jewish blood relations and his English compatriots and family. Daniel Deronda is entitled on the book cover as well as in the narrative because the Jewish signifier, the patronym of a devalued cultural identity, is in fact foreclosed. As Susan Meyer points out, "This novel by no means idealizes Jews. Instead, what this novel idealizes is the 'refined' Jew—the word is used repeatedly to describe Mirah and Mordecai."[74] Daniel passes as a well-born Englishman and Mirah, readers are reminded, could be mistaken for a Christian; Mordecai's consumption purifies him of his corporeality and endows him with transcendent virtue, while Leonora's illness only intensifies her embodied subjection.[75] It is no coincidence that Daniel's avowal of his hidden paternity occasions his departure from England and the novel to found a land for his people where this Jewish paternal metaphor and national inheritance can in theory enjoy full ascendancy. This gap reinforces the novel's covert anti-Semitism or, more accurately, its project to restore an ailing British nationalism with the remedy of religious and racial homogeneity. Where Eliot mythologizes Daniel's Judaism, this treatment is a flip side of the novel's obsessive castigation of Gwendolen. As Crosby observes, "Idealizing the Jews and punishing women are but two poles of the same problem, and both Jews and women are set up in *Daniel Deronda* only to confirm the everlasting unity of Man."[76]

Therefore, Daniel's role as confessor during Gwendolen's confession sponsors this "stronger something" expressly "for all men." The confession traces Gwendolen's murderous rebellion against male domination; it also marks her substitution of a benign master for a malevolent one. Gwendolen first poses a question to Daniel from which he retreats repeatedly throughout the confession; this equivocation fortifies Daniel's newfound role as father confessor, a figure of masculine power.

> "You know I am a guilty woman?"
> Deronda himself turned paler as he said, "I know nothing."
> He did not dare to say more.[77]

This initial exchange is paradigmatic for the entire confession. Gwendolen's power in the confession resides in her insistence on her guilt, her intention to slay Grandcourt, regardless of the precise choreography of her actions. Yet Daniel's authority overrides her own in his refusal to acknowledge her possible agency in the murder. Even the prospect of a woman murdering a man in a position of familial authority to her is nearly unthinkable, as *Lady Audley's Secret* demonstrates through Robert's efforts to obscure Lady Audley's confessed "mad" assault on her first husband. In this novel, Daniel's response advances a social necessity to commute judgment on Gwendolen from a legal verdict as a "guilty" murderess to a more muted diagnosis of hysterical confusion; thus Daniel bypasses Gwendolen's own narrative of an abiding "criminal desire" in favor of his view that in the spiritual struggle "her better will" won out. Regardless of her confession to the contrary, repeatedly Daniel refuses to recognize Gwendolen's capacity for murder; this denial effectively reiterates the novel's censure of resistance as a futile incursion on an established authority, whether a sadistic husband, a sexist patriarch, or a colonial power. Such repudiations finally reinforce the legitimacy of domination despite its random abuses.

Daniel's vested reading negates the possibility of deliberate criminal action and substitutes a psychic landscape of disorder: "It was with an inward voice of desperate self-repression that she spoke these last words, while she looked away from Deronda towards something at a distance from her on the floor. Was she seeing the whole event—her own acts included—through an exaggerating medium of delirium into which there entered a sense of concealment and necessity for self-repression? Such thoughts glanced through Deronda as a sort of hope. But imagine the conflict of feeling that kept him silent. She was bent on confession, and he dreaded hearing her confession." Like Lady Audley's confessor, Daniel seizes upon Gwendolen's disordered mind, "an exaggerating medium of delirium," as evidence to render her innocent and thus mitigate the possibility of her as "the guilty woman." To this end, Daniel pronounces his judgment of Gwendolen's confession: "You have not murdered him. You threw yourself into the water with the impulse to save him. Tell me the rest afterwards. This death was an accident that you could not have hindered."[78] By seizing interpretive power and imposing his own explanation, Daniel wards off this undesirable disclosure of a woman's violent retaliation against her husband's tyranny.

What is more important, however, is that Eliot's narration challenges the judgment of the confessor as well. At the end of the scene after Gwendolen has confessed that she has kept a knife in her traveling case in order to realize her murderous desire, and after she describes her momentary restraint from throwing the rope to her drowning husband, Daniel persuades himself of her "innocence": "It seemed almost certain that her murderous thought had no outward effect—that, quite apart from it, the death was inevitable. Still, a question as to the outward effectiveness of a criminal desire dominant enough to impel even a momentary act, cannot alter our judgment of the desire; and Deronda shrank from putting that question forward in the first instance."[79] The confession replays this dangerous defiance of a woman who appropriates the violent aggression of masculine physical mastery; yet the confessor recognizes this resistance only to suppress it. To offset this threat Daniel both overlooks the motive for murder and reads instead an intention of "murderous thought" rendered in mind only and without consequence or "outward effect."[80]

In another sense, the narrator at least allows for the possibility of Gwendolen's "criminal desire" to take radical measures, and this alternative perspective challenges the confessor's infallibility and his vested construction of truth. For the narrator implies that Daniel's own self-serving act of judgment is itself a transgression and so implicates him for not assessing the desire regardless of "outward effect." Gwendolen's compulsion to confess takes on a portentous power in Daniel's reluctant ears where her revelation of a secret "criminal desire" assumes a sexual valence. Daniel's aversion to hearing Gwendolen suggests a countermove of narrative foreclosure to disavow this assault on the paternal law. Clearly, Daniel regards Gwendolen's confession of odious scenes from her marriage as a burden of unwanted intimacy: "She was bent on confession, and he dreaded hearing her confession. . . . He was not a priest. He dreaded the weight of this woman's soul flung upon his own with imploring dependence."[81] Quite apart from his recently discovered Jewishness, Daniel as an Englishman avers he is "not a priest." The anti-Catholic rhetoric on the untoward familiarity of confession clarifies his preference for a proper distance to the sexualized intimacy of this woman's confidences. Such remoteness contributes to Daniel's masculine empowerment.

After Gwendolen's avowal of an intention to murder her husband, Daniel minimizes the import of Gwendolen's words: "And it has all remained in your imagination. It has gone on only in your thoughts." As articulated in his so-called seduction theories, Freud privileges psychic processes over historical events. By the same token, this confessor "insistently" reads the insinuation of sexual violence as fantasy only. To acknowledge any determination beneath Gwendolen's murderous wish would likewise require a recognition of the provocation, something not beyond Daniel's comprehension since his contempt for Grandcourt is frequently registered in the novel. By diminishing Gwendolen's intention to kill as a "momentary murderous will," Daniel also avoids passing judgment on another man before a woman, even a man as despicable as Grandcourt. Thus Daniel gives no reply to the few allusions to Grandcourt's violence that Gwendolen makes: "Sometimes I thought he would kill *me* if I resisted his will. But now—his dead face is there and I cannot bear it."[82] Where Gwendolen finds this psychic image intolerable, this predicament illustrates that paternal mastery escalates through death and absence; its authority is inviolable. And Daniel's aloof position as confessor intensifies this masculine domination.

Twice Daniel distances himself from Gwendolen: both at the close of her confession and at her final appearance in the novel. Daniel's words of consolation "widened his spiritual distance from her, and she felt it more difficult to speak: she had a vague need of getting nearer to that compassion which seemed to be regarding her from a halo of superiority, and the need turned into an impulse to humble herself more."[83] Cold comfort is such "compassion . . . from a halo of superiority" that compels Gwendolen's submission in effect as she experiences this "impulse to humble herself more." Whereas this passage betrays Gwendolen's impressions of his "spiritual distance from her," Daniel's delayed disclosure of his Jewish identity finally formalizes their relationship into one of precisely this "spiritual distance," both in terms of his religious difference and in terms of his intentions to marry someone else.

During their final scene together when Daniel makes his confessions of a different religious/national inheritance and of a different love than Gwendolen might have wished, he offers the dejected woman a mixed consolation indeed: "'I shall be more with you than I used to be,' Deronda said with gentle urgency, releasing her hand and rising from his kneeling posture. 'If we had been much together before, we should have felt our differences more, and seemed to get farther apart. Now we can perhaps never see each other again. But our minds may get nearer.' "[84] Daniel's movement from his knees alongside Gwendolen to an erect stance above her embodies the distance Gwendolen witnesses earlier. The shift in the positions of their bodies in the passage likewise suggests a movement from metonymy to metaphor, from affiliation to hierarchical difference. Daniel's words and posture underwrite the paternal metaphor to which he subscribes; their relationship "may get nearer," his symbolic impact on her will intensify, he suggests, through physical absence. In other words, Daniel enjoys the masculine right of transcendence; Gwendolen is imprisoned in the mundane difficulty of a narrowing material world.

All told, Gwendolen's confession to Daniel facilitates his own empowerment; Daniel's confession to Gwendolen, on the contrary, poses a violent disturbance of her knowledge of him and her assumptions about their relationship now and in the future. In striking contrast to her own protracted confession to Daniel, here Gwendolen does not wield an inquisitorial gaze or interpretive license. Indeed, she does not even anticipate a confession of this nature: Gwendolen thinks she is in a marriage plot, but discovers through Daniel's disclosure that she is a subsidiary character in another romance. Once more she is punished for presuming her knowledge wider than it happens to be. She has known nothing about Daniel's forays into Jewish history and culture or about his meeting with his mother, who reveals the Jewish heritage that finally enables Daniel to bind together these narrative threads. Gwendolen construes her blindness to this untold story—that is, untold to her—as yet another instance of her egoism for which she has suffered once through her marriage to Grandcourt and now though her exclusion from Daniel's marriage.

Interestingly, Hans Meyrick, Daniel's rival over his future wife Mirah, lambastes him for his trivialization of Gwendolen's loveless future. When Daniel questions whether it is "absolutely necessary that Mrs. Grandcourt should marry again," Hans replies: "You monster! . . . do you want her to wear weeds for *you* all her life—burn herself in perpetual suttee while you are alive and merry?"[85] Relegating to metaphor a custom of a culture under British imperialism, these words again intimate the male colonization of women by invoking a Hindu practice to reprove the sexism of a Christian-turned-Jewish man. As in the passages alluding to the Jamaican uprising, colonial discourse again mirrors domestic relations. As Jenny Sharpe asserts in her reading of the tropes of colonial women in *Jane Eyre*, the burning body of the Hindu woman substitutes for the domestic angel of the Victorian home so that "the silent passivity of the Hindu woman is the grounds for the speaking subject of feminist individualism."[86] This use of the subaltern woman as allusion lies beneath the stinging accusation of "perpetual suttee" to describe both Daniel's prerogative and Gwendolen's enforced sacrifice to dead or departed men. Hans insinuates a blatant inequality whereby Gwendolen as unfortunate widow is doomed to the torment of "burn[ing] herself in perpetual suttee" while Daniel, with whom Gwendolen entertained the possibility of a romantic future, can be "merry" and marry. Since Daniel's wholesale dismissal of Gwendolen in his romance plot results from his newly disclosed identity, the passage also implies another dubious correlation where untempered masculine power is assigned to other—that is, Hindu or Jewish—men.[87]

Daniel emerges from both Gwendolen's confession and his own revelation as upright master of the fate of their connection to one another. But Gwendolen's penance for her transgressive violence—whether in thought, word, or deed—toward male authority surfaces in this portrait of her physical submission that closes her confession scene: "He rose as he spoke, and she gave him her hand submissively. But when he had left her she sank on her knees, in hysterical crying. The distance between them was too great. She was a banished soul—beholding a possible life which she had sinned herself away from."[88] For Daniel's devotion to the "something stronger" of his Jewish inheritance harmonizes with his empowered position as a descendent of Jewish patriarchs. Yet for Gwendolen, Daniel's "spiritual distance" is punishment, and she construes the foreclosure of "a possible life" with him as her own fault. The outcome of both women's confessions strengthens Daniel's ascent and assent to paternal law predicated on precisely this "spiritual distance." At the same time, distance reinforces Leonora's and Gwendolen's inflexible bondage to the paternal metaphor that prevails, after all, through its absence.

"The Marriage of Our Souls":
Homosocial Bonding and Banishment

In Eliot's novel, confessions of domestic tyranny certify Daniel's masculinity, both through his mother's revelation of his Jewish patriarchal heritage and through his role as confessor passing judgment on each woman's transgressions against their familial masters. In this sense, the twin confessions promote Daniel's identification with and exercise of an empowering bond "for all men." Inscribing gendered arrangements of domination and submission, this model of confession foregrounds guilt and judgment, transgression and penance, which mediate relations between women and men. But *Daniel Deronda* presents yet another version of confession, this one specifically between men: a revelation fostering their affiliation to one another through an avowal of faith to the paternal metaphor whose privilege, as men, they can reap. The women's confessions unveil a paternal force that transmutes heterosexual bonds into a terror akin to rape; Daniel's confession of his Jewish identity to

Mordecai unveils a homosocial bond generating a mutual pleasure in a common cultural inheritance rather than the pain of psychological and physical subjugation. In Eliot's plot extolling the idea of a religious/national legacy, which I understand as the paternal metaphor magnified, she uses a male character to demonstrate that this "something stronger" affords a gratifying identification, while she disciplines two female characters for their efforts to resist the "something stronger" of exaggerated, masculinized, and transcendent authority.

The language of love shapes the narrative's depiction of the relationship between Daniel and Mordecai, even before Daniel's confession of his Jewish origins finally legitimates the blossoming bond between them: "In ten minutes the two men, with as intense a consciousness as if they had been two undeclared lovers, felt themselves alone in the small gas-lit book-shop and turned face to face, each baring his head from an instinctive feeling that they wished to see each other fully."[89] The intimacy of the setting as well as the erotics of "baring" define the private encounter between "two undeclared lovers." Unlike the gendered power dynamic in the confessions of Leonora and Gwendolen, here the mutuality of absolute revelation collapses a distinction between viewer and viewed through their desire "to see each other fully."

Encoding a narrative of a homospiritual transmission of a racialized Jewish culture, Mordecai's rhetoric deploys organic images of procreation and gestation to describe the union of Daniel's embodied soul with his own: "You must be not only a hand to me, but a soul—believing my belief. . . . You will be my life: it will be planted afresh; it will grow. You shall take the inheritance; it has been gathering for ages."[90] Here Daniel assumes a feminine role as helpmate and as pregnable body in whom Mordecai's life and inheritance "will be planted afresh; it will grow." Eliot is drawing on a frequent figuration in the Torah that likens the covenant of Jews with God to a marriage contract; in such passages, which Eliot liberally recasts in her novel, Israel is fashioned as the bride, God as the bridegroom. In Chasidic Judaism, a populist mysticism that first emerged in eighteenth-century Eastern Europe, prayer is often equated with sexual intercourse, even to the point of orgasm.[91] The erotic imagery that often pervades these depictions in Jewish scripture accentuates the pleasures of spiritual adoration; yet given the painful scenes of marriage the novel elsewhere witnesses, Eliot's rendition of religious matrimony seems ironic at best. Again in contrast to the terror of violent possession by dead men envisioned in the confessions of Leonora and Gwendolen, these sexualized images of penetration and procreation resound in tones of exquisite devotion.[92] This process of spiritual insemination and germination conducted between men suggests again a paternal metaphor, this time decked out in all its transcendental glory through the ties of religion, race, and nation. The repeated use of organic and reproductive tropes blends with Eliot's racialized concept of national inheritance where, as Mordecai tells Daniel, "the life of Israel is in your veins." To this end Mordecai reveals an embodied identity in various unknown and celebrated Jewish patriarchs: "I have pleased myself with a faint likeness between these poor philosophers and the Masters who handed down the thought of our race—the great Transmitters."[93]

Eliot's emphasis on spirituality in the relationship between Daniel and Mordecai participates in her effort to idealize Jews refined of any of their unsavory worldly, embodied qualities, "the Jewish tatters and gibberish" that Leonora detests. Says Mordecai, "I believe in a growth, a passage, and a new unfolding of life whereof the seed is more perfect, more charged with the elements that are pregnant with diviner form."[94] This extended metaphor for the transmission of a national inheritance further promotes a rarefied vision of Jewish culture to come; by the same token, the paternal metaphor is firmly installed in this dream of Daniel Charisi, the name of the (grand)father. For the bond between Mordecai and Daniel affirms the nearly severed affiliation between the effaced Leonora's father and son, while this union also replicates the religious brotherhood between Joseph Kalonymos and Daniel Charisi. The Jewish covenant signifies unity, transacted always and only between men in Eliot's novel, but with women as the crucial linchpins to secure this power.

Where Gwendolen's and Leonora's isolated confessions to Daniel convey images of female bodies subjected nearly to death, Daniel's confession of mutuality supports life-generating figures. And so Mordecai proclaims: "In the multitudes of the ignorant on three continents who observe our rites and make the confession of the divine Unity, the soul of Judaism is not dead. Revive the organic centre: let the unity of Israel which has made the growth and form of its religion be an outward reality."[95] In this initial call for "an outward reality" to a "national centre"—as Daniel later tells Gwendolen—for Jewish people, confession of spiritual faith shades into the twin discourses of nationalism and imperialism inasmuch as to "revive the organic centre" means displacing some of the current inhabitants of Palestine.[96] Ironically, this Jewish restoration in the eastern Mediterranean that Eliot attributes to her devout Jews was not widely embraced by European Jews, yet was championed by some English gentiles during the time of the novel's setting and Eliot's writing. Whereas a Jewish settlement in this region might enhance British imperial interests, for European Jews, living within the Ottoman Empire and under the rule of a Turkish sultan was a dangerous and unwelcome prospect. In the 1860s and 1870s, not all Zionists favored Palestine as the site for the relocation, and significant numbers of European Jews did not espouse the Zionist notion of return, referenced repeatedly in Jewish scripture, at all.[97]

Nevertheless, the novel's homospiritual figuration of nationalist politics glorifies men through a metaphysical role and diminishes women as merely a profane and technical function in the process of cultural inheritance. For

Mirah, or more precisely her body, is the necessary medium of exchange through which these men enact their homosocial union:

> The two men clasped hands with a movement that seemed part of the flash from Mordecai's eyes, and passed through Mirah like an electric shock. But Daniel went on without pause, speaking from Mordecai's mind as much as from his own—
>
> "We have the same people. Our souls have the same vocation. We shall not be separated by life or by death."[98]

This orgasmic "flash from Mordecai's eyes" or "electric shock" uses Mirah as a conduit. While her presence assumes the function of catalyst, this erotic-spiritual consummation unites the two men in body, mind, race, and soul. In Eve Sedgwick's study of homosocial attachment, she stipulates the position of women in this iconography of male bonding: "A tableau of legitimation of 'modern' class and gender arrangements . . . takes place on firmly male-homosocial terms: it is a transaction of honor between men over the dead, discredited, or disempowered body of a woman."[99] Just as Daniel's bond to his grandfather is transacted and revealed through the suffering body of his mother, so is the consummate moment of his union with Mordecai achieved through the silent presence of Mirah's body. Mirah functions as a mirror, as an instrument of reflection, through which these men can see themselves in each other. If Eliot's prescribed ideal of a national inheritance demands self-abnegation in this process of transmission, the effects of gender modify the meanings of such selflessness. For Daniel, such devotion of self to community also encompasses a glorification of patriarchal narcissism, a tribute to the paternal metaphor in this cultural project "for all men." In contrast to the condemnation of both Leonora's and Gwendolen's unbecoming egotism that underlies their attempts at resistance, this confession scene applauds Mirah's compliant submission to a benevolent master. In this scene, Mirah is merely the wiring for "the spark . . . like an electric shock" that passes between these men whose role as "the Great Transmitter" is exalted in an economy of exchange. Fixed in the realm of reproduction and denied the moral benefits of transcendence, all three women furnish the unadorned medium of transmission of male power.

At the same time, Mordecai's dying body, whose death finally closes the novel, authenticates the more privileged bond between these men: "It has begun already—the marriage of our souls. It waits but the passing away of this body, and then they who are betrothed shall unite in a stricter bond, and what is mine shall be thine. . . . I desire the body that I gave my thought to pass away as this fleshy body will pass; but let the thought be born again from our fuller soul which shall be called yours."[100] "What is mine shall be thine" implies not only that Mordecai's body, thought, and soul will pass into Daniel, but also that his Mirah shall become Daniel's as well. The metaphysics of death rarefies this process of exchange and so disguises without completely eliminating the more unsavory designation of Jews as usurers. Given the prevalence of such anti-Semitic tropes in Victorian culture, what better identity could Eliot find for her idealized portrait of cultural transmission?

These scenes of homospiritual bonding position Mirah's body as a medium of exchange. Her marriage to Daniel is the worldly and material complement to Daniel's spiritual marriage to Mordecai. While her resemblance to a prostitute is obscured by the pious grandeur of these passages, expanded notions of prostitution inform the transgressions of both Gwendolen and Leonora that compel their confessions. As Chapters 2 and 3 make evident, the image of the prostitute lies beneath representations of deviant femininity which various confessions spotlight. In *Daniel Deronda*, prostitution—along with the idea of nonreproductive exchange—frames the three confessional subjects under consideration. Gwendolen, whose surname resembles "harlot," explicitly marries for money not love; her debut in the novel locates her in a gambling casino where she embarks on an economy of exchange and becomes, as Gallagher puts it, "a commodity condemned to perpetual resale."[101] As the Alcharisi, the great stage lyricist, Leonora also assumes the sign of the prostitute where stagewalker and streetwalker converge figuratively; Leonora trades the sanctioned, familial love of one man for the adoration of many unfamiliar fans—"men followed me from one country to another."[102] Finally, Daniel is inserted into this symbolic landscape of the prostitute in his confession of his Jewish identity; yet unlike the cynical treatment of Gwendolen and Leonora as exchange commodities, Daniel is venerated for his participation in this process of cultural transmission.

In the erotics of the homospiritual confession between men, Daniel assumes a feminized position in his submission to paternal law, dramatized in his role as receptacle for Mordecai's body, mind, and spirit. This feminine attitude of devotion replicates the playing out of the Jewish covenant with God whereby men, not women, do the worshiping of and the submitting to their divine bridegroom. These scenes with Mordecai predetermine Daniel's eventual heterosexual role through his marriage to Mirah and his undertaking the mission of his forefathers. But if Daniel acts as object of impassioned possession by a paternal decree, this occupation signifies a sacred duty nourished by spiritual joy. Daniel's felicitous religious surrender to the paternal metaphor offsets a malevolent and secular version of subordination that both women's confessions unfold. By the same token, these romanticized confession scenes between two men and "for all men" displace a certain aversion to Jews that surfaces elsewhere in the novel.

For this culminating confession scene conjoins the discourses of imperialism, nationalism, and patriarchy that punctuate the narrative. As Crosby argues, in *Daniel Deronda* Jews and women alike are instruments to further male transcendence. Beneath the idealized trope of a Jewish "national family" returning to their "national centre" lies Eliot's more vested interest in restoring an English national inheritance sanitized by the exodus of other racialized social groups. All three confession scenes enable Daniel's ultimate promotion as the new Englishman—in Zionist disguise—whose submission to the "Invisible Power" of what is finally patriarchal law promises the reclamation of an ailing English culture. Eliot's culminating pitch for such national restoration may be embedded in a different paternal metaphor. "Deronda" intimates a metaphoric assimilation of Disraeli—also of occluded Jewish origins—who was again prime minister in 1874 when Eliot was writing *Daniel Deronda*.[103] Although some decades earlier Eliot had opposed Disraeli's political position against racial fusion and assimilation, by the 1870s she was more enthusiastic about the endorsement of traditional values that underwrote Disraeli's Tory platform. Where Eliot clearly supported Disraeli's nationalism in contrast to Gladstone's liberalism, Jews functioned for both Disraeli and Eliot as a paragon for the importance of preserving a national inheritance in contrast to liberal cosmopolitanism.[104] In *Daniel Deronda*, Jews are metaphoric models for transmitting the idea—and not the reality—of this supreme form of identification with a national community. Eliot registers in the novel this aspect of Disraeli's politics, yet she represents in more muted tones another facet: Disraeli refashioned and popularized a new imperialism built on Carlyle's legacy.[105] The paternal metaphor that prevails in all three confession scenes operates as a condensed trope for Eliot's politics that ultimately highlight a racialized, nationalized, and gendered bond of inheritance. Whereas one confession scene applauds self-determination for Jewish men who pledge to leave England, the other confession scenes condemn self-determination as petty egoism in women who attempt to defy the violent assertions of authority by their familial masters.

The potential for transgressive retaliation against male privilege in Lady Audley's confession is reduced to the level of fantasy or a mere "contrivance" against "something stronger" in both Leonora's and Gwendolen's confessions. At the same time, all three women's narratives establish grievances over transgressions against these confessional subjects. In *Villette*, anti-Catholicism disguises travesties against an unsupported woman in English patriarchal culture; in *Lady Audley's Secret* such injustices begin to emerge, but only in the context of a confession of a depraved woman, explicitly labeled a madwoman and implicitly figured as a prostitute, who is consequently locked up and killed off. Although treating wronged women as wrongful is largely the case in *Daniel Deronda*, Eliot is more explicit than either Brontë or Braddon about the psychological tyranny of male sexualized oppression of women. With *Tess of the d'Urbervilles*, however, Hardy takes up the subject of sexual violence against a young woman in bolder strokes, while he also attributes to his heroine the act of mortal retribution of her assailant, something denied by Braddon and Eliot. Again like Eliot's rendition of Mordecai and Daniel as elaborate symbols for a spiritually vital national legacy, and like her treatment of Leonora and Gwendolen as cautionary tales about the hazards of selfish, rebellious women, Hardy exploits Tess's rape as a metaphor for the editorial subjection of a male author.

THE UN-INTACT STATE

Tess of the d'Urbervilles and Confessions
of Sexual and Textual Violence

> The representation of violence is inseparable from the notion of gender, even when the latter is explicitly "deconstructed" or, more exactly, indicated as "ideology." I contend, in short, that violence is en-gendered in representation.
> —Teresa de Lauretis, "The Violence of Rhetoric"

In his "Preface to the Fifth and Later Editions" to *Tess of the d'Urbervilles*, Thomas Hardy elaborately defends his novel against what he construes as a vicious assault. He qualifies these critical assailants as "manipulators of *Tess*," "professed literary boxers," and "sworn Discouragers," all of whom "pervert plain meanings, and grow personal under the name of practising the great historical method."[1] By writing the four prefaces, Hardy too "grows personal," not just because he retaliates against his critics but because he fashions himself as writer into a figure resembling his heroine.

As the story of a woman's rape, *Tess of the d'Urbervilles* highlights the dilemma of representing sexual violence, a difficulty evident both within the narrative and in the novel's editing history to which Hardy's prefaces refer. Whereas Gwendolen's telegraphic and condensed confession in *Daniel Deronda* signals a cultural uneasiness with female retaliation against male violence, the textual blankness of Tess's rape and her confession of it indicate the rhetorical and ideological complications of representing sexual brutality toward women at the end of the nineteenth century. With this novel, confession and testimony converge; Hardy's heroine represents the exemplary confessional subject in that Tess transgresses by attempting to bear witness to the transgression of violence against her. Although "more sinned against than sinning," as her husband and confessor Angel tells her, Tess is still held accountable for the violent deed of another man. For Tess, "the question of a woman telling her story" of rape becomes "the heaviest of crosses to herself."[2] For Hardy, publishing this story of sexual crime against a woman likewise constitutes martyrdom inasmuch as this narrative of transgression trespasses social decorum about subjects deemed fit for fiction.

The narrative gaps—the blank spaces and metaphoric descriptions—that signify Tess's rape and her account of it thus make manifest an ideological contradiction. On the one hand, relating a tale of sexual violence becomes a transgression. On the other, according to Foucault's repressive hypothesis, the incitement to speak sex, to put sexuality into discourse, also compels this transgression into representation. Foucault maintains that power permeates sexuality; so too does power mediate textuality, in this case, the textuality of aggressive sexuality, of rape. But as Teresa de Lauretis cautions, representing violence cannot be dislodged from the concept of gender. While Hardy attempts to do precisely this in his various figurative uses of rape, the confession scene also certifies with painstaking precision how, as de Lauretis puts it, "violence is en-gendered in representation."[3] In addition to exploring Tess's confession and the representations of sexual crime within the novel, this chapter takes confession to a metanarrative level. For the editing history of the novel and Hardy's prefaces also open up questions about the textual production of a male author's fictional account of a female character's confession of rape. Tess is unable to voice her version of sexual crime within the novel; by the same token, forces of censorship effect the initial publication of *Tess* in serial form in the *Graphic* and in the subsequent book versions.

Pure Text and Pure Tess: The White Mythology of Power

Foucault asserts that confession is one of various discursive and institutional techniques to discipline the body; power does not silence sexuality but urges its articulation. The body that becomes the chief focus of confession is necessarily an "object and target of power."[4] Managed by such disciplinary measures, bodies are "docile," readily manipulated according to the systems of coercion that power puts into play. With his repressive hypothesis, however, Foucault theorizes about a generic body, one that overlooks the specific elements of gender and class power. Both Tess and *Tess*, both female character and text, are docile bodies, that is, bodies shaped through political forces; yet these bodies, and the voicing of the restraints of these bodies, are not equivalent. Although Tess's body, in one sense, amounts to linguistic representation, there is a difference between a fleshy referent for this figured body and the product of textuality, the novel itself. Even so, Hardy's prefaces attempt to narrow the distinction between wronged writer, wrecked text, and ruined woman.[5]

This convergence has to do with the metaphorics of power, an intricate system of figuration upon which Hardy draws to defend the purity of both his text and his Tess. Where Tess's rape alters her body into an "un-intact state," as phrased in the novel, Hardy likewise bemoans the loss of his "novel intact," "mutilated" by the *Graphic*'s editors.[6] Yet Hardy also claims both within and outside the novel that his heroine and his text, Tess and the narrative that constructs her, are "pure" despite these sexual and editorial emendations.[7] Hardy's insistence on an intrinsic, fundamental intactness mythologizes the body—both a body of work and a body of woman—beyond social forces. This notion of an integral sexual (or in the case of *Tess*, textual) body prior to its social configuration is what Foucault labels a "ruse of power," a ploy that guarantees compliance with rather than subversion of power. The textual blankness of Tess's rape and confession bespeaks this maneuver since it inscribes a gap that seems to fall outside language, beyond representation. The white spaces that substitute for the sexual violation of Tess's body and for her narrative of this aggression also integrate Hardy's twofold argument of Tess as "A Pure Woman," as the subtitle proclaims, and his novel likewise a pure text, as if sexuality and textuality can exist apart from power.

In Chapter 4 I used the concept of the paternal metaphor to explore the rhetorical significations of male authority in confession where domination works best through substitution, absence, and invisibility. To appreciate further how power works on the level of signification and language, I now turn to Jacques Derrida's "white mythology" as a way to understand these figurative effects of force in *Tess* that structure representations of the heroine's rape and confession, as well as Hardy's prefatory claims about his Tess and text. While the novel explores the meaning of "A Pure Woman," the prefaces wobble around the notion of a purity of meaning, the metaphysics of a pristine text whose fundamental sense precedes its material and interpretive violations. The novel offers a panegyric for the quintessential experienced virgin; the prefaces bemoan an equally absurd proposition—the purity of the unread text.

Both ideals promote what Derrida calls "white mythology," the linguistic imperialism of western culture that privileges the supposedly inviolate language of white men as "a proper origin [and] the virginity of a history of beginnings."[8] Derrida's white mythology theorizes the ruse of power to designate any claim of a natural, intrinsic state external to social influence. Yet neither Derrida nor Foucault specifically addresses the ideological construct of gender, a belief that invariably frames abstract representations of purity and imperfection, especially in the case of Hardy's novel, which arranges an aesthetic of purity alongside the sexual crime of rape. In any case, this notion of unadulterated or nonderivative meaning, this "original figure" untainted by the violence of inscriptions, elides the metaphorical status of "original figure" or the *Tess* that constitutes "A Pure Woman." In a related sense, Angel Clare envisions Tess prior to her confession as "a visionary essence of woman" and as "a vessel untinctured by experience."[9] Hardy's fantasy of his pure Tess and text, where the repeated vacancy of both the rape and Tess's confession of the rape means unalloyed truth, attempts to detach gender and power from rape and its consequences for the female subject of sexual violence.

To explain this metaphorized power, I want to consider briefly the description of Tess's rape, which poses a corollary to Derrida's white mythology. At this moment in the narrative, on the brink of Alec's assault, Tess and text collapse into a continuity of body and meaning, or what Derrida terms white mythology's "purity of sensory language."[10] "Why it was that upon this beautiful feminine tissue, sensitive as gossamer, and practically blank as snow as yet, there should have been traced such a coarse pattern as it was doomed to receive; why so often the coarse appropriates the finer thus, the wrong man the woman, the wrong woman the man, many thousand years of analytical philosophy have failed to explain to our sense of order."[11] Not only is Tess figured as text, "this beautiful feminine tissue," but she is also "practically blank as snow" so that these metaphors together render Tess a white page about to be stained with a seminal "coarse pattern." This figuration of rape as textual inscription likewise characterizes writing as an act of violence. Like *Tess* and Tess, novel and heroine, pure writing must necessarily appear transparent, invisible, white, and, as such, pure representation cannot be read, consumed, or appropriated.

Derrida describes a similar primal scene of inscription: "White mythology —metaphysics has erased within itself the fabulous scene that has procured it, the scene that nevertheless remains active and stirring, inscribed in white ink, an invisible design covered over in the palimpsest."[12] The purity of this "white ink," or the impossibility of true representation, offsets the violation intrinsic in the act of writing, like the originary purity of "invisible design" that "remains active and stirring" despite its obfuscation through layers of inscription. Occurring in the narrative as gaps between chapters, Hardy's blank representations of Tess's rape and Tess's confession of the rape, as well as Hardy's prefatory frame to the novel, all establish a palimpsestic text of *Tess* where the original, necessarily unread novel fades beneath the assaultive reinscriptions of editing readers.

I do not mean to imply that a woman's rape is merely a matter of meta-discursive graphics upon an already written text. Rather, I am interested in examining the value of such metaphorical practices that either represent sexual violence as inscription or sexualize writing. In *Daniel Deronda*, Eliot capitalizes on images that convey sexualized male domination over women in confessions of familial power relations; in *Tess*, Hardy expands rape into an elaborate metaphor that encompasses the industrialization of a rural English landscape and the editing of his text. Just as Hardy represents Tess's rape precisely as violent inscription, Derrida's own metaphorical lexicon deploys an unqualified "virginity" in his delineation of white mythology. While both are exquisitely attentive to the violence of the letter, neither Hardy nor Derrida considers gender as a critical component of violence, rhetorical or otherwise. Given this elision of gender, one might wonder about the political ramifications of persistently metaphorizing rape and virginity, especially since western culture has overdetermined women as sexual bodies. In terms of a late Victorian vernacular of sexual crime, the word "violation" appears frequently in contexts that might correspond to more recent usage of "rape." Although the legal definitions and terminology of sexual crimes have an elaborate history enveloping meanings of intention, consent, and embodied evidence, nevertheless, "violation" reinforces a metaphoric correspondence between text and female body as properties equally subject to injury.[13]

Hardy's approximation of sexual crime as textual inscription exposes a fundamental white mythology of purity that reifies the stakes of virginity as well as the stakes of its violent undoing, rape. In Hardy's prefaces, the author capitalizes on the metaphoric currency of purity to bemoan his defiled text. Crucial material distinctions between these docile bodies, between a botched manuscript and a sexually battered woman, collapse in Hardy's metaphorics of rape; the suggestion of textual tampering obscures and thus safeguards the more egregious aggression of sexual crime. These boundaries of white mythology furnish the terms of Hardy's defensive aesthetics. In the prefaces, Tess's purity substitutes for both the novel's integrity and the writer's virtue.[14] In the narrative of *Tess*, the heroine's rape functions metaphorically for the disfigurement of the pastoral countryside by the mechanical inscriptions of the Industrial Revolution. Hardy features this analogy between Tess and landscape: "A field-man is a personality afield; a field-woman is a portion of the field; she has somehow lost her own margin, imbibed the essence of her surrounding, and assimilated herself with it."[15] Here a vehicle/tenor distinction dissolves as Tess, the "field-woman" featured here, "somehow los[es] her own margin" and blends into the scenery. At the same time, both Hardy's prefaces and Tess's confession venture a white mythology of power that figuratively assimilates a woman's rape to issues of censorship and capitalism. According to Hardy's estimations of the *Graphic* production of his novel and of subsequent critical censures of *Tess*, his text is both pristine territory and violated representations, both underivative tongue of "original sense" and consumed commodity of circulated reinscriptions. Tess's confession, including its variant renditions in serial and volume forms, is pure white textual space, yet its present absence also makes graphic the glaring foreclosure of Tess's narrative of sexual violence.

Sex, Power, and Censorship:
The Multiple Versions of Hardy's *Tess*

Before turning to the prefaces Hardy appended to his controversial novel, let me review the publication history of *Tess of the d'Urbervilles*. Commissioning Hardy to write the novel in 1887, Tillotson's Fiction Bureau was also the first publisher to reject it in 1889.[16] Seemingly determined to get his narrative of "a woman's story" into print, Hardy made multiple submissions of different versions of the text to the *Graphic, Murray's Magazine*, and *MacMillan's Magazine*. Although the ironically titled *Graphic* accepted Hardy's projected novel in the fall of 1889, when the proprietor and editorial staff read the submitted manuscript in June 1890, they were appalled by Tess's rape, pregnancy, and childbirth and demanded alterations. Hardy then removed the section of Tess's rape as well as the midnight baptism of her child and managed to publish these chapters "more especially addressed to adult readers," as he notes in the 1891 preface to the first book edition, separately as "episodic sketches" in the *Fortnightly Review* and the *National Observer*. To explain Tess's child, Hardy substituted an account of a mock marriage that Alec stages in order to assert his sexual desires over the credulous Tess.

The novel first appeared in serial installments in the *Graphic* in 1891 and then was published in three volumes in December 1891 which reinstated much, but not all, of the excised portions. Simon Gatrell speculates that the second half of the novel following Tess's wedding-night confession may have been written "under a certain amount of constraint deriving from Hardy's knowledge of the prejudices of the *Graphic*'s editorial board."[17] Finally, the 1912 Wessex edition is regarded as the most recent version of the novel that Hardy endorsed in which he included many revisions.

Clearly the publishing history of the novel demonstrates that the textuality of a story of sexual crime is bound up with editorial and market power. While Hardy's prefaces provide a somewhat abstract narrative of the forces of domination in the literary marketplace, N. N. Feltes's Marxist account examines the ideology of production that shaped the *Graphic*'s editorial decisions. Considered a family journal drawing a wide lower-middle-class audience, the *Graphic* was a heavily illustrated newspaper with the weekly serial as the longest section of uninterrupted prose.[18] Feltes categorizes the *Graphic* as a "class" journal interpellating readers into a particular social audience. Consequently, the *Graphic* version of Hardy's narrative was subjected to constructions of class as well as class-specific notions of gender through the contents and illustrations of the magazine as well as through editorial practices. Rather than indicting Victorian priggishness, Feltes concludes that censorship and Grundyism were absorbed by a capitalist literary mode of production that rendered Hardy's novel a "commodity text."[19] By the same token, the novel fashions its heroine Tess a commodity, a product of nature appropriated by vile social and sexual forces.

Sixteen years earlier, another writer engaged in similar ideological battle with the *Graphic* over the issue of representing aggressive male sexual behavior toward a female character. When Wilkie Collins first published in serial form *The Law and the Lady* in the *Graphic* in 1875, the literary editor, whom Collins termed "a mouthpiece of his proprietors," objected to a scene in which Valeria Woodville describes an unceremonious physical encounter with Miserrimus Dexter.[20] Although the editor substituted a briefer, milder passage when the episode was initially printed, Collins had expressly stipulated in his contract that the *Graphic* must publish "verbatim" from his manuscript; as a result, the next installment included the "objectionable" description.[21]

In the controversy, the literary editor of the *Graphic* insisted that their publication should "give no offense to the family circle," an ideologically saturated construction of audience which Collins labeled "that British Domestic Inquisition."[22] I would suggest that "family circle" also signifies a ruse of power whereby a readership is constituted as natural, unburdened in its characterization by forces of domination and control. Such white mythology of power further disguises what Tony Bennett calls a "reading formation" by which readers encounter a text "already 'over worked,' 'over coded,' productively activated in a particular way as a result of its inscription within the social, material, ideological, and institutional relationships which distinguish particular reading relationships."[23] Hardy similarly employs a deceptively uncomplicated notion of writer, woman, and text in his prefatory protests of his novel's critical censure.

Prefacing Confessions: My Body/My Text/My Tess

Like the innocent and trusting Tess, in his 1892 preface Hardy humbles Tess's author into "a mere tale-teller" of "plain meanings" who might have "overlooked" and "by pure inadvertence have run foul of when in the least aggressive mood" the cultural values his detractors uphold. Also "in the least aggressive mood," Tess is asleep at the threshold of her rape. What is most remarkable about this prefatory regress to the act of literary genesis is the figure of the writer whose blameless "pure inadvertence" and vulnerability suggest the defiled Tess and the defaced text in which she appears. Tess, text, and "tale-teller" converge in this cover story to a story that tries to uncover "a true sequence of things"—as the first preface of 1891 states—about a raped woman whose plight resembles, in some sense, that of the disparaged writer. Altogether Hardy wrote four prefaces to *Tess*. The first, "Explanatory Note for the First Edition," dated November 1891, accompanied the initial publication of the novel in book form and briefly describes the editing history to date of *Tess*. In July 1892 Hardy appends "Preface to the Fifth and Later Editions," the lengthiest and most defensive of the four. In January 1895 he adds a paragraph in which he seems to regret his rather heated response to the critical reception of *Tess* "when a spirited public and private criticism of its points was still fresh to the feelings." Finally, the March 1912 passage for the Wessex edition discloses yet another textual deletion and reinstallment.

In an account of the modern body, one unmarked by gender distinctions, Francis Barker maintains that "the bourgeois subject substitutes for its corporeal body the rarefied body of the text."[24] The abstraction that Barker observes also cushions the metaleptic arrangement of the body of author, text, and heroine that Hardy encourages. As a writer whose acute sensitivity toward rebuke makes criticism almost a physical attack, Hardy navigates his identity with his text into a position analogous to Tess's body. Because Hardy is writing at the end of the century when social interest increases in "the woman question," this attention frames his identification as a maligned writer with the battered body and reputation of his heroine. Indeed, many readers declare that Hardy "identified" with Tess.[25] J. Hillis Miller, for instance, contends that Hardy's feelings for this heroine were "perhaps stronger than for any other of his invented personages" and that Hardy "even obscurely identified himself with her" so that the text seems to exclaim, "Tess, c'est moi" for its author.[26] For Margaret Higonnet, Tess's "postulated voice permits a creative extension of Hardy's own voice" and the "ventriloquistic illusion" in which the congruence of the voices of narrator and Tess facilitates the assimilation of a woman's story of sexual violence to a male author's philosophic fatalism.[27] Yet none of these readings trace the extended metaphors of purity and pollution that conjoins the prefaces and the novel, the writer and the heroine.

Hardy's prefaces declare a resemblance between his text, deformed through corrections enforced by publishing editors and hostile critics, and Tess's fallen body, altered through the act of rape and rejected by Angel as purveyor of social mores. Like Hardy's vexed revisions of "a woman's story," Tess's construction of her own history is supplemented and obstructed, curtailed and foreclosed, by the authorized and conventional readings of "fallen" women offered by the biblical text-painter, Alec, and Angel. In a way, the prefaces render Hardy's text immaculate at the core, although defiled by surface alterations, like Tess's vulnerable body. Structurally, the body of Tess in the text and the body of *Tess* as the text represent the always inadequate, incomplete representation of a transgression that remains essentially unnarratable.[28] This resonance between Hardy's novel and Tess's character begins on the title-page with the line beneath the title: "A Pure Woman Faithfully Presented by Thomas Hardy." The constancy embedded in the sense behind both "Pure" and "Faithfully" links Tess's womanhood and Hardy's text as the true presentation of this "Pure Woman." Tess is a "Pure Woman" and Hardy is "faithful" to her, unlike Angel. Hardy's book and Tess's body stand in figurative concert with Tess's body substituting for the body of Hardy's text. Beneath the subtitle is the novel's epigraph from *Two Gentlemen of Verona*: "Poor wounded name! My bosom as a bed / Shall lodge thee." Writer, heroine, and text collapse here under "wounded name." This epigraph alludes not only to the heroine's name, linguistically wounded from Teresa d'Urbervilles to Tess Durbeyfield, although the narrative and the title confuse in which direction the wound lies, but also to the damage her body and her reputation suffer.[29]

"Poor wounded name" also suggests the injuries that the sensitive writer felt had accrued to his text and to his signature as author. That Hardy bore criticism of his writing almost as bodily insults emerges in his autobiography. For instance, Hardy responds as follows to a review of *Tess*: "How strange that one may write a book without knowing what one puts into it—or rather, the reader reads into it. Well, if this sort of thing continues no more novel-writing for me. A man must be a fool to deliberately stand up and be shot at."[30] This sense of a menacing audience recurs in Hardy's speculations about the writer who is physically endangered by "that absolute want of principle in the reviewer which gives one a start of fear as to a possible crime he may commit against one's person, such as a stab or a shot in a dark lane for righteousness's sake."[31] Bennett's notion of a "reading formation" qualifies the power that Hardy would locate within individual, professional readers as well as with the more general phenomenon of audience-at-large. Framed in his autobiography, "the reader" that Hardy posits here is also a text overdetermined by various ideological, formal, and material relationships.[32]

Hardy's dramatic depiction of the writer at risk to his readers on whom he is also dependent repeats Tess's vulnerability to crime: while traveling alone at night she is raped by the very man who offers to protect and guide her. The juxtaposition of textual body with Hardy's material body under fire is reinforced in his postscript to his last novel, *Jude the Obscure*: "So much for the unhappy beginning of *Jude*'s career as a book. After these verdicts from the press its next misfortune was to be burnt by a bishop—probably in his despair at not being able to burn me."[33] These associations position Hardy as sacrificial writer, just as Tess and Jude suffer martyrdom. Although Hardy personifies criticism of his novel as assaults on his body, he never explicitly construes himself as raped, as a victim of the sexual crime that befalls his "pure" heroine. Yet he persistently compares himself to her; he likens his degraded text and honorable intentions to innocent Tess's disgraced body and "fallen" status. This simultaneous silence and juxtaposition suggest that rape is precisely what he cannot discuss or articulate. Instead, Hardy displaces the subject of sexual crime by capitalizing on its metaphoric power, by reconstituting both rape and its victim through images of textual injury and violence, such as "poor wounded name."

Implicitly, the epigraph to *Tess* refers to the history of the material body of the manuscript that had been abridged and rearranged in serial form, the "pure" textual body that successive book-length versions attempt to reconstruct. In Shakespeare's play, Juliet has ripped up a letter from her lover, but then rues her impetuous act and pieces together the letter signed "Love-wounded Proteus." Similarly, compelled to secure its appearance in print after three rejections, Hardy disassembled and rewrote portions of his manuscript to conform to the *Graphic*'s demands by expunging sections on the subjects of Tess's rape and the baptism of her illegitimate and dying baby and by substituting the mock marriage for rape. Like Juliet's reconstruction of her lover's letter, Hardy's publication of the book edition tries to restore its material integrity, what he calls "the novel intact." Thus the epigraph is also an epitaph for the "original" unread (and unwritten) text, repeatedly deformed and re-formed through Hardy's persistent editing, as well as a lament for an essentially pure Tess and *Tess*, character and text, that waft beyond social forces.

The opening paragraph to the 1891 "Explanatory Note to the First Edition" introduces this accretion of Tess and text by figuring the novel as a dismembered organic body: "My thanks are tendered to the editors and proprietors of those periodicals for enabling me now to piece the trunk and limbs of the novel together, and print it complete, as originally written two years ago." Yet the bibliographic history of *Tess* makes the location of an originary text impossible. This first edition of the novel, contrary to the author's assertion, is not "complete, as originally written two years ago." The 1912 preface to the Wessex edition contradicts Hardy's initial prefatory claim by disclosing one supposedly inadvertent omission, the episode of the dance at the hay-trusser's just prior to the rape scene.[34] But according to J. T. Laird's meticulous research, no original version of the novel ever existed intact due to Hardy's obsessive revisions, his continuous regrafting of alterations onto a manuscript itself in the process of being written: "Most of the text of the First Edition represents a conflation of readings from earlier texts—the *Graphic*, the manuscript, and two printed sketches—a number of readings are entirely new, and illustrate Hardy's continued interest in the novel, an interest that was to show itself again in the revisions of the 1892, 1895, 1902, and 1912 editions."[35] Both an originary pure Tess and an originary pure *Tess* are impossible referents, not unlike Derrida's white mythology of "a proper origin [as] the virginity of a history of beginnings." Purity in both contexts is an abstraction intricately bound to signification and power. Hardy attempts to assert his own untenable domination over competing constructions, variant readings, of

Tess and text, while at the same time upbraiding interpretations falling outside his purview, that is, forces that read Tess and text otherwise.

In "Preface to the Fifth and Later Editions," Hardy insinuates the mutilation, the textual and interpretive "violations" of Tess by editors and critics: "Manipulators of Tess were of the predetermined sort whom most writers and readers would gladly forget; professed literary boxers, who put on their convictions for the occasion; modern 'Hammers of Heretics'; sworn Discouragers, ever on the watch to prevent the tentative half-success from becoming the whole success later on; who pervert plain meanings, and grow personal under the name of practising the great historical method."[36] The author alludes here to the forces of control—the more conspicuous features of Bennett's reading formation—encountered at the Graphic and in truculent reviews that demand what Hardy elsewhere calls "unceremonious concession to conventionality."[37] Again, Hardy's contention implies a ruse of power whereby readers, writers, and texts evade ideological, material, and institutional influences by basking in some primordial light outside the reading formations in which Hardy too is inscribed. In a different sense, Hardy's emphasis on carping reviewers who "grow personal" under the pretext of would-be objective criticism illuminates his own inability to separate self from text, similar to the dilemma of his heroine, a wrongdoing Hardy attempts to correct through his subtitle. Only in Tess's case, social constructions of femininity oblige this conflation of body and self where the condition of sexual purity determines female morality.

By far the lengthiest of the four, the preface to the fifth edition of Tess functions in some sense as a confession, where the writer reluctantly and ambivalently concedes his shortcomings. Yet this confession reads more like an indictment as the author emphasizes the transgressions of his readers rather than his own unintended mistakes.[38] All chronicled by reviewers and cited here in the preface, his faults of impropriety, vulgarity, and blasphemy pale "by pure inadvertence" beside those of the novel's assailants whose interpretive violence is encoded in the words Hardy employs: "manipulators," "boxers," "Hammers." So too do Tess's transgressions—equivocally defined as her rape, her failure to make this disclosure before her marriage, and, finally, the wedding-night confession of these events—shrivel in proportion to the penance imposed on her.

Hardy's prefatory confession also exposes the author's demise in another way: the anticipated material death of the author that follows the earlier figurative death of textual mastery. While the prefaces try to maintain the writer's authority by defending the purity of his text and its heroine, this defense also becomes an admission of the writer's limited control over the distribution of meanings that "a mere tale-teller, who writes down how the things of the world strike him, without any ulterior intentions whatever, has overlooked, and may by pure inadvertence have run foul of when in the least aggressive mood." Whereas this authorial construction is Hardy's attempt to gain interpretive dominion, "pure inadvertence" also signifies a curtailment of mastery, a limitation that Hardy reasserts and literalizes in the 1895 preface: "Some of the critics who provoked the reply [the fervent 1892 preface] have 'gone down into silence,' as if to remind one of the infinite unimportance of both their say and mine." Death as the great leveler here dissolves the differences, so hotly described in the previous preface, between writer and reader. Yet this "silence" disturbingly recalls the textual muting of Tess's rape and confession, a dangerous political move in which suppression is construed as "infinite unimportance."

In both the prefaces and the novel they introduce, transgression occurs when the textual body and the female sexual body are read, edited, consumed. The prefaces etch out a figurative cross-dressing between defamed writer and slandered woman as they defend the innocence of text and Tess. On the one hand, Hardy's prefaces allow that his novel has been dismantled and reassembled by the author, sliced and sullied by editors and critics; on the other hand, these framing words also establish the paradox of a metaphysical text beyond marketplace and other ideological forces. Within the novel, Hardy stresses that Tess is injured not only by Alec's rape of her, but also by the production and circulation of its narrative representations ranging from idle gossip to blank confession. Both the rape and its replay, Tess's confession, are construed through metaphors of inscription, yet they are foreclosed as narratives from the narrative itself.

In this comparison between Tess and text, between maligned writer and wronged heroine, Hardy's confession is an empowering, authorial act where the "mere tale-teller" exonerates his unwitting errors and condemns in turn his critical adversaries. For Tess, confession merely accentuates and reinforces her own disempowerment, her own vanishing agency to which the textual blankness of her confession attests. As in *Daniel Deronda*, the significance and consequences of confession are gendered, a distinction further accentuated by the double confession scene within the novel of Angel and Tess. Hardy's association of author and text rehearses a more problematic slippage in Tess's story, in which rape collapses into sexual history and an incident of sexual crime signifies her principal biography.

Confession, Gender, Sexuality:
Silencing the "Endless Mill of Speech"

In "Candour in English Fiction," published during the period of *Tess*'s initial rejections, Hardy decries "the fearful price" the writer incurs for speaking the unspeakable, for representing the unrepresentable sexual crime of rape.[39]

Hardy titles the section of the novel following Tess's confession "The Woman Pays" to indicate the price exacted from her for representing, for confessing, rape. As I observed earlier, Tess's confession marks the ideological contradiction of a subject compelled to speak her "truth" by speaking her sexual history since this narrative is muffled, displaced onto a transmogrifying description of the room that witnesses the disclosure. Foucault theorizes about an "endless mill of speech" manifesting the compulsion to confess "through explicit articulation and . . . accumulated details."[40] Hardy actually underscores the wholesale omission of Tess's words from the reader's view by deploying abstractions: "Her narrative ended; even its reassertions and secondary explanations were done."[41] The irony of these passages illuminates patterns of gender and power that complicate further Foucault's idea that confession channels sex into discourse. Such speaking sex encounters ideological dilemmas and representational snafus where a woman is framed as speaking subject, her sexuality the confessional subject.

The sensation of Tess's disclosure in the twin confession scene at the center of *Tess* replaces the climax of marital consummation. Uncovering past sexual events—in Tess's case, her rape and the birth of her child—forestalls the uncovering of bodies customary on the wedding night. However, in the book edition, Tess's confession remains covered by the blank space that registers it in the text. Is this textual effacement a silencing of Tess as a speaking subject, as agent constructing her own story? Or does the elision signify protection from rebuke by silencing confession's "endless mill of speech," a vexed attempt at advocacy for the wronged woman (and wronged writer) inevitably punished for the offense of bearing testimony on a narrative of transgression? In any case, the glaring absence of Tess's words accentuates the power of the confessor, of masculine entitlement that reads, assesses, and assimilates a tale of female sexual violence into a culturally overdetermined representation of women as eloquent, voiceless bodies.

The matter of "a woman telling her story" is fraught with difficulties in the novel repeatedly before the confession scene itself. Prior to the wedding night, Tess's attempts to confess her sexual history to Angel are either interrupted by circumstances, truncated by Angel's insertion of his fairy-tale version of her past, or abandoned by her unsteady resolve to tell a story that her mother advises Tess not to disclose. A look at this maternal counsel exposes gendered lines of power underwriting confession of a sexual past. Daunted by Angel's persistent courtship and her uncertainty about marrying him, given her secret history of rape, Tess writes "a most touching and urgent letter to her mother," an appeal that is nevertheless foreclosed from the text. Substituting a "J" for the first person, Joan Durbeyfield writes back to her daughter: "But with respect to your question Tess J say between ourselves quite private, but very strong, that on no account do you say a word of your bygone

Trouble to him. J did not tell everything to your father, he being so proud on account of his respectability, which perhaps your Intended is the same. Many a woman, some of the Highest in the Land, have had a Trouble in their time; and why should you Trumpet yours when others don't Trumpet theirs? No girl would be such a fool, specially as it is so long ago, and not your Fault at all."[42] Although her mother encourages Tess to withhold her "bygone Trouble" from Angel, she also insinuates that the problem of confession is not so much this "Trouble," something many women—even "the Highest in the Land"—have had, but the dubious pride and "respectability" of male privilege. This advice between and about women as confessional subjects, about women as commonly subjected to a sexually encoded "Trouble," points to the gendered effects of power inherent in the act of confession.[43]

In contrast, Angel initiates the twin confessional scene of the newlyweds. He begins his story by preambling on church doctrine and citations from biblical scripture and Horace. With this veneer of philosophical support, the trappings of an intellectual legacy due to class and gender advantages that Tess lacks, Angel aligns himself with the moral system of his father and the church as he professes, before he confesses, to admire "spotlessness" and to despise "impurity." His confession breathes through the cleansing air of his own humility and signifies a redemptive fall from pride and self-righteousness (although the hypocrisy of Angel's self-righteousness lingers through his reaction to Tess's confession) to the humble position of human error: "Well, a certain place is paved with good intentions, and having felt all that so strongly, you will see what a terrible remorse it bred in me when, in the midst of my fine aims for other people, I myself fell."[44]

Unencumbered by Tess's reception as confessor, Angel's confession is succinct and contained in its effect, as well as entirely integrated with his view of himself, past and present. Divided into two paragraphs, the confession begins as paraphrase and ends as direct quotation, textual evidence of his control over this act of disclosure because his words, though somewhat abstract, do convey the secret of a sexual past. Like the quoted words, his story also assigns Angel an active role in this event of sexual initiation. Angel's generalized confession and Tess's unquestioning acceptance contrast strikingly with his subsequent demands for details about her history. In short, confession of his transgression makes Angel virtuous; its substance causes no disturbance to the text, to the narrative, to his confessor. The masculine subject of confession and the textuality of his speaking sex prevail "intact."

The irony of confession and of the idiom of the sexual fall surfaces in this narrative display of gender difference where Angel introduces both terms, "confession" and "fall." And yet his transgression, his account of a deliberate, if brief, lapse, dwindles in contrast to Tess's disclosure, even though in her case it is a man who transgresses by committing sexual violence on Tess's sleeping body. Hardy's point is that in both instances "The Woman Pays," that the gender ideology of Victorian England holds the woman ultimately responsible for the moral rectitude of any sexual act. In Angel's confession, the offending woman appears as "a stranger," as "her," otherwise nameless, voiceless:

> . . . he plunged into eight-and-forty hours' dissipation with a stranger.
>
> "Happily I awoke almost immediately to a sense of my folly," he continued. "I would have no more to say to her, and I came home. I have never repeated the offence."[45]

Rehearsing Tess's blank confession, this total exclusion of the woman's voice suggests a power imbalance implicit in the heterosexuality of storytelling along with the impossibility of a legitimate, meaningful female perspective on sex. If this "stranger" is presumably a London prostitute or an otherwise unsuitable "woman much older than himself,"[46] any implication of material circumstances mediating her position is effectively suspended. Such elision again suggests the white mythology of power whereby silences, blanks, and omissions augment masculine authority. Further, Angel downplays his illicit sexual encounter by his assessment of the incident as "offense"; within his own confessional act, he plays both confessing subject and judging confessor.

Before the trauma of Tess's revelation, the interlude between the confessions entertains the promise of resemblance between the two secrets and their reception by each confessor. This possibility bespeaks the romantic convention of twin subjectivities united through heterosexual love, something the narrative's attention to gender difference finally collapses. When Angel anticipates that Tess's confession "can hardly be more serious," she replies: " 'It cannot—O no, it cannot!' She jumped up joyfully at the hope. 'No, it cannot be more serious, certainly,' she cried, 'because 'tis just the same!' "[47] A perception of similarity is the crucial field on which difference unfolds, for divergence and otherness depend upon the possibility of resemblance. The words "because 'tis just the same!" are omitted in the expurgated *Graphic* version, therefore mollifying the harshness of Angel's response to Tess's confession.

Yet their confessions are far from "just the same": one is a man's narrative of witting, if regrettable, sexual initiation, the other a woman (not) telling her story of rape, with measureless consequences that far exceed anything resulting from Angel's "offence." Tess's spontaneous perception of this sameness imparts both her wisdom and ignorance as she sees a structural similarity but overlooks a cultural code that assigns vastly different meanings of sexuality to men and to women. Sandra Bartky suggests how gendered arrangements of confession can encourage the illusion of political equality: "The man's confession of fear or failure tends to mystify the woman's understanding not only of the power dimensions of the relationship between herself and this particular man, but of the relations between men and women in general."⁴⁸ In light of Bartky's observations here, Angel's confession only promotes Tess's misapprehension. Nevertheless, as the scene progresses, the gendered disparities accumulate around the construction, substance, and interpretation of these marital confessions.

While Angel maintains some sense of agency over his revelation, Tess's confession is entirely mediated through a description of the room along with the objects it contains. Nowhere do Tess's words appear in direct quotation or even indirectly through paraphrase, although the physical qualities of her voice and tone are included in the detached inventory. Kaja Silverman observes that in the confession scene sexual difference delimits figurative meaning; Angel's position is divided between spectacle and spectator, yet Tess is wholly spectacle with the "searchlight" of the narrator's gaze centered on her.⁴⁹ This panoptic vision recalls the disciplinary subject of confession. In contrast to Angel's narration, in this scene details of Tess's body are included in the inventory of objects contained within the narrator's specular glare. Angel speaks his confession while Tess and the surrounding scene embody hers. In this way, Tess's subjectivity is referenced to her body and its controversial "un-intact state." This contrast schematizes the gendered politics of confession where Foucault's "accumulated details" of confession's "endless mill of speech" are displaced from a speaking subject onto an embodied object. On the one hand, Angel can shift his position from confessee to confessor, from offender to judge. On the other hand, Tess's own judgment of her past is dismissed or foreclosed. Instead, the meaning of Tess's confession of someone else's transgression against her is rendered variously as textual blank space and as her own wrongdoing, her own tainted sexual history.

The textual description that surrounds Tess's blank confession is structured into two parts so that the temporal slot of her narrative falls precisely into the space between the two divisions of the novel, "Phase the Fourth" and "Phase the Fifth." This structural gap connects Tess's confession with the narrative instance of her rape, also a blank passage on the page falling between book phases. The first paragraph of the description, narratively coinciding with the beginning of her confession, focuses on Tess's body: "Their hands were still joined. The ashes under the grate were lit by the fire vertically, like a torrid waste. Imagination might have beheld a Last Day luridness in this red-coaled glow, which fell on his face and hand, and on hers, peering into the loose hair about her brow, and firing the delicate skin underneath. A large shadow of her shape rose upon the wall and ceiling. She bent forward at which each diamond on her neck gave a sinister wink like a toad's; and pressing her forehead against his temples she entered on her story of her acquaintance of Alec d'Urberville and its results, murmuring the words without flinching, and with her eyelids drooping down."⁵⁰ Although the "red-coaled glow" colors Angel's face and hand, it "peers into" and "fires" Tess's hair, brow, and skin; at the same time, these verbs also highlight the scrutinizing stare of the confessor. Because Tess's confession forces Angel to re-vision a Tess remote from his fantasy of her, it doubly "fires" Angel's image of Tess: the obliterated confession both erases his version of her and introduces a sexualized female body absent from his previous readings of Tess as "a fresh and virginal daughter of Nature."[51] The firelight exaggerating Tess's body into a monstrous shadow is a morphological symptom of her transformation in the eyes of Angel; Tess's unnarratable confession reconfigures her embodied history as this "large shadow" overwhelming Angel's reading of her based on his own projection.

Rape and Its Metaphors: The Semiotics of the Unspeakable

The ghoulish representation as Tess begins to confess registers her story as unassimilable to discrete language, at the same time that her wordless disclosure multiplies images and destabilizes the process of representation. Julia Kristeva defines the abject as "what disturbs identity, system, order. What does not respect borders, positions, rules. The in-between, the ambiguous, the composite."[52] Quite literally the "in-between, the ambiguous," Tess's foreclosed narrative renders the confessional subject of female sexual violence as the abject, the uncategorizable, a subject that is neither subject nor object.

Following the gap in the text, the next "Phase" of the novel opens with the frame of the confession's conclusion, again embodied through Tess's physical properties: "Tess's voice throughout had hardly risen higher than its opening tone; there had been no exculpatory phrase of any kind, and she had not wept." This summation assumes the dry contours of a brief report on Tess's delivery. However, the signifying consequences of the eclipsed words brought to light, although offstage, spill over onto random objects. "Pervert[ing] plain meanings," to recall Hardy's prefatory accusation, the scene of confession converts simple objects into freakish distortions: "But the complexion even of external things seemed to suffer transmutation as her announcement progressed. The fire in the grate looked impish—demoniacally funny, as if it did not care in the least about her strait. The fender grinned idly, as if it too did not care. The light from the water-bottle was merely engaged in a chromatic problem. All material objects around announced their irresponsibility with terrible iteration. And yet nothing had changed since the moments when he had been kissing her; or rather, nothing in the substance of things. But the essence of things had changed."[53]

Tess's confession of her rape puts in motion a spectacular semiotic catastrophe. The gaping shadows, produced both materially during Tess's confession and thematically through the implied substance of her transgression, inaugurate a reading crisis, or a fall from meaning, foregrounded by the blank space. This confession of a violent fall from sexual innocence induces a fall from language, not only the narrative foreclosure of Tess's story, but also the dislodged coherence between sense and referentiality, the unsettled connection between surface and depth, or "substance of things" and "essence of things." Dramatizing the impossible representation of Tess's rape, the narration executes the loss of a stable viewpoint, a momentary interpretive arrest that linguistically transfers the thematic indeterminacy of Tess's "fall" as an imposed transgression. Ellen Rooney holds that the elisions, silences, and ambiguities surrounding Tess's rape and confession indicate Hardy's "inability" to represent Tess's perspective as a subject of sexual violence at a historical moment authorizing only masculine readings of sexuality.[54] That both the transformed items in the scene and Tess are associated with announcements encourages a connection between the personified objects and Tess as objectified person: "her announcement progressed" and "material objects around announced their irresponsibility with terrible iteration." Even syntax bestows agency on the objects, while Tess's is elided. The displacement of her confession onto a catalogue of things in the room again defines Tess's subjectivity as problematically yet persistently fastened to the status of bodies, hers and the indifferent objects surrounding her.

The wrenching apart of signifiers and meaning in this passage also reveals the interpretive stranglehold of Angel's perspective so that the significance of Tess's narrative of sexual crime is assimilated into her masculine confessor's distressed and violent reading. The "transmutation," replicated in the inversion of substance and essence that mark the objects, corresponds with how Tess's "announcement" exposes Angel's perceptions of Tess as fantasy, just as the objects in the room "suffer" hallucinatory transposition. When Angel says, "You were one person; now you are another," he distinguishes Tess's transgression not as the sexual fall itself, but as her iterability into "another woman in your shape. . . . a grotesque—prestidigitation."[55] And yet this duplicity, projected onto the confessional subject of a raped woman, is more or less Angel's handiwork, impressed by the ideological, material, and social forces encoded in any act of reading, including Hardy's subtitled and prefatory assertions of an essentially "pure" Tess and text.

As in the prefaces to *Tess*, this semiotic nightmare exploits the figurative power of rape by conflating the sensation of a woman's sexual violation with its accompanying social implications and the more abstract problem of interpretation and critical regard that writers encounter. Like the novel's critics, Angel occupies the position of reader whose variant constructions of Tess overlook a mythologized innocence despite her sexual knowledge, the very meaning of Tess that the narrative advances. This scene framing a dramatic textual gap, the radical unraveling of Tess's merely "auricular impressions" uses a woman's unspeakable story of rape as metaphor for a premodernist distrust of the necessarily partial language of Victorian realism and the vested interests of Victorian critical discourse.[56] Given this metaphoric deployment of Tess's metalinguistic confession, the politics of the textual vacancy of an unspeakable confessional subject begin to emerge.

Catherine Belsey defines a literary text's ideological underpinnings through the absence at its center: "The text is divided, split as the Lacanian subject is split, and Macherey compares the 'lack' in the consciousness of the work, its silence, what it cannot say, with the unconsciousness Freud explored."[57] Whereas the absence of Tess's confession at the center of the novel is overdetermined by Hardy's ambivalent "concession to conventionality," Tess's voicelessness reinforces the purity of Tess and *Tess* at the same time that it equates silence with feminine speech so that Tess is both "Pure Woman" and purely a woman's body.[58] Thus this blaring blank space condenses the contradictions of truth, sexuality, and power for women since Tess's passivity, her sexual victimage as well as its foreclosed confession, is also the source of Hardy's defense of her virtue.

To understand the rhetorical value of Tess's absent confession, I compare the two versions: the description surrounding the blank space in the book edition and the *Graphic* rendition. Although no direct quotation appears in the *Graphic*, at least some detail of Tess's narrative does. She describes the subterfuge of a mock marriage in her account to Angel: "the visit with D'Urberville to the supposed Registrar's, her abiding sense of the moral validity of the contract, and her wicked flying in the face of that conviction by wedding again. She murmured the words without flinching, and with her eyes fixed on the fire."[59] Adjusting the transgression from rape in the manuscript to bigamy here, this confession in the *Graphic* condenses Tess's fuller disclosure to her mother earlier in the serial:

> Then Tess told. "He made love to me, as you said he would do; and he asked me to marry him, also just as you declared he would. I never have liked him; but at last I agreed, knowing you'd be angry if I didn't. He said it must be private, even from you, on account of his mother; and by special license; and foolish I agreed to that likewise, to get rid of his pestering. I drove with him to Melchester, and there in a private room I went through the form of marriage with him as before a registrar. A few weeks after, I found out that it was not the registrar's house we had gone to, as I had supposed, but the house of a friend of his, who had played the part of the registrar. I then came away from Trantridge instantly, though he wished me to stay; and here I am."[60]

It is worth noting the more elaborate confession in direct quotation Tess makes to her mother. Because both are vulnerable to the sexual and social powers of men, the mother, who has implied her share of "Trouble," represents a much less risky confessor than a father or husband. Thus Tess's mother cautions her daughter not to tell her "bygone Trouble" to her "Intended." Such warning against confession prefigures the gendered politics of disclosing sexual violence that heralds Tess's demise. Yet in the book version, this confession to her mother, like the later one to her husband, is collapsed to a vanishing point: "Then Tess went up to her mother, put her face upon Joan's neck, and told."[61] The next paragraph records the mother's reaction; Tess's actual confession, present in direct quotation in the *Graphic*, is twice absent in the book.

The complicated editing history of *Tess* indicates that the confession scenes in the book are a recollection of the earlier manuscript, which was dismantled with the controversial episodes excised as separately published sketches and patched up with the mock marriage for the *Graphic*. In one sense, the serial confessions Tess makes are decidedly more explicit, more textually present through direct quotation and paraphrase; in another way, this thematically ungraphic *Graphic* version covers over with the mock marriage explanation the more striking sexual crime of rape implicated in the book form. Hardy's insertion of the mock marriage presumably reforms a narrative of sexual crime into a story compatible with the ideology of a "family circle" readership. This alteration partially corresponds with a legal legacy in which, according to Hebraic and Saxon laws, rape is absorbed into marriage, a move that domesticates the transgression of sexual violation.[62] Despite the *Graphic*'s seemingly conventional treatment of the subject of sexual crime, the qualification of a counterfeit, rather than a genuine, marriage demystifies this legal conversion of rape.

Is the *Graphic* confession Hardy's capitulation to the material powers of publishers, the ideological forces of convention, for the more dangerous rape scene that can only be insinuated, but never explicitly remembered, in the book? Does the mock marriage confession protect both Tess and Hardy from the moral outrage that accrues around representations of fallen women, even while it protects masculine might by not exposing, however obliquely, a rapist's violent act? If the novel posits the unnarratable in a way the serial does not, does this absent center replicate another form of violence against women, one that censors a woman's perspective on sexual crime? Although the blankness of Tess's confession in the book protects her from humiliating specificity, it also denies her the privilege of speech. Where Tess does not author in words her confession in the book version, this disempowerment also coincides with her powerlessness in the transgression that the confession seeks to remember.

Whether advocating for Hardy's Tess, or his *Tess*, or his authorship of a plot revolving around rape, the blank space in the book version constitutes the difficulties of representing sexual violence. The textual gap resists absorbing, containing, or domesticating the essential dislocation and otherness of rape into narrative contiguity. The victim's version of this violent assault on a woman's body is neither appropriated through the narrator's paraphrase nor mimicked between quotation marks. Yet if Tess's voicelessness at this climactic juncture suggests the impossibility or the injustice of depicting rape, the metaphoric vacancy impresses a confession of sexual crime against a woman into service for the authority of a besieged author and the woes of the written word. As a result, the blank spaces of Tess's rape and confession ironically substitute for her purity, for Hardy's noble intentions, for his original text of immaculate integrity—in other words, for the notion of a pure origin that lies outside language, beyond social, material, and ideological forces. In the prefaces and the novel, Hardy offers a correlation between pure textual body and pristine female body. Both categories maintain their inviolate status as abstractions, as idealized constructions, that rectify the "unintact" states of a novel's forced editing and a woman's sexual battery. The rhetorical effects of confession in *Tess* disclose this white mythology of power, which assimilates the sensation of Tess's "transgression" into metaphors of inscription and interpretation that finally deflect altogether the subject of rape, the problem of sexuality and domination.

Given this elaborate metaphorical use of sexual violence, one might well wonder if confession can be a source of unambivalent power for women, or for anyone already disempowered in hierarchies of social relations. I have argued that in each instance where a woman confesses to a transgression, even one clearly not of her doing, she further trespasses in the very act of speaking out, of testifying to systematic injustices based on the privileges of gender and class. Keeping in view the political, social, and rhetorical dimensions of gender, the convergence of confession and testimony for women makes unfortunate sense all too often. The blank space of Tess's confession is consistent with the assiduous protection Hardy lavishes on his heroine, yet this textual hole also signals a woman's problematic ability to provide testimony for an act of aggression against herself. In each case of a confessional subject, from *Villette* and *Lady Audley's Secret* to *Daniel Deronda* and *Tess of the d'Urbervilles*, such textual stuttering occurs around this question of representing abuse, discrimination, resentment, or fear of familial and masculine power. Attempting to dislodge some narrative of discrimination, one that is sexualized in its depiction if not explicitly of a sexual nature, each heroine inevitably transgresses in the act of representing this condition of disempowerment. The lines of power so complicate the very rhetoric of violence that it becomes difficult to disengage the transgressed from the transgressive, the violated from the violator. Analyzing acts of confessing, implicated as they are in relations of power, illuminates our understanding of ideological constructions of deviance and transgression, necessarily informed by social categories such as gender.

NOTES

Introduction

1. While there are numerous examples of this complexion of cultural criticism, I only mention Ann Cvetkovich's *Mixed Feelings*; this astute reading of affect in Victorian sensational literature, including two novels that my study also covers, *Lady Audley's Secret* and *Daniel Deronda*, is predicated on the kind of opposition I am describing here. I return to Cvetkovich's readings in Chapters 3 and 4.

2. Foucault, *History of Sexuality*, p. 62.

3. Gilmore, *Autobiographics*, p. 112. Gilmore elaborates on Foucault's influence on her understanding of confession as a mutual process: "After Foucault, we can see how confessor and penitent are positioned in a differential power relationship, though they should not be thought of exclusively as producer/penitent and consumer/confessor of truth but also as enjoined in a mutually productive performance of truth telling" (p. 112). While Gilmore's point is well taken that this relationship generates both confession and truth, I would maintain that reducing the operations of confession to this synergism risks obliterating the very specifics of a "differential power relationship." Indeed, for this reason I have chosen to define as "confession" many scenes of transgressive self-disclosure. In Chapter 1 I explore further the ways in which gender marks this disparity.

4. Walter Reich, "The Monster in the Mists," *New York Times Book Review*, May 15, 1994, p. 35.

5. Racial politics clearly complicate gender politics in this instance of a woman's disclosure simultaneously regarded as testimony and confession, a point that applies as well—although with distinctions as well—to Clarence Thomas's testimony before the Senate Judiciary Committee. For a collection of essays that challenge a reading of Hill's testimony as confession in the sense of culpability, see Morrison, ed., *Race-ing Justice, En-gendering Power*. Also see Morris, *Bearing Witness*.

6. Tambling, *Confession*, p. 1.

7. Butler, *Gender Trouble*, pp. 1–7.

8. Foucault, *History of Sexuality*, p. 65.

9. The one exception is *Villette*, in which Lucy Snowe does confess to a Catholic priest in a Catholic church; yet even this confession can be read as an extended metaphor for the uncanny relationship Brontë establishes in the novel between the foreign and the domestic, between alienation abroad and isolation at home.

10. De Lauretis, "The Rhetoric of Violence," pp. 240–41.

11. Kucich, *Repression in Victorian Fiction*, p. 3.

12. Litvak, *Caught in the Act*, p. ix.

13. See Michie, *The Flesh Made Word*, especially chap. 1, for a discussion of these Victorian tropes for feminine passion. Also see Bordo, *Unbearable Weight*, especially the section entitled "Hunger as Ideology." Michie and Bordo discuss how diet and appetite function as metaphors for sexuality in Victorian culture.

14. Gagnier, *Subjectivities*, p. 31.

15. Since women were accorded limited or negligible legal status under Victorian law, the status of women as witnesses in mid-century courts of law offers a resourceful issue for related investigations.

16. Poovey, *Uneven Developments*, p. 17.

17. On March 14, 1995, the *New York Times* ran a series of articles responding to this story, including a front-page article entitled "After Killing, Hard Questions for Talk Shows." Also see the following cover stories: "Fatal Attraction," *People*, March 27, 1995, and "A Special Report: Are Talk Shows out of Control?" *TV Guide*, April 1–7, 1995.

Chapter One

1. While I qualify both Freud and Foucault as "master theorists," I do acknowledge their very different intellectual and professional relationships to confession. On the one hand, Freud founded and promoted a new discourse and institution of confession as a form of treatment, namely psychoanalysis. On the other hand, Foucault wrote critically about the discursive development of confession as an elaborate policing system. For a useful comparison of the theories of Foucault and Freud, see Patrick Hutton, "Foucault, Freud, and the Technologies of the Self."

2. Leigh Gilmore makes a similar point about confession as "relational." See Gilmore, *Autobiographics*, p. 112. Also see my Introduction, note 3.

3. Foucault, *History of Sexuality*, pp. 65–66.

4. I want to make clear that while my study focuses on one such social category in particular—that is, gender—I am alive to other identity constructions that must be considered in analyzing a discourse, like confession, structured by power relations. In the Victorian texts that I examine, class, religion, age, race, sexuality, and nationality come into play in varying degrees.

5. Rubin, "The Traffic in Women," pp. 267, 275.

6. Although I focus on this first volume of *The History of Sexuality*, I want to note that the other two volumes, often referred to collectively as the "late" (published later and posthumously) Foucault, have received more attention in recent years. These texts, *The Use of Pleasure* (vol. 2) and *The Care of the Self* (vol. 3), provide a more complicated, that is, more contradictory, version of identity and subjectivity than in the first volume. Indeed, the "late" Foucault opens up the possibility and potentiality of the concept of individual agency. Even so, Lynn Hunt observes Foucault's own admission that these later volumes analyze "the history of desiring man" from a male perspective. See Hunt, "Foucault's Subject in *The History of Sexuality*," p. 80.

7. Foucault, *History of Sexuality*, pp. 61, 59.

8. Ibid., p. 60.

9. Ibid., p. 59.

10. Ibid., pp. 66, 70.

11. Ibid., p. 62.

12. Foucault, *The Use of Pleasure*, p. 22.

13. Foucault, *History of Sexuality*, pp. 63, 104.

14. Williams, *Hard Core*, p. 48.

15. Foucault, *History of Sexuality*, p. 94.

16. Hartsock, "Foucault on Power," p. 170.

17. Besides Linda Williams and Nancy Hartsock, other feminists have offered useful

critiques of Foucault's theory of power and sex. See Bartkowski, Bartky, de Lauretis, Lydon, Martin, and Sawicki.

18. Foucault, *History of Sexuality*, pp. 31–32.

19. Rubin, "The Traffic in Women," p. 278.

20. See Michie and de Lauretis for related readings of the same passage. Michie contends that Foucault's use of the neutral aggregate "bucolic" conceals a persistently male viewpoint and overlooks "the potentially spectacular fact of sexual difference" (Michie, *Flesh Made Word*, p. 6). De Lauretis likens these "bucolic" acts to "the rape and sexual extortion performed on little girls by young and adult males." Stressing the implicit and contradictory power dynamics in Foucault's illustration, de Lauretis observes that Foucault overlooks the privilege of male sexuality as he focuses his analysis on the power of institutions (de Lauretis, *Alice Doesn't*, p. 94).

21. Foucault, *History of Sexuality*, p. 31.

22. Williams, *Hard Core*, pp. 53, 36.

23. While I recognize that some of the essays are attributed to Breuer, some to Freud, and some to both, I will continue to use "Freud" as the author in my reading of this material. Despite individual authorship, these theories can be brought under "Freud" as it refers to the theory, discourse, and institution of confession most commonly associated with this proper name, namely, psychoanalysis. The passage I am quoting here is actually attributed to Breuer in the standard edition of Freud's texts.

24. Freud, *Standard Edition*, 2:211, emphasis added.

25. Elsewhere in the series of essays on hysteria, Freud again associates abreaction with confession: "In other cases speaking is itself the adequate reflex, when, for instance, it is a lamentation or giving utterance to a tormenting secret, e.g., a confession" (ibid., 2:8). Speaking or "giving utterance" is the "adequate reflex," again suggesting something automatic or involuntary rather than deliberate. Not to confess becomes inadequate resistance; to confess is compulsion, coercion, even if displaced onto unconscious processes.

26. Another example of this implicit male standard occurs in Freud's categorization of clinical cases into two types, "anxiety neurosis" and "neurasthenia." Freud elaborates: "Now it was easy to establish the fact that each of these types had a different abnormality of sexual life as its corresponding aetiological factor: in the former, *coitus interruptus*, undischarged excitement and sexual abstinence, and in the latter, excessive masturbation and too numerous nocturnal emissions" (*Autobiographical Study*, p. 41). Given that this discussion appears in the context of hysteria and that Freud's hysteric patients were by and large women, his detailed etiology of the "abnormality of sexual life" seems ludicrous.

27. Freud, *Standard Edition*, 2:212–13.

28. See Freud, *Autobiographical Study*, p. 58.

29. Tracing the evolution of his theory of infantile sexuality, Freud relates the initial "error into which I fell" when he believed the stories of childhood incest so many of his patients reported. Freud notes that fathers were most frequently targeted in these theatricalized "scenes": "With female patients the part of seducer was almost always assigned to their father" (Freud, *Autobiographical Study*, p. 57). Even in conceding the occasional instance where sexual aggression in reality rather than fantasy causes the illness, Freud's revised view of this subject still tends to exonerate patriarchs, that is, *adult* males who would necessarily hold some degree of power in their culture: "Moreover, seduction during childhood retained a certain share, though a humbler one, in the aetiology of neuroses. But the seducers turned out as a rule to have been older children" (pp. 58–59).

30. Also see Susan Stanford Friedman's compelling argument in "Hysteria, Dreams, and Modernity." Friedman contends that "the early corpus of psychoanalysis can be read

intertextually to reveal a textual unconscious of sexual politics in which the male subject displaces the female subject" (p. 42).

31. Freud, *Standard Edition*, 20:188.

32. Ibid., 20:188–89, emphasis added.

33. Ibid., 2:117.

34. Freud, *Autobiographical Studies*, pp. 44, 68, emphasis added.

35. Foucault calls psychiatry "a confessional science" that exploits its power to turn sex into talk through a process of "many-sided extortion" (*History of Sexuality*, p. 64). I offer here a couple of references on Freudian tropes for the psychoanalyst as knife and ear. In a discussion of the patient's resistance in analysis, Freud remarks, "I always prick up my ears when I hear a patient speak so disparagingly of something that has occurred to him" (*Standard Edition*, 2:279–80). In defense of his profession, Freud draws a parallel between psychoanalytic technique and the surgeon's knife: "Honesty compels me to admit that the activity of an untrained analyst does less harm to his patients than that of an unskilled surgeon. The possible damage is limited to the patient having been led into useless expenditure and having his chances of recovery removed or diminished. Furthermore, the reputation of analytic therapy has been lowered. All this is most undesirable, but it bears no comparison with the dangers that threaten from the knife of a surgical quack" (20:233). This is yet another instance in which Freud both implies and disguises the power of the analyst; the implication of power is by virtue of the analogy between "analytic therapy" and the "knife"; yet the potential consequences of "the activity of an untrained analyst" is also contained through the contrast and through such disclaimers as "useless expenditure."

36. Freud, *Standard Edition*, 20:189.

37. Freud, *Dora*, pp. 77–78.

38. Lacan, "The Signification of the Phallus," in *Écrits*, p. 287. For another translation of this argument, also see Rose, "Introduction II," p. 82. For a feminist reading of Lacan's assertion, see Gallop, *The Daughter's Seduction*, especially chap. 2.

39. Freud, "Resistance and Repression," p. 287.

40. Freud, *Standard Edition*, 2:294.

41. Freud, "Resistance and Repression," p. 289.

42. While I realize that the Freudian notion of countertransference allows for the analyst's own resistance, and as such complicates the strict lines of power that my reading suggests here, this concept is not integrated into Freud's discussions of resistance in general.

43. Freud, *Standard Edition*, 2:301.

44. Foucault, *History of Sexuality*, pp. 95–96.

45. Gilmore, *Autobiographics*, pp. 112, 226. Gilmore's point here seems inflected by recent possibilities of resistance that have come out of cultural studies. For instance, Michel de Certeau's idea of poaching is similar to what Gilmore describes as a "raid" on dominant ideology, or, in Gilmore's words, "the discourses of truth and identity." De Certeau's notion of reading as poaching theorizes the reader's capacity for resistance: "The reader takes neither the position of the author nor an author's position. He invents in texts something different from what they 'intended.' . . . He combines their fragments and creates something un-known in the space organized by their capacity for allowing an indefinite plurality of meanings" (*The Practice of Everyday Life*, p. 169). As wily cultural consumers, readers, according to de Certeau, are also like travelers who "move across lands belonging to someone else, like nomads poaching their way across fields they did not write" (p. 174). My overall reservations about this notion of resistance applies to de Certeau as well, for who gets to decipher and determine such acts of interpretive poaching?

46. Lydon, "Foucault and Feminism," p. 136.

47. Cixous, "The Laugh of the Medusa," pp. 255, 257.

48. Kofman, *The Enigma of Women*, p. 44, emphasis added.

49. Bartkowski, "Epistemic Drift in Foucault," pp. 49, 45.

50. Martin, "Feminism, Criticism, and Foucault," p. 15.

51. Bernstein, "Confessing Feminist Theory."

52. See Lewin, "Negotiating Lesbian Motherhood," p. 337.

53. Gilmore also grants confession a liberating potential: "I would say that women find in confessional discourse a subject position that grants them the authority from which to make truth claims" (*Autobiographics*, p. 225). Although I would question the nature and status of such "truth claims," still I agree that even a rhetorical subject position carries some value.

54. Bordo, *Unbearable Weight*, p. 295.

55. Chapter 4 explores the different ways in which power and gender are constituted in confessions of faith and confessions of transgressions.

56. Butler, *Gender Trouble*, p. 145.

57. Gilmore, *Autobiographics*, p. 164.

58. Felman and Laub, *Testimony*, p. xix.

59. Ibid., pp. 15, 5, 163.

60. Ibid., pp. 14–15.

61. Even though I am not devoting attention to Paul de Man's deconstructive treatment of confession as effacement of self and responsibility, it is worth mentioning that his "Excuses (Confessions)" forms a crucial theoretical linchpin in Felman's sense of confession as an impossible discourse. If de Man suggests that confessions are paltry attempts to apologize for what can never be condoned, Felman—among many of de Man's defenders—wishes to redeem his very problematic "witnessing" of Naziism in his early wartime writings. See Felman's fifth chapter, "After the Apocalypse: Paul de Man and the Fall to Silence" (Felman and Laub, *Testimony*). By Felman's standards, de Man would qualify as such an authoritative reader, yet the reams of writing in recent years on de Man's suppressed collaborationist journalism in 1940s Belgium collectively represents a document on the rhetorical, theoretical, and historical complications of interpretation embedded in any act of reporting, including witnessing.

62. Daly, *Gyn/Ecology*, pp. 92, 435.

63. Bartky, *Femininity and Domination*, p. 115.

64. Felman and Laub, *Testimony*, p. 7.

65. Gugelberger and Kearney, "Voices for the Voiceless," p. 4.

66. See Menchú, *I . . . Rigoberta Menchú*.

67. Gugelberger and Kearney, "Voices for the Voiceless," p. 8.

68. See Yudice, "*Testimonios* and Postmodernism," p. 16.

69. "Postfictional" is John Beverley's term, quoted in Gugelberger and Kearney, "Voices for the Voiceless," p. 11. *Testimonios* have also been called "resource literature" and "resistance literature," according to Gugelberger and Kearney.

Chapter Two

1. Brockman, *Letter to the Women*, pp. 4, 2. The bibliographic material on the pamphlet is limited; the publisher is not indicated nor is the precise date of publication supplied. The copy I examined belongs to Widener Library, Harvard University. This document is of a piece, however, with many of the texts circulated in various forms and quantities that make

up the printed discourse of the "anti-Catholic excitement" of the period from the 1840s to the 1870s, especially in its emphasis on the particular vulnerability of women as confessional subjects. In another pamphlet issued by the Protestant Evangelical Mission, *From Windsor to Rome through Anglican Sisterhoods*, there is a note on the mission's mandate in which contributions are directed to "Lieut-Col. Brockman, 23 Cambridge Gardens, Notting Hill." It is entirely feasible that the author of *Letter to the Women of England* was a leading member of this mid-century Evangelical society intent on eradicating any traces of the Church of Rome in England.

2. John Haslam, "Feminine Confessions," *Considerations on the Moral Management of Insane Persons*, quoted in Skultans, *Madness and Morals*, p. 223.

3. Blakeney, *Popery in Its Social Aspects*, p. 171, emphasis added.

4. Franchot, *Roads to Rome*, p. xvii.

5. It would also be fascinating to examine other historical institutions of confession, such as secular forms of witnessing in courts of law. What kind of legal status, for example, did Victorian women have as witnesses? William Tait argues in *Magdalenism* against prostitutes testifying in court because of their supposed habits of dissimulation. See Anderson, *Tainted Souls and Painted Faces*, p. 61.

6. Owen Chadwick notes that the Church of England prayer book allowed confession "in agonies of conscience or sickness" and that private consultation with a clergyman often resembled confession. See Chadwick, *The Victorian Church*, pp. 503–9.

7. Without doubt, the English Catholic church expanded in the decades following the reestablishment of the Catholic hierarchy. Walter Arnstein reports that in the 1850s and 1860s in England this church was "transformed from a tiny, isolated, quietist vestige into a rapidly growing organization that demanded a major role in the political, social, and intellectual life of the nation and that emphasized rather than minimized the ties that bound it to the universal Catholic church centered in Rome" (Arnstein, *Protestant versus Catholic*, p. 40). Nevertheless, the expansion of the English Catholic church had more to do with Irish immigration and population growth than with an onslaught of conversions, although the much-publicized conversions of prominent Tractarians like Newman bolstered this viewpoint. See Wolffe, *The Protestant Crusade*, p. 116.

8. Wolffe, *The Protestant Crusade*, pp. 108, 119.

9. As a devoted Low Church Evangelical, Tonna continued to oppose Catholicism in England after emancipation in 1829 by denouncing the Tractarian movement in texts she wrote in the 1840s, including *Conformity* (1841), *Falsehood and Truth* (1841), and *The Church Visible in All Ages* (1844). Her spiritual autobiography, *Personal Recollections*, correlates her conversion to Evangelicalism with her zealous commitment against Catholicism. Yet Tonna's anti-Catholicism should not be regarded as extraordinary, but in keeping with a more pervasive attitude among Anglo-Protestants of the 1840s and 1850s. See Kowaleski, " 'The Heroine of Some Strange Romance,' " p. 148. Tonna's social protest writings include *Helen Fleetwood* (1839–41) on deplorable factory conditions, *The Perils of a Nation* (1843) on the condition of children in industry, and *The Wrongs of Woman* (1843–44).

10. See Wolffe, *The Protestant Crusade*, especially chap. 2.

11. Ibid., pp. 113–14, 127.

12. Quoted in Arnstein, *Protestant versus Catholic*, p. 43.

13. Titles of other tracts issued by the Protestant Evangelical Mission include "The Underground Railway to Rome," "Reasons for Abjuring Allegiance to the See of Rome," and "The Oxford and Roman Railway." See *From Windsor to Rome*, p. 16.

14. "Why Should We Fear the Romish Priests?," p. 469.

15. In his discussion of Christina Rossetti's "feminist" High Anglicanism, Antony Har

rison recognizes the considerable support from Englishwomen of "the Ritual movement" reviving sisterhoods, auricular confession, and open seating in churches, all innovations that compromise the values of Victorian patriarchy. See Harrison, "Christina Rossetti," p. 100.

16. Brockman, *Letter to the Women*, p. 2.

17. Quoted in Arnstein, *Protestant versus Catholic*, p. 95.

18. Wolffe, *The Protestant Crusade*, p. 123.

19. Quoted in ibid.

20. Quoted in Arnstein, *Protestant versus Catholic*, p. 90.

21. There are abundant documents claiming evidence of infanticide through hundreds of such illegitimate corpses. Maria Monk supposedly saw a register of almost two hundred infants born and put to death at a convent. In a diatribe against sisterhoods, the author of *From Windsor to Rome through Anglican Sisterhoods* cites witness after witness on this subject, including an excavator at the site of an abandoned nunnery who dug up hundreds of infant corpses. See *From Windsor to Rome*, p. 10. Also see Billington, *The Protestant Crusade*, p. 67. Franchot discusses the convent as the scene of anti-Catholic stories of seduction and sexual intrigue in her sixth chapter, "Cruel Convent and Family Love." In this protracted anti-Catholic rhetoric on the "familial atrocities of Rome," lime was supposedly poured on infant corpses to expedite disintegration. See Franchot, *Roads to Rome*, p. 160. Many mid-century English documents associate Catholicism, and its supposedly celibate orders, with epidemic and illicit sexual activity. See Nield, *Prostitution in the Victorian Age*, for examples of this cultural perception of the imbrication of venereal disease and prostitution with the Catholic conventual system. In Chapter 3, I expand upon associations between the Catholic church—dubbed the Whore of Babylon through anti-Catholic readings of the Book of Revelations—and the prostitute in Victorian culture.

22. Blakeney, *Popery in Its Social Aspects*, p. 246.

23. Altick, *The English Common Reader*, pp. 287–88.

24. See Hepworth and Turner, *Confession*, p. 116.

25. See Litvak, *Caught in the Act*, especially chap. 4, "Dickens and Sensationalism," on the meanings and uses of theatricality and sensationalism in Victorian culture during this period.

26. See Peggy R. Ellsberg, "Distant and Different," for an engaging account of these Victorian anti-Catholic fictions. Charlotte Elizabeth Tonna also contributed generously to the popularization of anti-Catholic discourse in fiction and in her autobiography. See note 9 above.

27. Foucault, *History of Sexuality*, pp. 10–11.

28. Arnstein, *Protestant versus Catholic*, p. 95.

29. Ibid., p. 93.

30. Newman, *Letters and Diaries*, 14:501–2.

31. Ray Allen Billington observes that the third edition of Gavin's book was published in London in 1773. During the American Revolution and again in 1812, it was reprinted in the United States as *A Master Key to Popery, Giving a Full Account of the Customs of the Priests and Friars and the Rites and Ceremonies of the Popish Religion*. This particular title—*The Great Red Dragon; or the Master-Key to Popery*—was used in the 1854 edition published in Boston. See Billington, *The Protestant Crusade*, pp. 67 and 80 n. 77.

32. Hepworth and Turner, *Confession*, p. 42.

33. I want to point out that I am not maintaining this distinction between private and public spheres. On the contrary, this anti-Catholic discourse makes evident that public and private, state and family, are interconnected; I use the idea of the domestic to emphasize the

ways in which these supposedly separate realms are aligned in contrast to an alien power such as the Roman Catholic church.

34. Gavin, *The Great Red Dragon*, pp. 19, 37, 25.

35. This figure of the Whore of Babylon, taken from the Apocalypse, was interpreted as "Popery" in much anti-Catholic exegesis circulating in England during the mid-nineteenth century. The extremities of misogyny surface in this vision in Revelations of the Whore of Babylon, who is beaten, killed, eaten, and burned. This association between the Whore of Babylon and the Catholic church capitalizes on the idea that Catholicism seduces its adherents. This interpretation of the gendered figuration of abusive power also exposes a widespread anxiety about the potential of otherwise marginalized social groups.

36. Gavin, *The Great Red Dragon*, p. 37.

37. Ibid., p. 51, emphasis added.

38. "On Confession," p. 444.

39. Hepworth and Turner, *Confession*, p. 47.

40. Also see Theodore Zeldin, "The Conflict of Moralities," for a more detailed context of nineteenth-century anti-Catholicism in France. Franchot discusses Michelet in the context of American anti-Catholicism in *Roads to Rome*, pp. 121–23, 395 n. 17.

41. "Michelet on Auricular Confession and Direction," p. 102.

42. Ibid.

43. Ibid.

44. In discussing the 1850s censure of the Catholic conventual system, a polemic by various Protestant societies in England, John Wolffe considers how the controversy over enforced celibacy was viewed primarily as "representing the hostility of the Victorian paterfamilias to a rival patriarchalism." Wolffe goes on to observe that many women supported this interpretation at the time, which Wolffe speculates to be an indication of "an embryonic feminism in the perceived resistance to sexual oppression in the form of priestly seduction and authoritarianism." See Wolffe, *Protestant Crusade in Great Britain*, p. 126.

45. "Michelet on Auricular Confession and Direction," pp. 105, 104.

46. Ibid.

47. Ibid., p. 105.

48. Ibid., pp. 104, 105, 106.

49. Wolffe, *The Protestant Crusade*, p. 35.

50. Blakeney, *Popery in Its Social Aspects*, p. 169.

51. Ibid., pp. 169–71.

52. In the final volume of the sociological study *London Labour and the London Poor*, first published in 1851, Henry Mayhew and Bracebridge Hemyng designate prostitution as the source of social disorder across all cultures throughout history. Of course, Mayhew is also quick to couple prostitution with the Roman Catholic church. For a fuller discussion of prostitution and Catholicism, see *London Labour*, chap. 3.

53. Blakeney, *Popery in Its Social Aspects*, pp. 174, 174–75, 178.

54. The Protestant Evangelical Mission issued a notice in its various tracts that related texts, including "Maria Monk," were available for distribution. In case an English reader was unable to pick up a copy of Monk's story, many anti-Catholic tracts quoted from it. See, for example, *From Windsor to Rome*, p. 16. For an excellent account of the American reception to *Awful Disclosures* and to Maria Monk's controversial fame, see Franchot, *Roads to Rome*, pp. 154–61. Also see Griffin, "Awful Disclosures," for another informed analysis of Monk's text as part of the genre of escaped nuns' stories in nineteenth-century American culture.

55. See Billington, *The Protestant Crusade*, pp. 99–108, and Franchot, *Roads to Rome*, pp.

160–61. Franchot covers the vehement debate in the United States that culminated in the exposure of Monk's imposture. A New York lawyer took it upon himself to investigate the Hotel Dieu Nunnery and published an account of his unexceptional findings there. Monk's mother also claimed that Maria had been demented as a child when a pencil was driven through her head and that a Protestant minister, who had himself impregnated Maria, asked her to attest to this fabrication about the Catholic convent. Franchot is mostly interested in the cultural significance of the enormous popularity of Monk's story in the United States, where it was a best-seller with 300,000 copies sold before the Civil War, a figure surpassed only by *Uncle Tom's Cabin*. While only Stowe's anti-slavery novel achieved similar popularity in England, *Awful Disclosures* was circulated and quoted generously in anti-Catholic documents issued by the Protestant Evangelical Mission. Griffin calls Monk's book "an international best-seller" ("Awful Disclosures," p. 95).

Franchot also discusses Rebecca Reed's *Six Months in a Convent* (1835) as another example of what she labels, along with *Awful Disclosures*, the "convent captivity narrative." Another contemporary text of this genre is *Rosamond: or, a Narrative of the Captivity and Sufferings of an American Female under the Popist Priests, in the Island of Cuba* (1836). In both *Awful Disclosures* and *Rosamond* the patriarchal threat is foreign to the United States, where both were published and widely disseminated. Just as the threat of popery in English anti-Catholic documents is relegated to Rome and other Catholic countries, in these two narratives, Cuba and Canada emanate the hazards of Catholicism.

56. Newman, *Letters and Diaries*, 14:504.

57. Monk, *Awful Disclosures*, pp. 173, 78, 14.

58. See Wolffe, *Protestant Crusade*, pp. 125–26. In this regard, *Awful Disclosures* bears resemblance to captivity, seduction, and slave narratives of mid-century United States and to Gothic and sensation fiction in England. Franchot elaborates upon the American genres that correspond with these visions of conventual life and confessional sacrament in anti-Catholic literature. Griffin mentions British, American, French, and Spanish forms of the escaped nun's tale; see Griffin, "Awful Disclosures," p. 94.

59. Franchot, *Roads to Rome*, p. 123; Griffin, "Awful Disclosures," p. 94.

60. Monk, *Awful Disclosures*, p. 14. This story is also quoted in *From Windsor to Rome*.

61. I want to make clear that I am not claiming that Charlotte Brontë purposefully set about utilizing these tropes of Victorian anti-Catholic propaganda so that she could cleverly camouflage through her depiction of a Catholic country a critique of gender privilege in English society. Instead, given the cultural determinants of what is speakable and unspeakable, what a middle-class Victorian woman was permitted to discuss and what she would be censured for addressing, I am suggesting that sanctioned discourses of protest—even ones clearly marked as bigotry—tend to absorb protests over what might be deemed illicit or off-limits subjects. This notion of the intersection of the speakable and unspeakable is crucial to my sense of how confessional discourse bears a testimonial value.

62. Brontë, *Villette*, p. 231. The phrase "suffer and be still," popularized by recent criticism on Victorian domestic ideology, comes from Sarah Stickney Ellis's pronouncement on a woman's "highest duty" in *The Women of England: Their Social Duties and Domestic Habits* (1839). Lucy Snowe utters a variation on this dictum with such terse commands as: "But I must not complain" (p. 155); yet the tenacity of her narrative also belies this gendered catechism.

63. In particular, see Clark-Beattie's "Fables of Rebellion."

64. Brontë, *Villette*, p. 122.

65. John Kucich's perspective on Victorian habits of repression sheds light on Lucy's customary reticence. Following Foucault, Kucich argues that in an era when any knowl-

edge about an individual bestows power on whomever captures this information, repression serves as a necessary defensive strategy. Kucich amplifies this position by maintaining that for Lucy Snowe—as well as other Brontë heroines—repression itself is a form of power, a kind of weapon; Lucy's talent for self-negation bespeaks something Kucich describes as "reserve's intimate, interpersonal power" that is then "eroticized in self-reflexive terms." See Kucich, *Repression in Victorian Fiction*, pp. 78, 90. The foil to this English and feminine repression is the foreign and Catholic expression that Brontë continually draws around her heroine; to my mind, the two positions are not as conflicting as one might presume. More than that, through the consequences that the narrative unfolds of self-expression and self-denial, neither is clearly desirable. Ginevra may not be respected for her indulgent deportment, but she gets her man and her material way paved in the end. Such closure is ambiguous for Lucy. If the ending of the novel is another instance of Kucich's notion of repression, of knowledge denied to the reader but power granted to the read, I have difficulty rallying around such a devious and immaterial rendition of power.

66. Brontë also genders this opposition with the binary "continental 'female'" and "insular 'female'" (*Villette*, p. 97). Yet even this distinction breaks down inasmuch as Ginevra signifies an alloy of the two profiles and the supposed superiority of the Englishwoman or "insular female" falters with the suffering brought on by Lucy's social and emotional insularity.

67. Ibid., p. 66.

68. I should also mention here that Brontë's equivocal closure bestows prosperity on her characters most problematically and insistently aligned with Roman Catholicism. The last sentences of the novel read: "Madame Beck prospered all the days of her life; so did Père Silas; Madame Walravens fulfilled her ninetieth year before she died. Farewell" (p. 618).

69. Ibid., pp. 524, 525.

70. Ibid., pp. 526–27.

71. Ibid., p. 143.

72. Brontë wrote to Gaskell on August 6, 1851, about Kingsley's drama. This date not only coincides with the period in which Brontë was writing *Villette*, but also with the flurry of invective—including Newman's inflammatory lectures on Achilli—denouncing Catholic church fathers as threats to the sexual virtue of vulnerable young women.

73. Brontë, *Villette*, p. 254.

74. *From Windsor to Rome*, p. 10. Also see note 21 above.

75. His photographs of Hannah Cullwick, a Victorian maidservant, are included in *The Diaries of Hannah Cullwick*, an edition of her diaries that she wrote at the behest of Munby. See Stanley, ed., *The Diaries of Hannah Cullwick*.

76. *From Windsor to Rome*, p. 15. Also see Charlotte Elizabeth Tonna, *Personal Recollections*. Tonna also writes of "the Great Harlot" as part of an elaborate sign system not only for Catholic religious sisters but also for the institution of the Catholic church itself. Also see note 9 above.

77. Brontë, *Villette*, pp. 83, 130–31.

78. Directly after relaying the legend of the nun, Lucy confesses her struggle with self-repression as she recalls stormy weather that "woke the being I was always lulling, and stirred up a craving cry I could not satisfy" (*Villette*, p. 134).

79. Ibid., pp. 193, 194. Lucy continues: "Well, each and all, take it your own way. I accept the sermon, frown, sneer and laugh; perhaps you are all right: and perhaps, circumstanced like me, you would have been, like me, wrong. The first month was, indeed, a long, black, heavy month to me." This defensive anticipation of harsh and unsympathetic readers

recalls the virulent criticisms of reviewers like Elizabeth Rigby (Lady Eastlake) over Brontë's *Jane Eyre* as "a decidedly vulgar-minded woman" whose words amount to "a murmuring against God's appointment—there is a proud and perpetual assertion of the rights of *man*, for which we find no authority either in God's word or in God's providence" (emphasis added). Rigby goes so far as to link the novel's "pervading tone of ungodly discontent" with the spirit of Chartism. See the December 1848 *Quarterly Review's* review of *Jane Eyre*, especially pp. 153–54. My point here is that Brontë is able to disguise even this sally against her detractors by framing the whole question of self-revelation in anti-Catholic rhetoric.

80. Other cryptic depictions of Lucy's circumstances include "the cravings of a most deadly famine," "peculiarly agonizing depression," and "a strange fever of the nerves and blood" (*Villette*, pp. 195, 197).

81. Ibid., pp. 199, 527, 174.

82. Ibid., pp. 199–200, 197.

83. Ibid., pp. 200, 201.

84. Ibid.

85. For one example, see Moglen, *Charlotte Brontë*, p. 209.

86. Ibid., pp. 201–2.

87. *From Windsor to Rome*, pp. 10–11, emphasis added.

88. Brontë, *Villette*, p. 233.

89. Ibid., p. 311.

90. Ibid., pp. 231–32. Earlier, during the confession scene, Père Silas counsels, "I see you are ill, and this church is too cold; you must come to my house" (p. 201).

91. From a letter dated 2 September 1843 and quoted in Brontë, *Villette*, p. 634.

92. Constantin Héger was Brontë's teacher of literature in Brussels where she was a pupil at Madame Héger's pensionnat from 1842 to 1843. Like much biographical criticism, this text reads Mme. Beck as Brontë's revenge on Mme. Héger, who was married to the man for whom Brontë revealed a tumult of passion, especially in letters written to him upon her return to England in 1844–45. The author of this book, Frederika Macdonald, claims to have been a student at Héger's school sometime after Brontë's residence there. Macdonald's purpose is twofold: to supply the precise nature of Brontë's confession to the Catholic priest and to rehabilitate the reputations of both M. and Mme. Héger. Macdonald bases her speculations on Brontë's supposed confession of love for this married man from letters Brontë wrote to Emily from Brussels and to Héger from Haworth. The second half of *The Secret of Charlotte Brontë*, called "Some Reminiscences of the Real Monsieur and Madame Héger," is largely Macdonald's recollection of her experiences as an English schoolgirl from 1859 to 1861 at the pensionnat when M. Héger was her literature professor. Although Macdonald takes painstaking care to argue that the Hégers do not deserve the fictionalized treatment Brontë delivers in *Villette*, her memoirs provide an interesting account of the severe regime of discipline that constituted the pedagogy of this boarding school for girls.

In this vein, another title that captured my attention is *The Confessions of Charlotte Brontë*, privately published in 1954, in which John Malham-Dembleby issues "the amazing revelation" that Charlotte Brontë is the actual author of all the texts attributed to her siblings, Branwell, Emily, and Anne. The sensationalism of this use of confession is quite remarkable, for the author frames this story of literary detection and unmasking through the popular tropes of stage melodrama with chapters entitled: "The Curtain Rises on the Masquerade" and "The Curtain Falls on an Astounding Confession."

Chapter Three

1. See Nield, ed., *Prostitution in the Victorian Age*, for five articles on the subject of prostitution that appeared in the *Westminster Review* in the context of the debate over and subsequent passage of the Contagious Diseases Acts of the 1860s. For a historical account of prostitution in Victorian England, see Walkowitz, *Prostitution and Victorian Society*. For a discussion of prostitution in Victorian culture and literature, see Michie, *Outside the Pale*, especially chap. 4: "'Those That Will Not Work': Prostitutes, Property, Gaskell, and Dickens." Also see Anderson, *Tainted Souls and Painted Faces*, chap. 1, for a comprehensive treatment of prostitution and the rhetoric of fallenness in the 1840s and 1850s. See Poovey, *Uneven Developments*, chap. 5, for an account of the ideological uses of representing prostitution in Britain in the 1840s. Poovey coordinates various cultural documents on prostitution with the figure of the governess in *Jane Eyre*. For a discussion of W. R. Greg's essay, see Poovey, "Speaking of the Body."

2. See Gagnier, *Subjectivities*, p. 79.

3. Greg's *Westminster Review* article was reprinted in 1853 in a pamphlet titled *The Great Sin of Great Cities*. Although generally a conservative on religious and social issues, Greg argued for the state regulation of prostitution with measures that anticipate the Contagious Diseases Acts of the 1860s: more lock hospitals, periodic examination of women suspected as prostitutes, and mandatory detention of infected prostitutes. See Fisher, *Scandal*, pp. 11–12. The first chapter of *Scandal* offers a cogent history of these prostitution debates.

4. Note that "The Prostitute Class Generally" in *London Labour and the London Poor* was written collaboratively by both Henry Mayhew and Bracebridge Hemyng, while the section "Prostitution in London" is attributed solely to Hemyng. In my discussions below of *London Labour* I alternate between citing Mayhew alone and Hemyng and Mayhew together.

5. Greg, "Prostitution," pp. 474–75, 449.

6. Victorian critics of the 1860s tended to regard Lady Audley as villain rather than victim. For example, in two 1865 reviews, W. F. Rae characterizes Lady Audley as "a female Mephistopheles" and Henry James calls her "diabolically wicked."

7. The enormous popularity of these novels anticipates more recent widespread fascination with tabloid tales that feature women whose sexuality occupies a position in the unlocking of each criminal case. The image of the prostitute, of the excessively sexual woman, figures in murder and assault cases that have become spectacular media events of the 1990s, from Amy Fisher and Tonya Harding to Susan Smith. Like their Victorian counterparts, these late-twentieth-century female celebrity victim-villains signify "indexical references with multiple meanings," according to Lorraine Delia Kenny in "Amy Fisher, My Story," a fascinating account of the cultural uses of these "media-saturated cultural obsessions." Kenny maintains that Amy Fisher has generated so much attention not because she is anomalous, but because "only a few degrees separate her from the more ordinary teenage girls" (p. 84).

8. See Chapter 2 for a fuller discussion of this correlation between nun and prostitute in Victorian anti-Catholicism, especially in Brontë's novel and in Millais's painting. Also see Franchot, *Roads to Rome*, pp. 155, 157, 161, for related discussions. Franchot examines Maria Monk as "the nun's alter-image, the prostitute" (p. 155).

9. Braddon, *Lady Audley's Secret*, pp. 1, 3.

10. Ibid., p. 374.

11. Franchot, *Roads to Rome*, pp. 182–83.

12. Again invoking the notion of a tenuous "boundary line," the narrator acautions, "What pleasure could have remained for Lucretia Borgia and Catherine de'Medici, when the dreadful boundary line between innocence and guilt was passed, and the lost creatures stood upon the lonely outer side? Only horrible vengeful joys, and treacherous delights were left for these miserable women." See Braddon, *Lady Audley's Secret*, p. 296.

13. Mayhew, *London Labour and the London Poor*, 4:201.

14. Much of the debate around prostitution was focused on the question of government intervention. Modeled on the French system of surveillance, a police network much discussed in Greg's account, the Contagious Diseases Acts were initially passed in England in 1864, amended in 1866 and 1869, and repealed in 1883. This legislation mandated the identification of prostitutes by undercover policemen and their subsequent examination and treatment, including detention in lock hospitals for months. This approach to the social problem of prostitution was advocated by W. R. Greg and William Acton, by Tory supporters of the military, by Liberals concerned with public health issues, and by police and other civil authorities. See Walkowitz, *Prostitution and Victorian Society*, for a detailed history of this legislation. See Fisher, *Scandal*, for an account that takes issue with Walkowitz's reading of the Contagious Diseases Acts and their repeal.

15. Chapman, "Prostitution," pp. 137–38.

16. Ibid., p. 138.

17. Greg, "Prostitution," pp. 458–59, 449.

18. Braddon, *Lady Audley's Secret*, pp. 9–10, 10–11.

19. Quoted in Skultans, *Madness and Morals*, pp. 228–29.

20. Chapman, "Prostitution in Relation to the National Health," p. 179.

21. Greg, "Prostitution," pp. 476, 491.

22. See Taylor, *Secret Theatre of Home*, p. 64.

23. Showalter, *The Female Malady*, p. 29.

24. James Prichard, quoted in ibid.

25. Showalter elaborates on definitions of sanity and insanity reproducing dominant ideologies of gender and class. In this sense, she qualifies the Victorian madwoman in terms of her resistance, refusal, or noncompliance with standards of proper femininity. Showalter reads Lady Audley's eponymous "Secret" of inherited madness in this spirit. See ibid., pp. 71–72. As I discuss in Chapter 1, I am uneasy with such interpretations that maneuver pathology into "resistance," a term too generously applied, too often without careful consideration of social, linguistic, and material power arrangements.

26. Stocking, *Victorian Anthropology*, p. 8. Also see my discussion of the cultural work of Victorian uses of degeneracy, particularly in relation to sensation fiction, in Bernstein, "Dirty Reading." This degeneracy argument tended to be harnessed to theories about the depravity of both the upper and lower classes; as such, this rhetoric attempted to bolster middle-class power.

27. Anderson, *Tainted Souls and Painted Faces*, pp. 51–52.

28. Greg, "Prostitution," p. 454.

29. A very partial list of these characters identified as or associated with streetwalkers include Esther Barton in *Mary Barton*, the title character in *Ruth*, Hetty Sorrell in *Adam Bede*, Alice Marwood in *Dombey and Son*, Lady Dedlock in *Bleak House*, Anne Catherick in *The Woman in White*, Isabel Vane in *East Lynne*, and Lydia Gwilt in *Armadale*. More interesting, perhaps, are the exceptions to this rule, which include Magdalen Vanstone in *No Name*. By the same token, the characters I take up in the next chapters, namely Leonora Halm-Eberstein, Gwendolen Harleth, and Tess Durbeyfield, are each structured through the tropes and identity of the prostitute. Also see Anderson, *Tainted Souls and Painted*

Faces, chaps. 2 and 3, for her treatment of fallen women in the novels of Dickens and Gaskell.

30. Quoted in Nield, "Introduction," *Prostitution in the Victorian Age*, n.p. Also see Anderson, *Tainted Souls and Painted Faces*, pp. 12, 49.

31. It is beyond the scope of this chapter to discuss how the discourse of cultural anthropology coincided with urban sociology and psychology in the construction of degenerate categories of social groups ranging from the female urban poor of England to those of nonwestern cultures. For a fascinating study on symbolic associations between the prostitute and the African woman, see Gilman, *Difference and Pathology*. Also see Stocking, *Victorian Anthropology*. The word "race" was used variously in Victorian discourses; sometimes it refers to nationality, class, or gender.

32. Greg, "Prostitution," p. 457.

33. Ibid., pp. 460, 458, emphasis added.

34. In her discussion of Henry Mayhew's treatment of prostitution, Anne Humphreys also notes that this love of vanity was the most popular explanation among Victorians for why women became prostitutes. See Humphreys, *Travels into the Poor Man's Country*, p. 131.

35. See Yeo and Thompson, *The Unknown Mayhew*, for selections from this particular number. Gagnier describes Mayhew's series in the *Morning Chronicle* as an attempt at "social reconciliation" in the wake of several events of the preceding year, 1848: the European revolutions, the failure of Chartism, and the cholera epidemic. See Gagnier, *Subjectivities*, p. 78.

As for Mayhew's stint as urban ethnographer, he published eighty-two "letters" in the respectable publication, the *Morning Chronicle*, from October 1849 to December 1850. These weekly numbers were reissued as *London Labour* in 1851–52 and contained within the third and final volume a lengthy discussion of prostitution. *London Labour and the London Poor* was published in 1861, including a fourth volume, "Those Who Will Not Work." In this last volume Mayhew, along with his collaborator Bracebridge Hemyng, devotes considerable space to prostitution. See Gagnier, *Subjectivities*, p. 66, and Yeo and Thompson, *The Unknown Mayhew*, pp. 476–77.

36. According to E. P. Thompson, "The revelations about prostitution among the needlewomen were perhaps the most sensational moment of the series." See Yeo and Thompson, *The Unknown Mayhew*, p. 24.

37. Gagnier claims that Mayhew wrote only the first thirty-seven pages of this volume of the 1861 *London Labour*. See Gagnier, *Subjectivities*, pp. 82, 90.

38. For an analysis of this reading of Mayhew, see Levy, *Other Women*, chap. 2.

39. Mayhew, *London Labour*, 4:35.

40. Quoted in Yeo and Thompson, *The Unknown Mayhew*, p. 147.

41. Quoted in ibid., p. 148. Greg's 1850 essay on prostitution incorporates large portions of Mayhew's letters, including much of this November 1849 installment of the stories of slopworkers and needlewomen. See Greg, "Prostitution," pp. 461–68.

42. Mayhew followed up on this initial group meeting with one some weeks later of 1,000 female slopworkers to whom Mayhew had directed a mass questionnaire published in the *Morning Chronicle* on December 4, 1849. The future Earl of Shaftesbury—Lord Ashley—and Sidney Herbert disrupted the meeting and said that there were 500,000 surplus slopworkers in England and there was a coincidental shortage of 500,000 women in Australia. This began a subscription list headed by Queen Victoria and Prince Albert. I rely here on Gagnier, *Subjectivities*, p. 79, and Yeo and Thompson, *The Unknown Mayhew*, pp. 24–25, for their discussions of this occasion. I also want to note the gendered impor

tance of Australia in the second chapter of Braddon's novel, "On Board the Argus," in which a middle-class "redundant" or "surplus" woman and Lady Audley's first husband both return to England from this colony. For Miss Morley, the governess, Australia represents a desperate opportunity to support herself legitimately, if meagerly, so that she might marry back in England. For George Talboys, who has deserted his wife and infant, Australia signifies a golden chance for adventurous speculation.

43. Quoted in Yeo and Thompson, *The Unknown Mayhew*, pp. 167–68.

44. Ibid., p. 168.

45. Resembling the power arrangements of viewer and viewed in Mayhew's scene of confession is the consulting room of psychoanalysis where Freud describes "my practice of requiring the patient to lie upon the sofa while I sat behind him, seeing him, but not seen myself." See Freud, *Autobiographical Study*, p. 47.

46. Braddon, *Lady Audley's Secret*, p. 345.

47. Ibid., p. 346.

48. Ibid., pp. 403–4.

49. Chapman, "Prostitution in Relation to the National Health," pp. 180–81.

50. See Welsh, *George Eliot and Blackmail*, p. 22, for a reading of Lady Audley's "secret" as her underclass origins.

51. This association also brings to mind another way in which Victorian discourse deploys the tropes of prostitution. By definition from the lower classes, actresses, in effect stagewalkers, were frequently viewed as a species of streetwalkers by virtue of their public performance of emotion and intimacy, their cosmetic embellishments, and their ability to assume different identities. All of these accomplishments contradicted the dominant ideology of femininity as natural and private. Because they tend to assume particular identities for their own material advantages, sensation heroines are either explicitly or implicitly associated with actresses and prostitutes. In Collins's *No Name*, Magdalen Vanstone's career, her given name, and her bout with insanity and illness all combine these cultural representations of deviant femininity.

52. Braddon, *Lady Audley's Secret*, p. 345.

53. Quoted in *Wilkie Collins*, ed. Page, p. 143.

54. The most obvious example of this trope of madwoman is Bertha Mason Rochester, the hidden wife in *Jane Eyre* who happens to be Creole as well as insane. This characterization of a non-European woman as both insane and sexually promiscuous exemplifies Cora Kaplan's observation about the interests of hegemonic discourses in merging representations of the primitive and the degraded feminine. See Kaplan, *Sea Changes*, pp. 166–67. This association of moral degeneracy and female eroticism also informs Edward Said's *Orientalism* and Jenny Sharpe's *Allegories of Empire*.

55. Braddon, *Lady Audley's Secret*, p. 350.

56. Chapman, "Prostitution in Relation to the National Health," pp. 181, 202.

57. For a slightly later medical account of inherited insanity, see Andrew Wynter, *The Borderlands of Insanity* (1876): "It is agreed by all the alienist physicians, that girls are far more likely to inherit insanity from their mothers than from the other parent. . . . The tendency of the mother to transmit her mental disease is . . . in all cases stronger than the father's; some physicians have, indeed, insisted that it is twice as strong . . . If the daughter of an insane mother very much resembles her in feature and in temperament, the chances are that she is more likely to inherit the disease. . . . for if the general physical aspect and the temperament are alike, it points to a similar likeness in the structure of the body and nerve" (quoted in Skultans, *Madness and Morals*, p. 235). Lady Audley's account of her mother's puerperal insanity, inherited from her own mother and in turn passed down to Lady

Audley herself, is compatible with this Victorian account of inherited madness particularly prevalent between mothers and daughters. However, the medical doctor who renders his professional judgment on Lady Audley's condition specifies that "madness is not necessarily transmitted from mother to daughter" (*Lady Audley's Secret*, p. 377).

58. Braddon, *Lady Audley's Secret*, p. 393. For a related discussion of lactational insanity, a diagnosis applied to the delirium afflicting poor mothers who excessively breastfed their babies to prevent conception and save money, see Showalter, *The Female Malady*, p. 54.

59. Braddon, *Lady Audley's Secret*, p. 205.

60. Quoted in Showalter, *The Female Malady*, pp. 57–58. See Showalter for a discussion of puerperal insanity, which Showalter equates with the way motherhood signified domestic entrapment and increased material hardships for poor women. Also see pp. 71–72 for Showalter's reading of Lady Audley's madness.

61. Braddon, *Lady Audley's Secret*, p. 353.

62. Ibid., p. 351.

63. Mayhew, *London Labour and the London Poor*, 4:35, 36.

64. Greg, "Prostitution," p. 471.

65. Braddon, *Lady Audley's Secret*, p. 353.

66. Poovey, *Uneven Developments*, pp. 129–31.

67. Unlike George's sudden desertion of his wife and infant, Lady Audley leaves her child in the care of her father and sends money as she is able. Braddon lays out a series of parallels between the domestic departures of this husband and wife that highlight the way the entitlement of gender both grants George more liberty and absolves him of responsibility.

68. Mayhew, *London Labour and the London Poor*, 4:219.

69. Braddon, *Lady Audley's Secret*, p. 353.

70. Mayhew, *London Labour and the London Poor*, 4:213.

71. For a sustained discussion of this Victorian "anxiety of assimilation" and sensation fiction, see Bernstein, "Dirty Reading," pp. 225–28.

72. Mayhew, *London Labour and the London Poor*, 4:214.

73. Braddon, *Lady Audley's Secret*, p. 353.

74. Mayhew, *London Labour and the London Poor*, 4:217.

75. Braddon, *Lady Audley's Secret*, p. 354.

76. See Anderson, *Tainted Souls and Painted Faces*, pp. 1–9, for a discussion of the way fallenness in Victorian rhetoric signifies a loss of control or attenuated agency.

77. Braddon, *Lady Audley's Secret*, pp. 350–51.

78. Quoted in Yeo and Thompson, *The Unknown Mayhew*, pp. 148–49.

79. Braddon, *Lady Audley's Secret*, p. 351.

80. Mayhew, *London Labour and the London Poor*, 4:219–20.

81. For a discussion of commodity fetishism in *Lady Audley's Secret*, see Cvetkovich, *Mixed Feelings*, pp. 68–70.

82. Lady Audley's confessional history also anticipates aspects of Chapman's representation of prostitutes in his essays published several years after Braddon's novel.

83. Braddon, *Lady Audley's Secret*, pp. 375, 376.

84. By the same token, some paragraphs later Dr. Mosgrave reads Robert's secret suspicion: "Your face has told me what you would have withheld from me; it has told me that you *suspect!*" (ibid., p. 378).

85. Ibid., pp. 376, 378.

86. Ibid., p. 377.

87. See Showalter, *The Female Malady*, p. 29.

88. Braddon, *Lady Audley's Secret*, p. 377.

89. Ibid., p. 379.

90. Ibid., pp. 380–81, 382, 388, 391, 384–85. Interestingly, Robert invokes the image of a Catholic convent in response to Lady Audley's accusation that he has placed her in a "living grave." He says, "You will lead a quiet and peaceful life, my lady, such a life as many a good and holy woman in this Catholic country freely takes upon herself, and happily endures unto the end" (p. 391). Note once again this association between profligate woman and pious nun so popular in anti-Catholic discourse.

91. Quoted in Skultans, *Madness and Morals*, pp. 236–37.

92. From 1850 to 1875, the miles of railway lines doubled in England. This proliferation of the railway system is correlated to a rise in the national wealth of Victorian England at mid-century. See Freeman and Aldcroft, *Atlas of British Railway History*.

93. Braddon, *Lady Audley's Secret*, p. 381.

94. Foucault, *Discipline and Punish*, p. 19.

95. Chapman, "Prostitution in Relation to the National Health," p. 179.

Chapter Four

1. Eliot's treatment of "the Jewish question" in *Daniel Deronda* and her overall position on Jews is complex and difficult to categorize, a subject that is beyond the scope of my project here. Like Harriet Beecher Stowe's overriding concern in *Uncle Tom's Cabin*, the abolitionist novel that was a source of inspiration for *Daniel Deronda*, Eliot's chief interest lies in the spiritual and moral health of English society; anti-Semitism, like slavery and racism in *Uncle Tom's Cabin*, functions as an emblem for this cultural condition that Eliot wants to rectify. Similarly, Eliot's treatment of Gwendolen and Leonora, including the representations of male domestic tyrants and self-centered heroines, might also be understood in terms of this loftier vision. For detailed and divergent analyses on Zionism and imperialism in the novel, see Ragussis, *Figures of Conversion*, pp. 260–90, Said, *The Question of Palestine*, pp. 60–68, and Meyer, " 'Safely to Their Own Borders,' " pp. 748–53. What interests me primarily in Eliot's representations of Jews and women is how paternal metaphors operate in the respective confession scenes and how paternal metaphors also inform discourses of nationalism and imperialism.

2. Hall, *White, Male, and Middle-Class*, p. 33.

3. Eliot, *Daniel Deronda*, p. 479.

4. Ibid., pp. 456–57.

5. See Linehan, "Mixed Politics," for a more extensive version of this argument.

6. Eliot, *Daniel Deronda*, pp. 745, 477. For a suggestive reading of the language of pain to which I am referring, see Carpenter, " 'A Bit of Her Flesh.' "

7. Eliot, *Daniel Deronda*, p. 481.

8. Higgins and Silver, *Rape and Representation*, p. 5.

9. See ibid., pp. 24–27. See Gallagher, "George Eliot and *Daniel Deronda*," for an excellent discussion of the tropes of prostitution and usury through which rebellious women and Jews are associated in the novel.

10. Given his status as English and implicitly Christian for much of the novel, rather than Jewish, Daniel is finally both assimilated and self-affirming, that is, the ideal English gentleman, if by virtue of his romanticized devotion to Jewish nationalism. His departure for "the East" ostensibly marks Daniel's self-affirmation as a Jew, just as the revelation of his ancestry begins to dismantle his excessive, if not by his own design, assimilation. On the whole, the novel is divided on the issue of assimilation. Certainly Mirah and Mordecai's

father and Leonora are all assimilated Jews whom the novel seems to disparage on this score; yet Daniel too, if not deliberately, passes throughout much of the novel.

11. Eliot, *Daniel Deronda*, p. 760, initial emphasis added.

12. For a brief discussion of Lacan's paternal metaphor, see Rose, "Introduction II," pp. 36–40. Also see Lacan, "The Function and Field of Speech and Language in Psychoanalysis" and "On the Possible Treatment of Psychosis," in *Écrits*.

13. Note that "father-in-law" in the context of Gwendolen's familial relations is equivalent to "stepfather" in more recent usage. Obviously, the father of one's spouse and the spouse of one's mother are both fathers by virtue of law.

14. Gallop, *Reading Lacan*, p. 163. See Lacan, "Subversion of the Subject and the Dialectic of Desire," in *Écrits*, p. 310.

15. See Eliot, *Daniel Deronda*, p. 91.

16. Wilt, " 'He Would Come Back.' "

17. See Davis, "Introduction: Paternity Suite," *The Paternal Romance*, pp. 1–21.

18. Higgins and Silver, *Rape and Representation*, p. 3.

19. Butler maintains that " 'the paternal Law' in Lacan, as well as the monologic mastery of phallogocentrism in Irigaray, bear the mark of a monotheistic singularity that is perhaps less unitary and culturally universal than the guiding structuralist assumptions of the account presume." Butler, *Gender Trouble*, p. 29.

20. Crosby, *The Ends of History*, pp. 17–18.

21. I use "race" here in the sense that Victorians used it to encompass such identity categories that more recently fall under the rubric of ethnicity. "Race" was a ubiquitous term in circulation well before the nineteenth century to designate specific social groups of class, gender, nationality, and religion.

22. Eliot, *Daniel Deronda*, pp. 691, 702, 699.

23. Lacan, "On the Possible Treatment of Psychosis," in *Écrits*, p. 199.

24. Eliot, *Daniel Deronda*, p. 693.

25. Ibid., pp. 689, 692.

26. Note the inverse representations of Mirah and Leonora: Leonora disobeys her father and eschews the domestic role of Jewish daughter, wife, and mother in order to pursue a stage career; Mirah shrinks from the public display her disagreeable father makes of her body and yearns for the privacy and respectability of family and home. If Mirah is the dutiful daughter and Leonora's father the lofty Jewish patriarch, Leonora is the insubordinate daughter and Mirah's father the evil, money-grubbing Jew.

I do not construe as "confession" Mirah's account of her unhappy history to Mrs. Meyrick. For Mirah never appears to transgress. In contrast to the unfeminine egoism that undergirds the transgressions of Gwendolen and Leonora, Mirah reveals her pure victimage. Because of this chaste status, Mirah submits her story to the maternal judgment of Mrs. Meyrick rather than the male panoptic scrutiny that is reserved for Gwendolen and Leonora, whose victimage seems a consequence of their transgressive selfishness.

27. See Meyer, " 'Safely to Their Own Borders,' " pp. 745–46.

28. Eliot, *Daniel Deronda*, pp. 695, 694. This passage is also one of the subtle indications of the stereotyped femininized Jewish man, a feature that furthers Eliot's parallels between transgressive women and Jewish men.

29. Ibid., p. 698.

30. The function of the paternal name in Leonora's story is worth further consideration. Leonora's ambivalence in choosing her son's name with respect to the name-of-the-father is at least twofold. While she does change Daniel's surname, she chooses instead a name from "a branch of the family my father had lost sight of who called themselves Deronda."

Although the father's gaze no longer beholds it, or has "lost sight" of it, the name still bears traces of the patronymic tree. In addition, Leonora assigns and maintains her father's given name Daniel through the name of her son. When Daniel asks if his name is "real," Leonora answers, "Oh, as real as another . . . The Jews have always been changing their names." Following this vexed practice, Leonora both changes and does not change her son's name as well as her own. Anti-Semitism and the compulsion to assimilate reinforce this habit of name-changing that actually renders unstable the Jewish name-of-the-father. See Eliot, *Daniel Deronda*, p. 701.

31. Ibid., p. 726.

32. Ibid., p. 699.

33. Ibid., pp. 727, 726.

34. Ibid., p. 94.

35. James, "*Daniel Deronda*," p. 990.

36. Eliot, *Daniel Deronda*, pp. 392, 465.

37. Ibid., pp. 68, 756, 753.

38. Ibid., pp. 755–56.

39. Ibid., p. 756.

40. Madam Laure in *Middlemarch*, whose confession is embedded in Lydgate's history, is a precursor to Gwendolen as would-be husband-killer. Both women intend to kill, but their actual agency in relation to the act is ambiguous. See Rose, *Sexuality*, pp. 107–9, for a discussion of this doubleness to murder and not to murder at the same time as correlative with the ambivalent structure of hysteria. I am interested in the repeated narrative hesitancy that surrounds each act of murder associated with confessing women from Lady Audley and Gwendolen to Tess. Interestingly, in my vain search for an equivalent word for "uxoricide," I discovered that not only does there not exist in the English lexicon a signifier for "husband-killer," but that "husband" is only a subsidiary meaning for Latin words whose primary meaning is man (*vir*) or, pertaining to marriage, love (*maritus*). "Wife" as well as "wife-killing" are both firmly established entries in the English and Latin languages, while "husband" is only a secondary and less frequent category, just as the matrimonial phrase "man and wife" suggests. The narrative stuttering around husband-killing in these Victorian novels, therefore, bears out a similar imprecision in the language.

41. Eliot, *Daniel Deronda*, p. 757.

42. Ibid., p. 760.

43. Ibid., pp. 760, 761.

44. Ibid., p. 694.

45. See Rose, *Parallel Lives*, pp. 127–28, for her discussion of Harriet Taylor's co-authorship of Mill's work, including *The Subjection of Women*. Rose acknowledges Alice Rossi's scholarship on the protracted refusal to recognize even the possibility of this collaboration. Because of my attention to Mill's involvement in the Governor Eyre controversy, I follow the convention—while recognizing its problems—and refer only to Mill as the author of the essay.

46. In providing this historical background, I am indebted to Semmel, *Jamaican Blood and Victorian Conscience*, and Hall, *White, Male, and Middle-Class*.

47. See Paxton, "Mobilizing Chivalry," p. 8, and Sharpe, *Allegories of Empire*, p. 4.

48. Cvetkovich, *Mixed Feelings*, p. 160.

49. To a limited extent I am alluding to Edward Said's reading of Eliot's treatment of Zionism and "the East," an interpretation Cvetkovich and Meyer reiterate. I want to clarify that I am recounting Eliot's construction here and not generalizing on the complexities of nineteenth-century Zionist thinking, which was divided and varied among European Jews

until the end of the century when Theodore Herzl's 1896 pamphlet, "The Jewish State," solidified this thought into the Zionist movement per se.

50. Hall, *White, Male, and Middle-Class*, p. 33.

51. See Semmel, *George Eliot*, pp. 6–11, for a more elaborate explanation of Eliot's politics here.

52. Said, *Culture and Imperialism*, pp. 66–67. The premise of Said's study focuses on the roughly simultaneous development of the novel and imperialism, especially in Great Britain. Arguing that the novel and imperialism "fortified each other," Said examines the narrative constructions of imperialism and resistance.

53. See Sharpe, *Allegories of Empire*, pp. 47–54, for a similar reading of Brontë's use of colonized women to affirm Jane Eyre's racial superiority despite her class and gender inferiorities. Eliot uses other colonized groups as tropes elsewhere in *Daniel Deronda*: "the Caribs" (p. 246) and "the Bosjesman," Dutch for Bushman (p. 370).

54. See Hall, *White, Male, and Middle-Class*, pp. 272–89, for a summary of these positions on the Governor Eyre controversy.

55. George Henry Lewes, Eliot's domestic partner, took Mill's position against Eyre's colonial policies. See Rose, *Parallel Lives*, p. 264.

56. See ibid., pp. 42–44, 243–59, for a portrait of Carlyle's marriage to Jane Welsh, itself a study in domestic domination. Interestingly, Rose closes her study of five Victorian marriages with a brief account of the Eyre controversy in order to shore up the relationship between politics and sex, between the family and the state. Rose notes: "The men who backed Eyre tended to uphold strong male authority within the family and to expect submissiveness from wives" (p. 265).

57. Mill, *The Subjection of Women*, p. 31.

58. Eliot, *Daniel Deronda*, p. 376.

59. Ibid., p. 655.

60. Quoted in Hall, *White, Male, and Middle-Class*, p. 283.

61. Eliot, *Daniel Deronda*, pp. 744–45.

62. This logic of the same is also upheld in the one alliance of difference, the marriage between the wealthy English Catherine Arrowpoint and the struggling German Jew Herr Klesmer. Catherine, whose voice reveals her distinction both musically and intellectually earlier in the narrative, is rendered voiceless after she marries; her words never appear in song or in dialogue once she becomes "Mrs" (and not "Frau") Klesmer. The marriage thus entrenches her English and feminine status. Similarly, assimilated Jews like Mirah's father are frequently inferior to devout Jews, like Mordecai, according to the racialist terms of the novel.

63. Crosby makes a related observation about the correlation between Eliot's notion of history as the "Invisible Power" and the necessity of yielding to this paternal metaphor, to the inevitability of tradition and narrative. Crosby, *The Ends of History*, p. 18.

64. Gallagher, "George Eliot and *Daniel Deronda*," p. 50.

65. Interestingly, Lady Audley's confessor and nephew Robert undergoes a similarly gendered transformation with the confession scene as the culmination of his newly achieved masculine status. This difference suggests that to a certain extent confession is empowering for men, but disempowering for women. Chapter 5 will return to this question in more detail in the case of the twin confessions of Angel and Tess.

66. Leonora's confession offers an inversion of another Victorian confession scene between mother and son. In Gaskell's *Ruth*, the mother's motivation, in contrast to Leonora's, to tell her young child about her sexual fall devolves from Ruth's maternal devotion, from her desire to soften the effects of the inevitable disclosure and to preserve the bond

between them that must suffer under the blow of revelation. The scene occasions a mutual confession of love between mother and son, something for which Daniel yearns unrequitedly. What Ruth uncovers to Leonard is his illegitimacy; what Leonora divulges restores Daniel's legitimacy.

67. Eliot, *Daniel Deronda*, pp. 726–27.

68. Semmel, *George Eliot*, pp. 6–14. Also see pp. 117–32 for Semmel's reading of *Daniel Deronda* in relation to this value of a national inheritance.

69. I will use "religious/national" occasionally to signify the association Eliot implicitly makes between the Jewish tradition and the idea of an English national inheritance. As an illustration, when Daniel tells Gwendolen about his Zionist mission, he mentions his intention to found "a national centre, such as the English have" (Eliot, *Daniel Deronda*, p. 875).

70. See Meyer, " 'Safely to Their Own Borders,' " pp. 733–38, for an elaboration of this critical contradiction in *Daniel Deronda*.

71. Eliot, *Daniel Deronda*, p. 727.

72. Ibid., pp. 636–37.

73. Ibid., p. 731.

74. Meyer, " 'Safely to Their Own Borders,' " p. 746. The readability of the Jewish signifier here may depend on the relative familiarity of Ashkenazic over Sephardic names. Yet *Daniel Deronda*'s implied Christian identity for much of the novel also suggests the historical phenomenon of crypto-Jews in post-Inquisition Spain, a subject of much interest to Eliot in *The Spanish Gypsy* (1868). Like Walter Scott and Edward Bulwer-Lytton, in this earlier novel Eliot turned to fifteenth-century Spain for a model of nationality rooted in racial and religious homogeneity. See Ragussis, *Figures of Conversion*, chap. 4.

75. At times, the novel endorses Jews who have passed as Christians, that is, the "refined" Mirah and Daniel; at other times, the novel condemns assimilated Jews like Mirah's father and Leonora. Eliot's ambivalent depiction conflates two divergent ideals of European Jews that were evolving in the mid-nineteenth century: Zionism and the Jewish Enlightenment movement. Adherents of the Enlightenment, a movement whose strongest expression occurred in Germany where Eliot and Lewes spent much time, wanted to divest Judaism of its differences in order to divest Jews of their despised, marginalized status. In contrast to the incipient Zionist ideal of the period, the Enlightenment movement, a forerunner of Reform Judaism, excised references to "longing for Zion" from the liturgy and maintained that Jews should be citizens of their country in public and Jews only in the privacy of their homes.

76. Crosby, *The Ends of History*, p. 14.

77. Eliot, *Daniel Deronda*, p. 753.

78. Ibid., pp. 753–54.

79. Ibid., pp. 761–62.

80. According to Wilt's reading, Gwendolen commits the crime. But what is more important, I think, is the ambiguity that surrounds the circumstances of Grandcourt's death, or more precisely, the haziness superimposed over the narratological attempt to recover or reconstruct the event. This recession of "truth" necessarily renders the object of confession—to bring to light a transgression—a complicated, fraught endeavor that defies the convention of the confessor's fixing or categorizing the crime and the nature of the criminal.

81. Eliot, *Daniel Deronda*, p. 754.

82. Ibid., pp. 756, 758.

83. Ibid., p. 759.

84. Ibid., p. 878.

85. Ibid., p. 871.

86. Sharpe, *Allegories of Empire*, pp. 54–55.

87. For another instance of Eliot's metaphoric appropriation of the practice of suttee, see her 1855 essay "Thomas Carlyle," in which she likens Carlyle's books to sacrificial wives: "It is an idle question to ask whether his books will be read a century hence: if they were all burnt as the grandest of Suttees on his funeral pile, it would be only like cutting down an oak after its acorns have sown a forest" (p. 187). Finally, in her Theophrastus Such essay "The Modern Hep! Hep! Hep!" that articulates her views on Jews, Eliot writes, "The Hindoos also have doubtless had their rancours against us . . . perhaps they do not admire the usual English profile" (p. 138). The passage also stresses the futility of resistance to British imperial power, again promoting the implicit English design beneath Eliot's support of a project of national inheritance.

88. Eliot, *Daniel Deronda*, p. 767.

89. Ibid., p. 552.

90. Ibid., p. 557.

91. See Biale, "Ejaculatory Prayer," p. 21.

92. Spiritual ardor rings of erotic sublimity elsewhere in Eliot's novels. One salient example in the prelude to *Middlemarch* is the invocation of Saint Theresa to figure the unsung passions of "later-born Theresas" such as Dorothea Brooke.

93. Eliot, *Daniel Deronda*, p. 633, 580.

94. Ibid., p. 585.

95. Ibid., p. 592.

96. Here I take note of Said's reading of Daniel's Zionist project of "restoring a political existence to my people, making them a nation again" (Eliot, *Daniel Deronda*, p. 875). Said contends that in this quest, representing early Zionist thought, Daniel views such unqualified territory as "essentially empty of inhabitants, not because there were no inhabitants . . . but because their status as sovereign and human inhabitants was systematically denied" (Said, *The Question of Palestine*, p. 66). Yet not all inhabitants in Palestine at the time Eliot writes were Arabs, as Said implies. Jewish presence was equally as strong in Jerusalem, for instance. In this sense, Said is as equivocal as Eliot in mythologizing a representation of a geographical space with a more complicated history than either writer allows.

I also want to register a distinction between imperialism and nationalism per se. The concept of imperialism usually entails a sovereign power colonizing another nation in order to extend its political interests and enhance its economic resources; since Jews did not constitute a sovereign political entity in the nineteenth century, "nationalism" seems a more accurate qualification of Daniel's goal here. I refer to the overlapping discourses of both nationalism and imperialism in the context of Eliot's novel because it seems to me that her overall interest is in English national inheritance and that Jews and Zionism provide a powerful metaphor for this ideal.

97. See Meyer, " 'Safely to Their Own Borders,' " pp. 747–50, for this brief historical summary. Also see Hertzberg, ed., *The Zionist Idea*, for a collection of essays on divergent ideas about Zionism by European Jews, such as Moses Hess, from the middle to the end of the nineteenth century. In terms of opposition to the notion of return, I am referring to the Jewish Enlightenment movement, discussed in note 75 above.

98. Eliot, *Daniel Deronda*, pp. 816–17.

99. Sedgwick, *Between Men*, p. 137.

100. Eliot, *Daniel Deronda*, p. 820.

101. Gallagher, "George Eliot and *Daniel Deronda*," p. 51.

102. Eliot, *Daniel Deronda*, pp. 688–89.

103. Benjamin Disraeli, along with his family, converted to the Church of England during his childhood. In her letters of the 1840s Eliot voiced her anti-Semitism by such comments as "Everything *specifically* Jewish is of a low grade," a remark made in opposition to Disraeli's praise of Jewish culture in two novels of his political trilogy, *Coningsby, Sybil,* and *Tancred.* Yet later, Eliot came around to endorsing his anti-assimilationist politics. In a letter to Harriet Beecher Stowe, Eliot writes about the bigotry directed "not only towards the Jews, but towards all oriental peoples with whom we English come in contact" in terms of "a spirit of arrogance and contemptuous dictatorialness" that constitutes "a national disgrace" (quoted in Ragussis, *Figures of Conversion,* p. 267). Where Grandcourt exemplifies this detestable attitude in the novel, it becomes clear that Eliot is most interested in rehabilitating English moral and spiritual welfare rather than in eradicating anti-Semitism per se. See Semmel, *George Eliot,* pp. 118–20.

104. Semmel, *George Eliot,* p. 129.

105. Hall, *White, Male, and Middle-Class,* p. 286.

Chapter Five

1. Hardy, *Tess of the d'Urbervilles,* p. 3. All references are to the Oxford edition of the novel unless otherwise noted.

2. Ibid., pp. 229, 182.

3. De Lauretis, "The Violence of Rhetoric," p. 240.

4. Foucault, *Discipline and Punish,* p. 136.

5. Winifred Woodhull cautions that embodying the subject of rape requires historicizing, gendering, and classing the subject of sexual violence. See Woodhull, "Sexuality, Power, and the Question of Rape," p. 174. As I elaborate on in Chapter 1, Foucault's generic body is implicitly male, the default gender of western culture.

6. Hardy, *Tess,* p. 330; Hardy, *Life and Work,* p. 29.

7. Margaret Higonnet uses the phrase "sexual lexicon" for Hardy's word choices describing the condition of his text. In this way, Higonnet points out the implicit analogy drawn between textual censorship and a woman's rape. See Higonnet, "Fictions of Feminine Voice," p. 214.

8. Derrida, "White Mythology," p. 229.

9. Hardy, *Tess,* p. 134.

10. Derrida, "White Mythology," p. 211.

11. Hardy, *Tess,* p. 77.

12. Derrida, "White Mythology," p. 213.

13. Ferguson, "Rape and the Rise of the Novel."

14. Lynn Parker notes that Hardy fashioned his revisions to reinforce Tess's purity; see Parker, " 'Pure Woman' and Tragic Heroine," p. 278; Ellen Rooney makes a similar point in " 'A Little More Than Persuading,' " p. 95.

15. Hardy, *Tess,* p. 93.

16. See Gatrell, "Note on the Text," pp. xxv–xxx.

17. Ibid., p. xxviii. Gatrell also discusses the American serialization of *Tess* in *Harper's Bazaar,* which presents yet another version of Hardy's text. He deleted the false marriage inserted in the *Graphic* narrative and briefly outlined the rape in The Chase.

18. See Taylor, "Note on the Text."

19. Feltes, *Modes of Production,* pp. 69, 74.

20. Taylor, "Note on the Text," p. 416.

21. See Taylor's "Note on the Text" and Appendix for more information on Collins's conflict with the *Graphic*'s censorship practices over the passage in *The Law and the Lady*. While Collins's text was eventually printed in the newspaper as he desired, this note appeared at the end of the 30 January 1875 episode: "The editor of this journal suppressed a portion of the paragraph on the grounds that the description originally given was objectionable. Mr Wilkie Collins having since informed us, through his legal advisors, that, according to the terms of his agreement with the proprietors of *The Graphic* his proofs are to be published *verbatim* from his MS, the passage in question is here given in its original form" (p. xxv). Another note, indicating editorial disapproval, appears after the final installment of the novel.

22. Quoted in Taylor, "Note on the Text," p. 417.

23. Bennett, "Text, Readers, Reading Formations," p. 224. With Bennett's "reading formation" in mind, it would be interesting to compare the *Graphic* and British versions of the rape and confession scenes with the rendition of the same that Hardy submitted for the American serialization of the novel in *Harper's Bazaar*. Bennett's reading formation is also discussed in Feltes, *Modes of Production*, pp. 68–69.

24. Barker, *The Tremulous Private Body*, p. 62.

25. Some interpretations of Hardy's investment in this heroine speculate on romantic associations. As reported by J. T. Laird, Bernard Paris believed that Hardy was "in love" with Tess; see Laird, *The Shaping of "Tess,"* p. 122. Lois Deacon speculates that Tess was modeled after Hardy's cousin (or niece), Tryphena Sparks, with whom Hardy may have fallen in love and been engaged to, and whose child he may have fathered during the betrothal period. She subsequently married someone else and died in March 1890 as Hardy was writing *Tess*; also see Laird, *The Shaping of "Tess,"* pp. 120–22. Penny Boumelha argues that the narrative silences of both the rape scene and the initial truncation of marital consummation permit the narrator, whom she identifies as "Hardy," to be the sole "possessor" of Tess (Boumelha, *Thomas Hardy and Women*, p. 12). Laura Claridge also notes "Hardy's intense identification with his heroine" (Claridge, "Tess," p. 354).

26. Miller, *Fiction and Repetition*, p. 119.

27. Higonnet, "Fictions of Feminine Voice," pp. 213, 211.

28. Rooney likewise argues that as a subject of sexual violence, Tess's subjectivity is "radically unreadable"; Rooney, among others, also notes "Tess' paralysis as a speaking subject." See Rooney, " 'A Little More Than Persuading,' " pp. 97–100.

29. Ronald D. Morrison discusses Hardy's epigraph and the project of restoring Tess's wounded name; see Morrison, "Reading and Restoration in *Tess*," p. 28.

30. Hardy, *Life and Work*, p. 259. Interestingly, these lines come from an entry written on "Good Friday, April 15, 1892," a day commemorating the ultimate Christian martyrdom. Hardy's perception of himself as sacrificial writer is encoded in such telling notations.

31. Ibid., p. 255.

32. According to Michael Millgate's introduction to *The Life and Work of Thomas Hardy*, Hardy attempted to control another representation of himself by ghostwriting his biography. Although published over Florence Hardy's name after her husband's death, this text is critically regarded as a third-person autobiography in which the author's wife functioned as his amanuensis. Supposedly Hardy was motivated to contrive this "authorized biography" to be published posthumously by his discovery after his first wife's death of Emma's secret memoirs containing entries "hostile" to him. Hardy's autobiography through his second wife repudiates the unpublished version of Hardy by his first wife as much as it attempts to forestall any future representations unsavory to the writer. Clearly he was obsessed with repeatedly refining his image as author. Perhaps more than anything else,

such preoccupation reinforces that, despite Hardy's uneasiness with institutional and so-cial forces of control, he believed that he could finally circumvent such management and produce an unsullied, essential portrait of himself, much as he intended for his heroine.

33. Hardy, *Jude the Obscure*, p. xxxvi.

34. Even more glaring is the contradiction between the first and last sentences of this very short 1912 preface, which opens with "The present edition of this novel contains a few pages that have never appeared in any previous edition" and concludes with "The novel was first published complete, in three volumes, in November 1891."

35. Laird, *The Shaping of "Tess,"* p. 18. Laird does posit an *ur*-text in his discussion of the novel's bibliographic history. But his own observations about Hardy's writing process and strategies of revision also belie the material existence of such an original document. Therefore, the status of textual purity becomes hypothetical only.

36. Hardy, *Tess*, p. 3.

37. Hardy, *Life and Work*, p. 291.

38. Rooney makes a related observation on Hardy's ambiguous use of Latin in his final preface of 1912 as he confesses his mistaken choice of the novel's subtitle. She reads this admission of guilt, "Melius fuerat not scribere," as a "disingenuous disclaimer"; see Rooney, " 'A Little More Than Persuading,' " p. 95.

39. Hardy, "Candour in English Fiction," p. 19.

40. Foucault, *History of Sexuality*, p. 18.

41. Hardy, *Tess*, p. 225.

42. Ibid., p. 192.

43. Although one might interpret Joan Durbeyfield's third-person voice of "J" as a sign of her class position and inferior education, it is also possible to see this cipher as a mark of a woman's rhetorical subjection, her estrangement from an immediate "I." On a different note, Joan observes about Tess that it "be your childish nature to tell all that's in your Heart." This perception renders Foucault's compulsion to confess something to which the guileless might submit, but that others might resist.

44. Hardy, *Tess*, p. 221. Boumelha cites Mary Jacobus's findings of discrepancies between earlier and later versions of Angel's confession. Evidence suggests that initially Angel was to confess a loss of faith rather than a sexual fall. This earlier rendition would have underscored "the varieties of heterodoxy available to (intellectual) man and (sexual) woman"; see Boumelha, *Thomas Hardy and Women*, p. 122. The vestiges of this dichotomy remain here since Angel's confession appears in words, while Tess's is displaced onto a description of lugubriously transformed physical objects.

45. Hardy, *Tess*, p. 221.

46. Ibid., p. 121.

47. Ibid., pp. 221–22.

48. Bartky, *Femininity and Domination*, p. 115.

49. See Silverman, "History, Figuration, and Female Subjectivity in *Tess*," p. 20.

50. Hardy, *Tess*, p. 222.

51. Ibid., p. 124. Again and again Angel reads and writes Tess through the appearances of her body and face: "Clare regarded her attentively, conned the characters of her face as if they had been hieroglyphics" (p. 176). Angel fashions Tess into the imaginary romantic mold he has construed, so this line about his future intentions are ironic: "after I have made you the well-read woman that I mean to make you" (p. 190). Indeed, Tess is already the much *read*, if not accurately or "purely," woman.

52. Kristeva, *Powers of Horror*, p. 4. Kristeva's other definitions of the abject: "A massive

and sudden emergence of uncanniness . . . radically separate, loathsome. . . . A weight of meaninglessness" (p. 2).

53. Hardy, *Tess*, p. 225.

54. Rooney, " 'A Little More Than Persuading,' " p. 97. Rooney maintains that as a subject of sexual violence Tess's perspective is impossible to represent due to the "cultural constructedness of perception itself," as Catharine MacKinnon's work on sexuality, rape, and law explores (p. 90). In the 1988 film *The Accused*, based on the rape of a New Bedford, Massachusetts, woman, the narrative flashes back to represent the rape only when a male witness is testifying and not during the testimony of the character who is raped. Like Tess almost a century earlier, the raped woman, perhaps more than her assailants, is "the accused."

Unlike Tess's execution for murdering her rapist, the January 1994 acquittal of Lorena Bobbitt, tried for cutting off her abusive husband's penis, suggests the unfolding of a legitimate female perspective on sexual crimes. However, the insanity defense on which Bobbitt was acquitted indicates the limitations on such legitimation. Angel Clare, upon hearing Tess's confession of her rape, says, "Am I to believe this? From your manner I am to take it as true. O you cannot be out of your mind! You ought to be!" (p. 225). With Tess's death, which closes the novel, Hardy joins Eliot in offering a bleak vision about the possibilities for female retribution against male aggression.

55. Hardy, *Tess*, p. 226.

56. This metaphoric meaning of rendering rape and its consequences does not have any "pure" origin in Hardy's novel. For instance, Terry Castle reads Clarissa's mad discourse following her rape as "traumatic loss of faith in articulation, and the power of the letter to render meaning" (Castle, *Clarissa's Ciphers*, p. 43).

57. Belsey, "Constructing the Subject," p. 56. Lacan contends that the ideal of American ego psychology of an integrated, whole self is impossible because every subject is "split" through the operations of language, through the gap between the word as signifier or sound or textuality and the referent, always elusive or absent, to which it refers. The unconscious, in Lacan's theory, is an effect of this division enforced through language.

58. Higonnet, who makes a similar observation, also locates passages in the narrative in which silence operates for Tess as a positive strategy. See Higonnet, "Fictions of Feminine Voice," p. 206.

59. See Skilton, "Textual Notes," *Tess of the d'Urbervilles*, pp. 512–13.

60. Ibid., p. 503.

61. Hardy, *Tess*, p. 69.

62. See Ferguson, "Rape and the Rise of the Novel," p. 92, which states: "Marriage recasts rape, so that marriage is a misunderstanding corrected, or rape rightly understood."

BIBLIOGRAPHY

Altick, Richard. *The English Common Reader*. Chicago: University of Chicago Press, 1957.

Anderson, Amanda. *Tainted Souls and Painted Faces: The Rhetoric of Fallenness in Victorian Culture*. Ithaca: Cornell University Press, 1993.

Armstrong, Nancy. *Desire and Domestic Fiction: A Political History of the Novel*. New York: Oxford University Press, 1987.

Armstrong, Nancy, and Leonard Tennenhouse, eds. *Literature and the History of Violence*. New York: Routledge, 1989.

Arnstein, Walter. *Protestant versus Catholic in Mid-Victorian England*. Columbia: University of Missouri Press, 1982.

Bakhtin, Mikhail. "Epic and Novel." In *The Dialogic Imagination*. Translated by Caryl Emerson and Michael Holquist. Austin: University of Texas Press, 1981.

Barker, Francis. *The Tremulous Private Body*. New York: Methuen, 1984.

Bartkowski, Frances. "Epistemic Drift in Foucault." In *Feminism and Foucault*, edited by Irene Diamond and Lee Quinby. Boston: Northeastern University, 1988.

Bartky, Sandra. *Femininity and Domination*. New York: Routledge, 1991.

Belsey, Catherine. "Constructing the Subject, Deconstructing the Text." In *Feminist Criticism and Social Change*, edited by Judith Newton and Deborah Rosenfelt. New York: Methuen, 1985.

Benjamin, Walter. "Theses on the Philosophy of History." In *Illuminations*. Translated by Harry Zohn. New York: Schocken Books, 1969.

Bennett, Tony. "Text, Readers, Reading Formations." *Literature and History* 9, no. 2 (Fall 1983): 214–27.

Bernstein, Susan David. "Confessing Feminist Theory: What's 'I' Got to Do with It?" *Hypatia* 7, no. 2 (Spring 1992): 120–47.

——. "Dirty Reading: Sensation Fiction, Women, and Primivitism." *Criticism* 36, no. 2 (Spring 1994): 213–41.

Biale, David. "Ejaculatory Prayer: The Displacement of Sexuality in Chasidism." *Tikkun* 6, no. 4 (July–August 1991): 21–89.

Billington, Ray Allen. *The Protestant Crusade*. Chicago: Quadrangle Books, 1938.

Blakeney, Richard. *Popery in Its Social Aspects*. London: Protestant Educational Institute, 1852.

Bordo, Susan. *Unbearable Weight: Feminism, Western Culture, and the Body*. Berkeley: University of California Press, 1993.

Boumelha, Penny. *Thomas Hardy and Women*. Totowa, N.J.: Barnes and Noble Books, 1982.

Braddon, Mary Elizabeth. *Lady Audley's Secret*. New York: Oxford University Press, 1987.

Brockman, W. J. *Letter to the Women of England on the Confessional*. London: n.p., [1870?].

Brontë, Charlotte. *Villette*. New York: Oxford University Press, 1990.

Butler, Judith. *Gender Trouble*. New York: Routledge, 1990.

Carpenter, Mary Wilson. "'A Bit of Her Flesh': Circumcision and 'The Signification of the Phallus' in *Daniel Deronda*." *Genders* 1 (Spring 1988): 1–23.

Castle, Terry. *Clarissa's Ciphers: Meaning and Disruption in Richardson's "Clarissa."* Ithaca: Cornell University Press, 1982.

Chadwick, Owen. *The Victorian Church*. Part 1. London: Adams and Charles Black, 1971.

Chapman, John. "Prostitution: Government Experiments in Controlling It." *Westminster Review* 37 (1870): 119–79. Reprinted in Nield, *Prostitution in the Victorian Age*.

——. "Prostitution in Relation to the National Health." *Westminster Review* 36 (1869): 179–234. Reprinted in Nield, *Prostitution in the Victorian Age*.

Cixous, Hélène. "The Laugh of the Medusa." In *New French Feminisms*. Edited with an introduction by Elaine Marks and Isabelle de Courtivron. New York: Schocken Books, 1981.

Claridge, Laura. "Tess: A Less Than Pure Woman Ambivalently." *Texas Studies in Literature and Languages* 28, no. 3 (1986): 324–38.

Clark-Beattie, Rosemary. "Fables of Rebellion: Anti-Catholicism and the Structure of *Villette*." *English Literary History* 53 (1982): 821–47.

Collins, William Wilkie. *The Law and the Lady*. New York: Oxford University Press, 1992.

Crosby, Christina. *The Ends of History*. New York: Routledge, 1991.

Culbertson, Rosamond. *Rosamond: or, a Narrative of the Captivity and Sufferings of an American Female under the Popist Priests, in the Island of Cuba*. New York: Leavitt, Lord & Co., 1836.

Cvetkovich, Ann. *Mixed Feelings: Feminism, Mass Culture, and Victorian Sensationalism*. New Brunswick: Rutgers University Press, 1992.

Daly, Mary. *Gyn/Ecology*. Boston: Beacon Press, 1978.

Davies, Charles Maurice. *Philip Paternoster, a Tractarian Love Story*. London: Bentley, 1858.

Davis, Robert Con. *The Paternal Romance: Reading God-the-Father in Early Western Culture*. Urbana: University of Illinois Press, 1993.

De Certeau, Michel. *The Practice of Everyday Life*. Translated by Steven Rendall. Berkeley: University of California Press, 1984.

De Lauretis, Teresa. *Alice Doesn't: Feminism, Semiotics, Cinema*. Bloomington: Indiana University Press, 1984.

——. "The Rhetoric of Violence: Considerations on Representation and Gender." In *Literature and the History of Violence*, edited by Nancy Armstrong and Leonard Tennenhouse. New York: Routledge, 1989.

De Man, Paul. "Excuses (Confessions)." In *Allegories of Reading*. New Haven: Yale University Press, 1979.

Derrida, Jacques. *Of Grammatology*. Translated with an introduction by Gayatri Spivak. Baltimore: Johns Hopkins University Press, 1974.

——. "White Mythology: Metaphor in the Text of Philosophy." In *Margins of Philosophy*. Translated by Alan Bass. Chicago: University of Chicago Press, 1982.

Eliot, George. *Daniel Deronda*. New York: Penguin Books, 1987.

——. "The Modern Hep! Hep! Hep!" In *The Impressions of Theophrastus Such*. Rutland, Vt.: Charles E. Tuttle Co., 1995.

——. "Thomas Carlyle." In *Selected Critical Writings*. New York: Oxford University Press, 1992.

Ellsberg, Peggy R. "Distant and Different: Catholics and Anti-Catholics in Some Victorian Novels." In *This Sacred History*, edited by Donald S. Armentrout. Cambridge, Mass.: Cowley Press, 1990.

Felman, Shoshana, and Dori Laub. *Testimony: Crises of Witnessing in Literature, Psychoanalysis, and History*. New York: Routledge, 1992.

Feltes, N. N. *Modes of Production of Victorian Novels*. Chicago: University of Chicago Press, 1989.

Ferguson, Frances. "Rape and the Rise of the Novel." In *Misogyny, Misandry, and Misanthropy*, edited by R. Howard Bloch and Frances Ferguson. Berkeley: University of California Press, 1989.

Fisher, Trevor. *Scandal: The Sexual Politics of Late Victorian Britain*. Phoenix Mill, Eng.: Alan Sutton Publishing, 1995.

Foucault, Michel. *The Care of the Self*. Translated by Robert Hurley. New York: Vintage Books, 1988.

——. *Discipline and Punish*. Translated by Alan Sheridan. New York: Vintage Books, 1980.

——. *The History of Sexuality*. Translated by Robert Hurley. New York: Vintage Books, 1979.

——. *The Use of Pleasure*. Translated by Robert Hurley. New York: Vintage Books, 1985.

Franchot, Jenny. *Roads to Rome: The Antebellum Protestant Encounter with Catholicism*. Berkeley: University of California Press, 1994.

Freeman, Michael, and Derek Aldcroft. *The Atlas of British Railway History*. Dover, N.H.: Croom Helm, 1985.

Freud, Sigmund. *An Autobiographical Study*. Translated by James Strachey. New York: W. W. Norton, 1983.

——. *Dora: An Analysis of a Case of Hysteria*. Edited by Philip Rieff. New York: Collier Books, 1963.

——. "Resistance and Repression." In *Introductory Lectures*. Translated by James Strachey. New York: W. W. Norton, 1966.

——. *The Standard Edition of the Complete Psychological Works of Sigmund Freud*. 24 vols. Translated by James Strachey. London: Hogarth Press, 1953–74.

Friedman, Susan Stanford. "Hysteria, Dreams, and Modernity: A Reading of the Origins of Psychoanalysis in Freud's Early Corpus." In *Rereading the New: A Backward Glance at Postmodernism*, edited by Kevin J. H. Dettmar. Ann Arbor: University of Michigan Press, 1992.

From Windsor to Rome through Anglican Sisterhoods. London: Protestant Evangelical Mission and Electoral Union, 1873.

Gagnier, Regenia. *Subjectivities: A History of Self-Representation in Britain, 1832–1920*. New York: Oxford University Press, 1991.

Gallagher, Catherine. "George Eliot and *Daniel Deronda*: The Prostitute and the Jewish Question." In *Sex, Politics, and Science in the Nineteenth-Century Novel*, edited by Ruth Bernard Yeazell. Baltimore: Johns Hopkins University Press, 1986.

Gallop, Jane. *The Daughter's Seduction: Feminism and Psychoanalysis*. Ithaca: Cornell University Press, 1982.

——. *Reading Lacan*. Ithaca: Cornell University Press, 1985.

Gatrell, Simon. "Note on the Text." In *Tess of the d'Urbervilles* by Thomas Hardy. New York: Oxford University Press, 1988.

Gavin, Anthony. *The Great Red Dragon; or the Master-Key to Popery*. Boston: Samuel Jones, 1854.

Gilman, Sander. *Difference and Pathology: Stereotypes of Sexuality, Race, and Madness*. Ithaca: Cornell University Press, 1985.

Gilmore, Leigh. *Autobiographics: A Feminist Theory of Women's Self-Representation*. Ithaca: Cornell University Press, 1994.

Greg, W. R. "Prostitution." *Westminster Review* 53 (1850): 448–506. Reprinted in Nield, *Prostitution in the Victorian Age*.

Griffin, Susan M. "Awful Disclosures: Women's Evidence in the Escaped Nun's Tale." *PMLA* 3, no. 1 (January 1996): 93–107.

Gugelberger, Georg, and Michael Kearney. "Voices for the Voiceless: Testimonial Literature in Latin America." *Latin American Perspectives* 18, no. 3 (Summer 1991): 3–14.

Hall, Catherine. *White, Male, and Middle-Class: Explorations in Feminism and History*. New York: Routledge, 1992.

Hardy, Thomas. "Candour in English Fiction." *New Review* 2 (January–June 1890): 15–21.

———. *Jude the Obscure*. New York: Oxford University Press, 1985.

———. *The Life and Work of Thomas Hardy*. Edited by Michael Millgate. Athens: University of Georgia Press, 1985.

———. *Tess of the d'Urbervilles*. Edited by David Skilton. New York: Penguin, 1978.

———. *Tess of the d'Urbervilles*. New York: Oxford University Press, 1988.

Harman, Barbara Leah. "In Promiscuous Company: Female Public Appearance in Elizabeth Gaskell's *North and South*." *Victorian Studies* 31 (Spring 1988): 351–76.

Harrison, Antony H. "Christina Rossetti and the Sage Discourse of Feminist High Anglicanism." In *Victorian Sages and Cultural Discourses*, edited by Thaïs Morgan. New Brunswick: Rutgers University Press, 1990.

Hartsock, Nancy. "Foucault on Power: A Theory for Women?" In *Feminism / Postmodernism*, edited by Linda J. Nicholson. New York: Routledge, 1990.

Heller, Tamar. *Dead Secrets: Wilkie Collins and the Female Gothic*. New Haven: Yale University Press, 1992.

Helsinger, Elizabeth K., Robin Lauterbach Sheets, and William Veeder. *The Woman Question: Society and Literature in Britain and America, 1837–1883*. Vol. 3. Chicago: University of Chicago Press, 1983.

Hepworth, Mike, and Bryan S. Turner. *Confession*. Boston: Routledge and Kegan Paul, 1982.

Hertzberg, Arthur, ed. *The Zionist Idea: A Historical Analysis and Reader*. New York: Atheneum, 1973.

Higgins, Lynn A., and Brenda R. Silver, eds. *Rape and Representation*. New York: Columbia University Press, 1991.

Higonnet, Margaret. "Fictions of Feminine Voice." In *Out of Bounds: Male Writers and Gender*, edited by Laura Claridge and Elizabeth Langland. Amherst: University of Massachusetts Press, 1990.

Hughes, Winifred. *The Maniac in the Cellar*. Princeton: Princeton University Press, 1980.

Humphreys, Anne. *Travels into the Poor Man's Country: The Work of Henry Mayhew*. Athens: University of Georgia Press, 1977.

Hunt, Lynn. "Foucault's Subject in *The History of Sexuality*." In *Discourses of Sexuality*, edited by Domna C. Stanton. Ann Arbor: University of Michigan Press, 1992.

Hutton, Patrick H. "Foucault, Freud, and the Technologies of the Self." In *Technologies of the Self*, edited by Luther H. Martin, Huck Gutman, and Patrick H. Hutton. Amherst: University of Massachusetts Press, 1988.

James, Henry. "*Daniel Deronda*: A Conversation." In *Henry James: Essays on Literature, American Writers, English Writers*. New York: Library of America, 1984.

Kaplan, Cora. *Sea Changes: Culture and Feminism*. London: Verso, 1986.

Kenny, Lorraine Delia. "Amy Fisher, My Story." *Socialist Review* 24, no. 3 (1995): 81–127.

Kofman, Sarah. *The Enigma of Women*. Translated by Catherine Porter. Ithaca: Cornell University Press, 1985.

Kowaleski, Elizabeth. " 'The Heroine of Some Strange Romance': The *Personal Recollections* of Charlotte Elizabeth Tonna." *Tulsa Studies in Women's Literature* 1, no. 2 (Fall 1982): 141–53.

Kristeva, Julia. *Powers of Horror*. Translated by Leon S. Roudiez. New York: Columbia University Press, 1982.

Kucich, John. *Repression in Victorian Fiction*. Berkeley: University of California Press, 1987.

Lacan, Jacques. *Écrits*. Translated by Alan Sheridan. New York: W. W. Norton, 1977.

Laird, J. T. *The Shaping of "Tess of the d'Urbervilles."* New York: Oxford University Press, 1975.

Langbauer, Laurie. *Women and Romance: The Consolations of Gender in the English Novel*. Ithaca: Cornell University Press, 1990.

Levy, Anita. *Other Women: The Writing of Class, Race, and Gender, 1832–1898*. Princeton: Princeton University Press, 1991.

Lewin, Ellen. "Negotiating Lesbian Motherhood: The Dialectics of Resistance and Accommodation." In *Motherhood: Ideology, Experience, and Agency*, edited by Evelyn Nakano Glenn, Grace Chang, and Linda Rennie Forcey. New York: Routledge, 1994.

Linehan, Katherine Bailey. "Mixed Politics: The Critique of Imperialism in *Daniel Deronda*." *Texas Studies in Literature* 34, no. 3 (Fall 1992): 323–46.

Litvak, Joseph. *Caught in the Act: Theatricality in the Nineteenth-Century English Novel*. Berkeley: University of California Press, 1992.

Loesberg, Jonathan. "The Ideology of Narrative Form in Sensation Fiction." *Representations* 13 (Winter 1986): 115–38.

Lydon, Mary. "Foucault and Feminism." In *Feminism and Foucault*, edited by Irene Diamond and Lee Quinby. Boston: Northeastern University Press, 1988.

Macdonald, Frederika. *The Secret of Charlotte Brontë*. London and Edinburgh: T. C. and E. C. Jack, 1914.

Malham-Dembleby, John. *The Confessions of Charlotte Brontë*. Bradford, England: n.p., 1954.

[Mansel, Henry]. "Sensation Novels." *Quarterly Review* 113 (April 1863): 481–514.

Martin, Biddy. "Feminism, Criticism, and Foucault." In *Feminism and Foucault*, edited by Irene Diamond and Lee Quinby. Boston: Northeastern University Press, 1988.

Mayhew, Henry. *London Labour and the London Poor*. Vol 4. London: Frank Cass and Co., 1967.

Menchú, Rigoberta. *I . . . Rigoberta Menchú: An Indian Woman in Guatemala*. Edited by Elisabeth Burgos-Debray. Translated by Ann Wright. London: Verso, 1984.

Meyer, Susan. " 'Safely to Their Own Borders': Proto-Zionism, Feminism, and Nationalism in *Daniel Deronda*." *English Literary History* 60, no. 3 (Fall 1993): 733–58.

"Michelet on Auricular Confession and Direction." *Foreign Quarterly Review* 30 (April 1845): 101–7.

Michie, Elsie. *Outside the Pale: Cultural Exclusion, Gender Difference, and the Victorian Woman Writer*. Ithaca: Cornell University Press, 1993.

Michie, Helena. *The Flesh Made Word: Female Figures and Women's Bodies*. New York: Oxford University Press, 1987.

Mill, John Stuart. *The Subjection of Women*. Edited by Sue Mansfield. Arlington Heights, Ill.: Harlan Davidson, 1980.

Miller, D. A. "*La Cage aux folles*: Sensation and Gender in Wilkie Collins' *The Woman in White*." *Representations* 14 (Spring 1986): 107–36.

Moglen, Helen. *Charlotte Brontë: The Self Conceived*. New York: W. W. Norton, 1976.

Monk, Maria. *Awful Disclosures of Maria Monk*. New York: Howe & Bates, 1836.

Morris, Celia. *Bearing Witness: Sexual Harassment and Beyond—Everywoman's Story*. Boston: Little, Brown and Co., 1994.

Morrison, Toni, ed., *Race-ing Justice, En-gendering Power: Essays on Anita Hill, Clarence Thomas, and the Construction of Social Reality*. New York: Pantheon Books, 1992.

Morrison, Ronald D. "Reading and Restoration in *Tess of the d'Urbervilles*." *Victorian Newsletter* 82 (Fall 1992): 21–35.

Newman, John Henry. *The Letters and Diaries of John Henry Newman*. Vols. 14 and 15. New York: Thomas Nelson and Sons, 1963.

Nield, Keith, ed. *Prostitution in the Victorian Age*. Westmead, Eng.: Gregg International, 1973.

"On Confession." *Christian Observer*, n.s., 163 (July 1851): 443–47.

Page, Norman, ed. *Wilkie Collins: The Critical Heritage*. Boston: Routledge & Kegan Paul, 1974.

Parker, Lynn. " 'Pure Woman' and Tragic Heroine? Conflicting Myths in Hardy's *Tess of the d'Urbervilles*." *Studies in the Novel* 24, no. 3 (Fall 1992): 273–81.

Paxton, Nancy L. "Mobilizing Chivalry: Rape in British Novels about the Indian Uprising of 1857." *Victorian Studies* 36, no. 1 (Fall 1992): 5–30.

Poovey, Mary. "Speaking of the Body: Mid-Victorian Constructions of Female Desire." In *Body/Politics: Women and the Discourse of Science*, edited by Mary Jacobus, Evelyn Fox Keller, and Sally Shuttleworth. New York: Routledge, 1990.

———. *Uneven Developments: The Ideological Work of Gender in Mid-Victorian England*. Chicago: University of Chicago Press, 1988.

Ragussis, Michael. *Figures of Conversion: "The Jewish Question" and English National Identity*. Durham: Duke University Press, 1995.

Rooney, Ellen. " 'A Little More Than Persuading': Tess and the Subject of Sexual Violence." In *Rape and Representation*, edited by Lynn Higgins and Brenda Silver. New York: Columbia University Press, 1991.

Rose, Jacqueline. "Introduction II." In *Feminine Sexuality* by Jacques Lacan. Edited by Juliet Mitchell and Jacqueline Rose. Translated by Jacqueline Rose. New York: W. W. Norton, 1985.

———. *Sexuality in the Field of Vision*. London: Verso, 1986.

Rose, Phyllis. *Parallel Lives*. New York: Vintage Books, 1983.

Rubin, Gayle. "The Traffic in Women: Notes on the 'Political Economy' of Sex." In *Toward an Anthropology of Women*, edited by Rayna R. Reiter. New York: Monthly Review Press, 1975.

Said, Edward. *Culture and Imperialism*. New York: Vintage Books, 1994.

———. *The Question of Palestine*. New York: Vintage Books, 1992.

Sawicki, Jana. *Disciplining Foucault: Feminism, Power, and the Body*. New York: Routledge, 1991.

Sedgwick, Eve Kosofsky. *Between Men: English Literature and Male Homosocial Desire*. New York: Columbia University Press, 1985.

Semmel, Bernard. *George Eliot and the Politics of National Inheritance*. New York: Oxford University Press, 1994.

———. *Jamaican Blood and Victorian Conscience; The Governor Eyre Controversy*. Boston: Houghton Mifflin, 1963.

Sharpe, Jenny. *Allegories of Empire: The Figure of Woman in the Colonial Text*. Minneapolis: University of Minnesota Press, 1993.

Showalter, Elaine. *The Female Malady*. New York: Pantheon Books, 1985.

———. *A Literature of Their Own*. Princeton: Princeton University Press, 1977.

Sigsworth, E. M., and T. J. Wyke. "A Study of Victorian Prostitution and Venereal Disease." In *Suffer and Be Still*, edited by Martha Vicinus. Bloomington: Indiana University Press, 1972.

Silverman, Kaja. "History, Figuration, and Female Subjectivity in *Tess of the d'Urbervilles*." *Novel* 8, no. 1 (Fall 1984): 5–28.

Skilton, David. "Textual Notes." In *Tess of the d'Urbervilles*. New York: Penguin Books, 1978.

Skultans, Vieda. *Madness and Morals: Ideas on Insanity in the Nineteenth Century*. Boston: Routledge & Kegan Paul, 1975.

Stanley, Liz, ed. *The Diaries of Hannah Cullwick, Victorian Maidservant*. New Brunswick: Rutgers University Press, 1984.

Sternbach, Nancy Saporta. "Re-membering the Dead: Latin American Women's 'Testimonial' Discourse." *Latin American Perspectives*. 18, no. 3 (Summer 1991): 91–102.

Stocking, George W., Jr. *Victorian Anthropology*. New York: Free Press, 1987.

Tambling, Jeremy. *Confession: Sexuality, Sin, the Subject*. New York: University Press, 1990.

Taylor, Jenny Bourne. *In the Secret Theatre of Home: Wilkie Collins, Sensation Narrative, and Nineteenth-Century Psychology*. New York: Routledge, 1988.

———. "Note on the Text." In *The Law and the Lady* by Wilkie Collins. New York: Oxford University Press, 1992.

Trollope, Frances. *Father Eustace: A Tale of the Jesuits*. New York: Garland, 1975.

Walkowitz, Judith. *Prostitution and Victorian Society: Women, Class, and the State*. Cambridge: Cambridge University Press, 1980.

Welsh, Alexander. *George Eliot and Blackmail*. Cambridge: Harvard University Press, 1985.

"Why Should We Fear the Romish Priests?" *Fraser's Magazine for Town and Country* 37, no. 220 (April 1848): 467–74.

Williams, Linda. *Hard Core: Power, Pleasure, and the Frenzy of the Visible*. Berkeley: University of California Press, 1989.

Wilt, Judith. " 'He Would Come Back': The Fathers of Daughters in *Daniel Deronda*." *Nineteenth-Century Literature* 42, no. 3 (1987): 313–38.

Woodhull, Winifred. "Sexuality, Power, and the Question of Rape." In *Feminism and Foucault*, edited by Irene Diamond and Lee Quinby. Boston: Northeastern University Press, 1988.

Wolffe, John. *The Protestant Crusade in Great Britain 1829–1860*. New York: Oxford University Press, 1991.

Yeo, Eileen, and E. P. Thompson. *The Unknown Mayhew*. New York: Pantheon Books, 1971.

Yudice, George. "*Testimonios* and Postmodernism." *Latin American Perspectives* 18, no. 3 (Summer 1991): 15–29.

Zeldin, Theodore. "The Conflict of Moralities: Confession, Sin, and Pleasure in the Nineteenth Century." In *Conflicts in French Society: Anticlericalism, Education, and Morals in the Nineteenth Century*. London: George Allen and Unwin, 1970.

INDEX

Achilli, Giacinto, 51, 59
Acton, William, 83, 94
Agency: of confessional subjects, 13, 23, 32, 183 (n. 40); as theorized by Foucault, 17–18; as theorized by feminists, 30, 32–33, 36–38, 131–32; and testimony, 33; and *testimonios*, 38
Anderson, Amanda, 82–83
Anti-Catholicism: discourse of, in propaganda tracts, x–xi, 41–49, 51–52, 60; and gendered power relations, x–xi, 172 (n. 35); history of, in nineteenth century England, 6, 40, 44–45; in *Villette* (C. Brontë), 7–8, 61–62, 66–67, 173 (n. 61); and domesticity, 10, 41–49; and "priestcraft," 46, 63–64; confessors as characterized in, 47–49, 55–61, 77, 105; in Victorian novel, 49–50; "No Popery" movement, 50–51, 57; in *Lady Audley's Secret* (Braddon), 76–77, 79. *See also* Anti-Catholic texts
Anti-Catholic texts: *Popery in Its Social Aspects* (Blakeney), 43, 48, 57–58; *The Divine Warning to the Church* (Bickersteth), 45; *The Rockite* (Tonna), 45; "Why Should We Fear the Romish Priests?," 46; *From Windsor to Rome through Anglican Sisterhoods*, 46, 65, 68–69; *Letter to the Women of England* (Brockman), 46–47; *Philip Paternoster* (Davies), 47; "The Confessional Unmasked" (Murphy), 48, 50; *Father Eustace* (F. Trollope), 50; *The Great Red Dragon* (Gavin), 51–53, 54; "Michelet on Auricular Confession and Direction," 54; *Manual of the Romish Conspiracy* (Blakeney), 57; *Awful Disclosures of the Hotel Dieu Nunnery* (Monk), 59–61,

64, 172–73 (n. 55); *Convent Education and Nunnery Victims*, 64–65. *See also* Anti-Catholicism
Anti-Semitism: and gender, 116; and English nationalism, 130–31, 139–41; Jewish patriarch, characterization of, 130–31, 182–83 (n. 30); Eliot's position on, 181 (n. 1), 187 (n. 103). *See also* Jewish identity
Anxiety of assimilation, 95, 180 (n. 71)
Arnstein, Walter, 50
Auricular confession. *See* Confession

Bakhtin, Mikhail, 44
Barker, Francis, 150
Bartkowski, Frances, 1, 31
Bartky, Sandra, 36, 157
Belsey, Catherine, 161
Benjamin, Walter, 41, 42
Bennett, Tony, 149, 151, 153
Blakeney, Richard, 48, 57–58, 59
—*Popery in Its Social Aspects*, 43, 48, 57–58
Bobbitt, Lorena, xii, 176 (n. 7), 190 (n. 54)
Bordo, Susan, 32
Braddon, Mary Elizabeth, 73
—*Aurora Floyd*, 75
—*Lady Audley's Secret*, xii, 8, 71, 72, 87, 107, 131, 140; as sensation fiction, 11, 73, 98–99, 103; degeneracy and, 11, 74, 80–98, 99–100, 102–3; prostitution figured in, 11, 76–77, 79–80, 81–87, 87–98, 102–3; madness depicted in, 75, 81–98, 99–100, 102–3; secular confession in, 76, 101; anti-Catholicism in, 76–77, 79
Breuer, Josef, 22, 24

Brockman, W. J.: *Letter to the Women of England on the Confessional*, 41–42, 46–47

Brontë, Charlotte, 64; letter to Emily Brontë (1843), 70; makes confession, 70

—*Villette*, 7, 8, 58, 60–72, 76, 140; anti-Catholicism in, 7–8, 10, 61–62, 66–67, 173 (n. 61); as critique of patriarchal power, 61–69, 70–72

Butler, Judith, 5, 33, 112, 182 (n. 19)

Carlyle, Thomas, 124–26, 140, 184 (n. 56); defense of Governor Eyre, 124, 125; Eliot on, 186 (n. 87)

Catholicism: Oxford movement, 6, 44–45; history of, in nineteenth century England, 44–46, 170 (n. 7); and Church of England, 45; Irish, 45–46, 57; "whore of Babylon," depicted as, 52, 65, 77, 172 (n. 35); in France, 54–56, 57; and social unrest, 57–58; contradictory representations of, 60–61; as depicted in *Villette*, 61–62, 66; and national identity, 62; and anti-Protestantism, 63; as depicted in *Lady Audley's Secret*, 76–77, 79; as sexually repressive, 77–79; and prostitution, 78–80. *See also* Anti-Catholicism; Nuns; Priests

Catnach, James, 49

Chapman, John, 78, 90–91, 103

—"Prostitution in Relation to the National Health," 90–91

Cixious, Hélène, 30–31

Collins, Wilkie: censorship conflict with *Graphic*, 149, 188 (n. 21)

—*Armadale*, 75

—*The Law and the Lady*, 149

—*No Name*, 75, 90

Confession: and autobiography, ix; and gendered power relations, ix–xiii, 1–7, 13, 15–40, 27, 29, 46–47, 64, 67–72, 127–35, 154–59, 165 (n. 3); secularized, x, xi, 17, 21–22, 40, 42–43, 69, 72, 76, 77, 99–101; and pleasure, x–xii, 16–21; as testimony, xi, xii–xiii, 4–6, 10, 12, 13, 27–33, 34–40, 67, 75, 86–87, 103, 123, 163, 173 (n. 61); as relational, xi, 3–4, 9–10, 12–13, 15–16, 31, 37–38, 66; as

discourse, xi, 9, 20, 98, 169 (n. 61); and "truth," xi, 88–89, 185 (n. 80); in popular culture, xi–xii, 13, 49–50; as transgression, xii, 3, 66–67, 69–70, 97–98, 140–41, 143–44; as coercive, 1, 7, 31, 113; feminist theories of, 1, 10, 22–33; defined by author, 1–2, 32; as resistance, 2, 8, 27–33, 30–31, 38–39, 54–57; as theorized by Foucault, 2–3, 4, 5, 9–10, 15–21, 39–40, 144–45, 155, 158; as surveillance, 2–3, 7, 13, 21, 107, 158; and identity, 3; and recovered-memory therapy, 3–4; and sexuality, 3–4, 5, 8, 10, 16, 22–23, 47–49, 50, 52–53, 55–56, 59–61, 155–59; and psychoanalysis, 4, 10, 17, 21–23, 25, 56, 168 (n. 35); and repression, 6–7, 9–10, 28; and power, 8, 9–10, 16–17, 36, 87–88, 154; as theorized by Freud, 9–10, 15–16, 21–26, 39–40; and patri-archal power, 10, 41–42, 47, 48–49, 51–58, 60, 69–70, 105–6, 156; as threat to domesticity, 10, 46–48, 50–51, 52–53, 71–72; and Jewish identity, 11–12, 106, 107, 115–17, 127–35, 135–40; and agency, 11–13, 23, 32, 163; and sexology, 18–19; female body as, 18–19, 30–31; Roman Catholic, 21–22, 24–25; as corruption, 43, 57–58; his-tory of, in nineteenth century England, 44–46; criminal, 49, 51, 59–60; conse-quences of, 55–58, 69–70, 163; repre-sentations of, in Victorian fiction, 58–72; as indoctrination, 59, 67–69; made by men, 135–41, 156–58; 184 (n. 65); and linguistic violence, 159–63. *See also* Anti-Catholicism; Anti-Catholic texts; Catholicism; Confessor; Gen-dered power relations

Confessional subjects: women as, xii, 1–2, 9, 25–26, 41–44, 45–47, 55–56; as unspeakable, 3–4, 160–61; trans-gressions, 4–5, 13, 33, 36–37; sexual violence, 7, 12, 24, 143–44, 146–47, 154–55; defined, 13; sex, 31, 47–49, 155–58; political violence, 37–38; crime, 49–51; Lucy Snowe (*Villette*), 61–72; Lady Audley (*Lady Audley's*

Secret), 73, 87–103; Daniel Deronda, 106–7, 135–40; Gwendolyn Harleth (*Daniel Deronda*), 107–13, 117–21, 130–35; Leonora Halm-Eberstein (the Alcharisi, in *Daniel Deronda*), 113–17, 127–30; Tess Durbyfield (*Tess of the d'Urbervilles*), 143–44, 154–55, 157–59, 159–63; Angel Clare (*Tess of the d'Urbervilles*), 155–58. *See also* Confession

Confessor, 15–16; medical, xi, 42–43, 69, 72, 99–101; and patriarchal power, 6, 46–47, 127–35; as authorized interpreter, 7, 12–13, 17–18, 28, 29–30, 35–36, 131–34, 155, 160; as agent, 17–18; psychoanalyst as, 21–22, 26; as seducer, 25, 41–44, 46–47, 48, 51; and resistance, 28; Roman Catholic priest as, 41–44, 50–51, 55–61, 77; as threat to domesticity, 43, 51–58; political power of, 57–58; reader as, 66; secular, 76, 77, 99–101; as spy, 105–6. *See also* Agency; Anti-Catholicism; Confession

"Considerations on the Moral Management of Insane Persons," 42–43

Contagious Diseases Acts, 78, 177 (n. 14)

Crosby, Christina, 131, 139–40

Cvetkovich, Ann, 122, 165 (n. 1), 180 (n. 81)

Daly, Mary, 36

Davis, Robert Con, 111

Degeneracy: and material conditions, 11, 75, 84; moral, 47–48, 82, 100–101; prostitution as, 75, 80–87; madness as, 80–87, 90–91, 102–3

De Lauretis, Teresa, 6, 144

Dens, Peter: *Theologia Moralis et Dogmatica*, 48

Derrida, Jacques: white mythology as theorized by, 12, 145–47

Disease: and prostitution, 74–75, 78, 80–87, 103; venereal, 74–75, 81–82, 91, 103; as paternal revenge, 113–15; gendered meanings of, 130–31. *See also* Female body

Disraeli, Benjamin, 140, 187 (n. 103)

Domesticity, 92, 171–72 (n. 33); Victorian

ideas on, 5–6, 10; threat to, confession perceived as, 10, 46–48, 50–51, 52–53, 71–72; and fictional confessions, 71–72; and secularized confessions, 76; depicted as incarceration, 101–2; depicted as slavery, 124–25; and rape, 162. *See also* Paternal metaphor; Patriarchal power

Domination. *See* Gendered power relations; Patriarchal power

Eliot, George: and Benjamin Disraeli, 140, 187 (n. 103); "Jewish question," treatment of, 181 (n. 1), 187 (n. 103); on Thomas Carlyle, 186 (n. 87)

—*Daniel Deronda*, xii, 71, 143, 154; gendered power relations in, 11, 106–9, 117–21, 124–27, 127–35; homosocial bonding in, 11, 135–41; nationalism in, 11–12, 106, 112, 118, 137–41, 186 (n. 87); racialism in, 11–12, 106–7; as psychological realism, 103; patriarchal power depicted in, 105–41; Jews depicted in, 106, 112–13, 115–16, 130–31, 140, 181 (n. 1), 182 (n. 26), 185 (n. 75); and rape, fear of, 110, 112, 114–15; patriarchal revenge in, 113–17; symbolic patricide in, 113–17; marriage depicted in, 117–21; and imperialism, 120–21; and Caliban, allusion to, 125–26; masculinity, construction of, depicted in, 127–35; confessor as authorized interpreter in, 131–34

Eyre, Governor Edward John, 122, 124–26

Felman, Shoshana, 34–37, 39

Feltes, N. N., 148–49

Female body: and medical science, 18–19; as confession, 18–19, 30–31; and madness, 90–91; and lactational insanity, 91; in pain, 113–14; as site of male bonding, 138–39; as textuality, 144–45, 154, 158–59, 189 (n. 51). *See also* Disease; Sexuality

Feminist theory: and confession, theories of, 1, 10, 29–33, 36–40; Foucault, responses to, 29–30, 31–32, 39–40; and resistance, concept of, 29–33; and significations of power, 29–33, 35–40; and agency, concept of, 30, 32–33, 36–38; Freud, responses to, 30, 34–35, 39–40; *l'écriture féminine*, 30–31; and *testimonios*, 37–38

Fénélon, Bishop, 68

Fisher, Amy, xii, 176 (n. 7)

Foucault, Michel, xi, 1, 4, 7, 8, 113, 166 (n. 1), 168 (n. 35); confession as theorized by, 2–3, 4, 5, 9–10, 15–21, 39–40, 144–45, 155, 158; power as theorized by, 2–4, 11, 16–17, 27, 108, 144; resistance as theorized by, 3, 29; agency, as theorized by, 17–18; "repressive hypothesis" of, 43, 50

—*The Care of the Self*, 166 (n. 6)

—*The History of Sexuality*, x, 16–17, 18, 19–20

—*The Use of Pleasure*, 18, 166 (n. 6)

Franchot, Jenny, 44, 60, 77

Freud, Sigmund, x, xi, 34–35, 52, 166 (n. 1); "seduction theory," xi, 3, 24, 133, 167 (n. 29); confession as theorized by, 9–10, 15–16, 21–26, 39–40; and patriarchal power, 21–22, 24, 27; on resistance and repression, 28–29; on psychoanalytic technique, 168 (n. 35)

—"The Question of Lay Analysis," 24

—"Resistance and Repression," 28

—"Studies on Hysteria," 22, 23, 28

From Windsor to Rome through Anglican Sisterhoods, 46, 65, 68–69

Gagnier, Regenia, 8

Gallagher, Catherine, 127, 139

Gallop, Jane, ix, 110

Gatrell, Simon, 148

Gavin, Anthony: *The Great Red Dragon*, 51–53, 54, 59

Gender: indeterminacy of, 5; essentialism, 16, 31; in Foucault, 18. *See also* Gendered power relations

Gendered power relations, ix–xi, 2, 5–6, 11, 32, 74, 107, 144, 166 (n. 4); and repression, 9–10; and social difference, 12–13; in confession, 15–40, 41–42, 43, 67–72, 88–89, 127–35, 154–59, 163, 165 (n. 3), 184 (n. 65); and "race-

gendering," 123–24; and imperialism, 126; and nationalism, 126–27, 129–30. *See also* Female body; Feminist theory; Paternal metaphor; Sexual violence; Surveillance; Testimony

Gilmore, Leigh, 4, 29, 33, 168 (n. 45)

Girard, René, 6

Greg, William Rathbone, 74, 78, 80, 81, 83–84, 85, 92, 98, 102

Griffin, Susan, 60

Hall, Catherine, 107, 123

Harding, Tonya, xii, 176 (n. 7)

Hardy, Thomas: censorship of *Tess of the d'Urbervilles* by *Graphic*, response to, 147, 148–49, 149–54; relation to readers, 150–51, 153–54; critical reviews, response to, 151–52; authorial authority, defense of, 153–54

—"Candour in English Fiction," 154–55

—*Jude the Obscure*, 151

—Prefaces to *Tess of the d'Urbervilles*: "Preface to the Fifth and Later Editions," 143, 149–50, 153–54; "Explanatory Note for the First Edition," 149–50, 152; preface of 1895, 150; preface to Wessex edition, 150, 152, 189 (n. 34, 38)

—*Tess of the d'Urbervilles*, 2, 71, 140–41; sexual violence in, 8, 12, 143–44, 146–47; editing history, 12, 143–44, 146, 152; honeymoon confessions in, 143–44, 144–47, 154, 155–59, 159–63; censorship and, 144, 148–49; female body as text, representation of, 144–45, 158–59; power, metaphors of, in, 145–47; idea of purity in, 145–47, 150–54; publishing history of, 148–49; serialization of, in *Graphic*, 152, 161–62

Hartsock, Nancy, 19

Hemyng, Bracebridge, 78, 85, 93

Hepworth, Mike, 52

Higgins, Lynn, 108, 111

Higonnet, Margaret, 150

Hill, Anita, 4

Homospirituality, 135–41

Imperialism: and patriarchal power, 118; and Jamaican uprising of 1865, 121–27; and Indian mutiny of 1857, 122; and racialism, 125–26; and gendered power relations, 126, 134–35; Disraeli as supporter of, 140; and novel, 184 (n. 52); distinguished from nationalism, 186 (n. 96). *See also* Nationalism

Insanity. *See* Madness

Jamaica Committee, 124; J. S. Mill's leadership of, 124

Jamaican uprising of 1865, 11; history of, 121–22; reference to, in *Daniel Deronda*, 121–27; and Governor Eyre controversy, 124

James, Henry, 118

Jansenists, 54

Jesuits, 54

Jewish identity: as depicted in *Daniel Deronda* (Eliot), 11–12, 106, 112–13, 115–16, 130–31, 140, 181 (n. 1), 185 (n. 75); confession of, 106, 107, 115–17, 127–35, 135–40; and assimilation, 109, 137, 181–82 (n. 10), 182–83 (n. 30), 184 (n. 62), 185 (n. 75); and English nationalism, 117, 140–41, 187 (n. 103); as national inheritance, 128–30, 185 (n. 69). *See also* Zionism

Kingsley, Charles: *The Saint's Tragedy; or, The True Story of Elizabeth of Hungary*, 64

Kofman, Sarah, 31

Kristeva, Julia, 159

Kucich, John, 6–7

Lacan, Jacques, ix, 11, 26; on patriarchal power, 26; *le sujet supposé savoir*, concept of, 35–36; paternal metaphor, concept of, 108–10; Name-of-the-Father, concept of, 110; paternal law, 182 (n. 19); split subject, concept of, 190 (n. 57)

Laird, J. T., 152

Laub, Dori, 34–35

Law-of-the-Father. *See* Paternal metaphor

Litvak, Joseph, 7

Lydon, Mary, 29–30

Maddock, Alfred Beaumont, 80

Madness: and prostitution, 11, 75, 80–87; puerperal insanity, 81; and sexuality, 81; inherited, 81–82, 90–91, 179–80 (n. 57); moral deviation as, 82–83, 102; and material conditions, 88, 92–98; as contagion, 89–92; lactational insanity, 91; and venereal disease, 92; intermittent, 92, 94–96; as theorized by Foucault, 102; in Victorian female characters, 177 (n. 25); as legal defense, 190 (n. 54). *See also* Degeneracy

Mayhew, Henry, 11, 91, 92, 94, 95, 97, 98; prostitution, news columns on, 74, 84–87; surveillance used by, 86; interviews with prostitutes, 86–87

—*London Labour and the London Poor*, 74, 77–78, 85, 94–95, 98, 172 (n. 52), 176 (n. 4)

Martin, Biddy, 31

Menchú, Rigoberta, 37

Meyer, Susan, 130

Michelet, Jules: *Du Prêtre, de la Femme, et la Famille*, 54, 55–57

Mill, John Stuart: Jamaica Committee, leader of, 124

—*The Subjection of Women*, 121, 124–25

Millais, John Everett: *The Vale of Rest*, 65, 76

Miller, J. Hillis, 150

Monk, Maria, 59–61, 171 (n. 21), 172 (n. 54), 172–73 (n. 55)

—*Awful Disclosures of the Hotel Dieu Nunnery*, 59–61, 62, 172–73 (n. 55)

Munby, Arthur, 65

Murphy, William, 50–51

—"The Confessional Unmasked," 50

Name-of-the-Father. *See* Paternal metaphor

Nationalism, 117, 187 (n. 103); and antiCatholicism, 54–58; and religion, 62–63; and confession, 100, 106, 137–38; and patriarchal power, 123; and gendered power relations, 126–27; and anti-Semitism, 130–31, 139–41; of Disraeli, 140; and Zionism, 140–41. *See also* Imperialism; Zionism

Newman, John Henry Cardinal, 44, 45, 50, 59, 60; Newman-Achilli case, 51
—*Lectures*, 51
—"The Present Position of Catholics," 51
Newman-Achilli case, 51, 59
Nuns, 48; depicted in *Villette*, 59–64; depicted in Victorian culture, 64–66, 77, 171 (n. 21); and prostitution, 76, 181 (n. 90)

Oliphant, Mrs., 90
Oxford movement, 10, 44, 45

Panopticon. *See* Surveillance
Parent-Duchâtelet, Alexandre, 83
Paternal metaphor, 11; Lacan's concept of, 108–10; meanings of, 110, 112; and surveillance, 110–11, 117–21; and paternity, 112; and symbolic patricide, 114, 116; and patronym, use of, 115–16; divine power, construed as, 116, 119–20; and enslavement, 121–27; and national inheritance, 129–36; and absence, 133–35
Patriarchal power: in Freudian psychoanalysis, 3, 21–22, 24, 167 (n. 29); and repression, 6–7; in confession, 10, 41–42, 46–47, 48–49, 51–58, 60, 69–70, 105–6, 156; as theorized by Lacan, 26; and testimony, 36, 86; of Roman Catholic confessors, depicted in anti-Catholic propaganda, 41–44, 50–51; Charlotte Brontë's critique of, in *Villette*, 70–72; and nationalism, 107, 123, 140–41; and violence, 108, 118; as provisional, 111; and revenge, 113–17; and resistance, 120; and male confessors, 127–35; suttee, 134–35; and male confession, 135–41. *See also* Domesticity; Imperialism; Paternal metaphor; Surveillance
Patriarchy. *See* Patriarchal power
Poovey, Mary, 9, 94
Power: domination, differentiated from, 1; and narrative authority, 2–3, 153–54; as theorized by Foucault, 2–4, 11, 16–17, 27, 108, 144, 145–46, 149, 153; and resistance, 3, 28, 168 (n. 42); and con-

fession, 8, 16–17, 87–88, 163; of confessor, 15–16, 17–19, 53; and psychoanalysis, 21–22, 27; and testimony, 35; metaphors of, 75, 145–47; and madness, 87–88; of maternal word, 111; and sexuality, 144–45; and white mythology, Derrida's concept of, 145–46, 147, 149, 163; of readers, 151. *See also* Gendered power relations; Patriarchal power
Priests: as confessors, 41–44; depicted as sexual offenders, in anti-Catholic propaganda, 50–51, 55–61, 77
Pritchard, John, 82, 100
Prostitution: in Victorian culture, 11, 74–75, 78, 80; and madness, 11, 75, 81–87; and disease, 74–75, 78, 80–87, 103; and Catholicism, 76–79, 181 (n. 90); cicisbeism, 79; marriage as, 79–80, 85, 92–93, 96; as transient state, 83, 94–96; causes of, 83–86, 178 (n. 34); as metaphor, 85; social climbing as, 90, 96; and governessing, 94; anxiety of assimilation, 95; invisibility of, 95–96. *See also* Mayhew, Henry
Protestantism, 62–63
Psychoanalysis: as confession, 4, 10, 17, 21–22, 25; and power, 21–22, 27; abreaction, 22–23, 67, 167 (n. 25); resistance, 27–29; and testimony, 34–35; and "truth," 35; and *le sujet supposé savoir*, Lacan's concept of, 35–36; as technique, 168 (n. 35). *See also* Foucault, Michel; Freud, Sigmund; Lacan, Jacques
Psychological realism, 11, 103
Purity: metaphors of, 150–54; textual, 150–54. *See also* Virginity; White mythology
Pusey, William, 44

Rape: Victorian representations of, 3–6, 162–63; confession of, 12, 27, 144; in Newman-Achilli case, 51; fear of, 108, 110–12, 114–15, 125–26; as textual inscription, 146; as metaphor, 146–47, 151, 160–61; censorship and editing as, 149–54, 187 (n. 7); and marriage, 162. *See also* Sexual violence

Recovered-memory therapy, 3–4, 13

Repression: and patriarchal privilege, 6–7; in Victorian culture, 6–7; and confession, 6–7, 9–10; and gendered power relations, 9–10, 64; and resistance, 28; as theorized by Freud, 28–29; "repressive hypothesis," Foucault's concept of, 43, 50; as defensive strategy, 173–74 (n. 65)

Resistance: feminist theories of, 1, 22–33, 177 (n. 25); and confession, 2, 27–33, 38–39, 167 (n. 25); and power, 3, 28, 168 (n. 42); as theorized by Foucault, 3, 29; and agency, 13, 23, 30, 32–33, 36–38, 131–32, 183 (n. 40); as theorized by Freud, 27–29; and repression, 28; as relational, 29; silence as, 29–30; and social change, 32–33; and testimony, 32–33; domestic, 54–57; and imperialism, 123–24, 126

Rooney, Ellen, 160

Rubin, Gayle, 16

Said, Edward, 123, 186 (n. 96)

Schneiderman, Stuart, ix

Screen discourse, 60

The Secret of Charlotte Brontë (1914), 70

Sedgwick, Eve, 138

Semmel, Bernard, 129; national inheritance, concept of, 129

Sensation fiction, 11, 98–99, 103, 165 (n. 1), 179 (n. 51); as genre, 73; heroines in, 75; and anxiety of assimilation, concept of, 95, 180 (n. 71)

Sexuality: and confession, 3–4, 5, 8, 10, 16, 22–23, 47–49, 50, 52–53, 55–56, 59–61, 155–59; and violence, 5–6; repression of, in Victorian culture, 6–7; and pleasure, 16, 19–20; and crime, 81; and madness, 81; and textuality, 144; and power, 144–45

Sexual violence: disclosure of, by women, 4–6; and male domination, 8; representations of, 12, 143–44, 162–63, 190 (n. 54); as unspeakable, 36–37, 118–20, 154–63, 159; Catholic confession and, 41–44; and imperialism, 118. *See also* Rape

Sharpe, Jenny, 134

Silver, Brenda, 111

Silverman, Kaja, 158

Slavery, 124–25

Smith, Susan, xii, 176 (n. 7)

Spivak, Gayatri, 123

Surveillance: confession as, 2–3, 7, 13, 21, 107, 158; and patriarchal power, 2–3, 105–6, 108; in Victorian culture, 7; of prostitutes, 78, 86; and madness, 89; fear of, 108–9, 118–20; and paternal metaphor, 110–11, 117–21

Tambling, Jeremy, 5

Testimonios, 37–38, 169 (n. 69)

Testimony: confession as, xii–xiii, 4–5, 10, 12, 13, 27–33, 34–39, 75, 86–87, 98, 123, 163, 173 (n. 61); of Anita Hill, 4; and resistance, 32–33; and agency, 33, 37; and Holocaust, 34; psychoanalytic theory and, 34–35; "unconscious," 34–35, 39; and "truth," 35, 38, 39; "bearing witness," compared to, 36; etymology of, 36; as theorized by feminists, 36–40; as violence, 37–38; and autobiography, 38. *See also Testimonios*

Tonna, Charlotte Elizabeth, 59, 170 (n. 9)

—*The Rockite*, 45

"To Tell the Truth," xi

Tractarians. *See* Oxford movement

"Truth": as effect of power relations, 17; and testimony, 35, 38, 39; in history and fiction, 43–44; in confession, 88–89, 155, 185 (n. 80); and paternal authority, 111

Turner, Bryan, 52

Violence: defined, 5–6; domestic, 5–6; and sexuality, 5–6; confession and, 7, 12–13; and women, 9, 11; testimony as, 37–38; and paternal metaphor, 110–12; as psychological control, 116–17; in heterosexual relations, 118–19; symbolic patricide as, 118–19; and gendered power relations, 144, 147; censorship and editing as, 149–54, 162, 187 (n. 7); linguistic, 159–63. *See also* Rape; Sexual violence

Virginity, 146–47. *See also* Purity

White mythology, 163; as theorized by
Derrida, 145–46; and power, 145–46,
147, 149, 163; and "truth," 146; and
purity, 147, 152; and domesticity,
149
"Whore of Babylon": Catholicism
depicted as, 52, 65, 77, 172 (n. 35).
See also Anti-Catholicism

Williams, Linda, 19, 21
Wilt, Judith, 111
Witnessing. *See* Testimony
Wolffe, John, 47
Wynter, Andrew, 102

Zionism, 181 (n. 10), 183–84 (n. 49), 185
(n. 75), 186 (n. 96, 97); and nationalism,
123, 137–38, 185 (nn. 69, 74); and anti-
Semitism, 181 (n. 1)